BlackBerry Java Application Development
Beginner's Guide

Build and deploy powerful, useful, and professional Java mobile applications for BlackBerry smartphones, the fast and easy way

Bill Foust

BIRMINGHAM - MUMBAI

BlackBerry Java Application Development
Beginner's Guide

Copyright © 2010 Packt Publishing

All rights reserved. No part of this book may be reproduced, stored in a retrieval system, or transmitted in any form or by any means, without the prior written permission of the publisher, except in the case of brief quotations embedded in critical articles or reviews.

Every effort has been made in the preparation of this book to ensure the accuracy of the information presented. However, the information contained in this book is sold without warranty, either express or implied. Neither the author, nor Packt Publishing, and its dealers and distributors will be held liable for any damages caused or alleged to be caused directly or indirectly by this book.

Packt Publishing has endeavored to provide trademark information about all of the companies and products mentioned in this book by the appropriate use of capitals. However, Packt Publishing cannot guarantee the accuracy of this information.

First published: July 2010

Production Reference: 1190710

Published by Packt Publishing Ltd.
32 Lincoln Road
Olton
Birmingham, B27 6PA, UK.

ISBN 978-1-849690-20-1

www.packtpub.com

Cover Image by Parag Kadam (paragvkadam@gmail.com)

Credits

Author
Bill Foust

Reviewers
Richard Evers
Jason Reese

Acquisition Editor
David Barnes

Development Editor
Mehul Shetty

Technical Editor
Namita Sahni

Indexer
Monica Ajmera Mehta

Editorial Team Leader
Akshara Aware

Project Team Leader
Priya Mukherji

Project Coordinator
Ashwin Shetty

Proofreader
Jeff Orloff

Production Coordinators
Alwin Roy
Adline Swetha Jesuthas
Kruthika Bangera

Cover Work
Alwin Roy

About the Author

Bill Foust has been developing software for over fifteen years in a variety of fields and technologies. He began working with BlackBerry devices in 1999—before they even had built-in cellular phones! During that time, he created and sold applications, and helped several companies develop product offerings for BlackBerry.

With the release of the BlackBerry 5810 in 2002, the development environment changed from C++ to Java Micro and Bill started pursuing other opportunities, including .NET, and has continued to do development as a consultant professionally since then.

In 2004, he authored the book Mobile Magazine Guide to BlackBerry with Que Publishing (`http://www.amazon.com/Mobile-Guide-BlackBerry-Bill-Foust/dp/0789733439`). This book was a success and lead to Bill being a founding member of the Mobile Computing Authority podcast with two other book authors.

Bill is currently working with a consulting company in Kansas City and continues to opine about BlackBerry and the mobile computing industry in general through the Mobile Computing Authority blog and podcasts.

Acknowledgement

First, I need to thank God, the Father, for everything that He has done throughout my life and for the grace, favor, and peace to get this book done. The opportunity to write this book came about at a time in my life that was not very convenient. I was looking at moving cross country and a job change to help take care of my ailing mother. In spite of this, the many challenges we faced to complete this book were never overwhelming and in the end, were overcome.

Secondly, I need to thank my wife, Angela, and family for their continual support throughout the entire process. Even as deadlines were missed and evenings were spent writing instead of playing with the kids, my wife was understanding and supportive in seeing this done.

I also need to give special thanks to the staff at Packt Publishing for their patience and understanding with me through all of the issues and delays we faced.

I'd like to dedicate this book to my mother, who passed away during the writing of this book. We will miss you Mom.

About the Reviewers

Richard Evers develops software in many languages across several platforms, and has extensive experience developing for Oracle, DB2, Informix, MySQL, and SQL Server.

He has been the editor of five magazines, publisher of two magazines, author of thousands of software products, and publisher of eight educational websites.

Richard has been helped create books such as the Professional BlackBerry (Wrox), Mobile PC Guide to BlackBerry (Que), the BlackBerry For Dummies series (Wiley), four BlackBerry Certification Program self-study guides, the Civics Canada Online Textbook, The Complete Commodore Inner Space Anthology, and The Transactor Book of Bits and Pieces.

Richard worked for Research In Motion for more than 7 years, and recently left RIM to work for BlueCat Networks as a senior software engineer.

> I would like to thank my wife, Donna, and my children, Stephanie, Samantha, and Adam, for their love and support through countless years of hiding behind a computer screen.

Jason Reese has spent 12 years working in the telecommunications and wireless industries managing global mobility projects, device deployments, support, and application development on all major mobile platforms. Jason is a regular contributor to the technology site `GearDiary.com`. When he's not working, Jason enjoys traveling and spending time with his wife, Stephanie, and their 5 year-old Boston Terrier, Sophie.

> I would like to thank my wife, Stephanie, who has been incredibly supportive (and patient!) through many years and projects.

Table of Contents

Preface	**1**
Chapter 1: Introducing BlackBerry Application Development	**7**
Expectations of this book	8
General device capabilities	9
Two different approaches to application development	10
Choosing an SDK version	10
What you can expect	12
Summary	14
Chapter 2: Installing the Development Environment	**15**
System requirements	16
Development Environments	16
Downloading and installing Java	17
Time for action – downloading the Java Development Kit	17
Time for action – installing the Java Development Kit (JDK)	20
Introducing the BlackBerry Developer Zone	22
Downloading and installing Eclipse	23
Time for action – downloading Eclipse with the JDE plugin	24
Time for action – installing the JDE plugin for Eclipse Full installer	26
Installing other JDE component package versions	28
Time for action – installing other JDE component packages over-the-air	28
Summary	36
Chapter 3: Getting Familiar with the Development Environment	**37**
Starting the Eclipse IDE	37
Time for action – launching Eclipse for the first time	38
Importing the hello world project	42
Time for action – importing the HelloWorldDemo sample application	42
Running the application	46
Time for action – running an application in the simulator	47

Table of Contents

Debugging the application	**49**
Time for action – starting the debugger	**50**
Introducing Eclipse perspectives	**52**
Time for action – changing the perspective	**52**
Getting some help!	55
Time for action – displaying the Help	**55**
Summary	**58**
Chapter 4: Creating your First BlackBerry Project	**59**
Choosing the SDK version	**59**
Creating a new project	60
Time for action – creating a new project	**60**
Adding a package to the new project	62
Time for action – creating a new project	**63**
Start at the beginning	**65**
Application and UiApplication	65
Time for action – adding the UiApplication class	**65**
A closer look at the code	68
Time for action – expanding TipCalcApplication	**69**
MainScreen	71
Time for action – adding a MainScreen	**72**
Determining your screen requirements	73
Time for action – expanding the TIpCalcMainScreen	**74**
Time for action – adding more to the MainScreen	**75**
Adding a menu to the application	78
Time for action – adding a menu to the MainScreen	**78**
Setting the SDK version	81
Time for action – selecting the right component package	**81**
Testing it out	84
Time for action – running your new application	**84**
Giving TipCalc some polish	**86**
Adding an icon to TipCalc	87
Time for action – adding an icon	**88**
Time for action – changing the application title	**92**
Fixing the Bill Amount field	93
Time for action – fixing the bill amount field	**93**
Disabling the save prompt	94
Time for action – disabling the "save" dialog	**94**
Summary	**95**

Chapter 5: Learning the Basics About the UI	**97**
Getting to know other Field classes	97
SeparatorField	101
Time for action – creating a SeparatorField	101
LabelField	102
Time for action – creating a LabelField	102
BitmapField	103
Time for action – creating a BitmapField	104
ChoiceField	105
ObjectChoiceField	106
Time for action – creating an ObjectChoiceField	106
NumericChoiceField	108
Time for action – creating a NumericChoiceField	108
GaugeField	109
Time for action – creating a GaugeField	110
DateField	113
Time for action – creating a DateField	114
CheckboxField	116
Time for action – creating a CheckboxField	117
RadioButtonField	118
Time for action – creating a RadioButtonField	119
TextField	122
BasicEditField	122
Time for action – creating a BasicEditField	124
EditField	126
Time for action – creating an EditField	126
PasswordEditField	127
Time for action – creating a PasswordEditField	127
EmailAddressEditField	128
Time for action – creating an EmailAddressField	128
AutoTextEditField	129
Time for action – creating an AutoTextEditField	129
ActiveAutoTextEditField	131
Time for action – creating an ActiveAutoTextEditField	131
RichTextField	133
Time for action – creating a RichTextField	133
ActiveRichTextField	136
Time for action – creating an ActiveRichTextField	137
Summary	139

Chapter 6: Going Deeper into the UI — 141
- ButtonField — 142
- Time for action – creating a ButtonField — 142
  - ListField — 145
- Time for action – creating a ListField — 145
- TreeField — 149
- Time for action – creating a TreeField — 150
- MapField — 154
- Time for action – creating a MapField — 154
- Displaying another screen — 155
- Time for action – creating an "About Screen" — 156
- Displaying a dialog — 158
- Time for action – collecting information with a common dialog — 159
- Time for action – collecting information with custom buttons on a dialog — 160
- Time for action – collecting information with a list on a dialog — 162
- Listeners and callbacks — 164
- Layout managers — 164
  - Special considerations for touchscreens — 165
  - TouchEvents and TouchGestures — 166
- Summary — 168

Chapter 7: Storing Data — 171
- Laying the ground work — 171
- Creating a data class — 172
- The Java way: RMS — 172
- Time for action – creating and opening a RecordStore — 174
- Time for action – adding a record — 177
- Time for action – retrieving records — 179
- Time for action – deleting records — 182
- The BlackBerry way: Persistent Store — 184
- PersistentStore and PersistentObject — 184
- Time for action – preparing the JournalEntry class — 185
- Time for action – getting a PersistentObject — 186
- Time for action – accessing the PersistentObject data — 188
- Time for action – accessing the PersistentObject data — 189
- Accessing removable storage — 192
  - Connector and FileConnection — 193
- Time for action – storing data to a file — 193
- Time for action – reading data from a file — 198
- Summary — 202

Chapter 8: Interfacing with Applications — 203
Introducing PIM — 204
Why is all so generic? — 204
- PIMLists — 205
- PIMItems — 205
Laying the ground work — 206
Time for action – creating test contacts — 206
Expanding your test contacts — 212
Time for action – adding telephone numbers — 212
Expanding even more — 215
Time for action – adding e-mail addresses — 215
Finishing the test contacts — 217
Time for action – adding e-mail addresses — 217
Embedding the address book into your application — 220
Time for action – embedding the address book — 220
Adding the event to your calendar — 224
Time for action – adding an event to the calendar — 225
Recurring events — 227
Sending e-mail — 229
Time for action – sending an e-mail from an application — 230
Summary — 233

Chapter 9: Networking — 235
Threading — 236
Connector class — 236
HTTP basics — 237
HTTP GET requests — 238
Time for action - HTTP Basics — 238
HTTP POST requests — 244
Time for action – calling a web service — 245
Time for action – parsing the response — 250
The transport—so many possibilities — 255
- Direct TCP/IP — 255
- MDS/BES — 256
- BIS-B — 256
- Wi-Fi — 257
- WAP — 257
  - WAP 1.X — 257
- WAP 2.0 — 258
Debugging with the MDS simulator — 258
Testing for availability of transports — 262
Time for action – testing for availability — 263

Moving beyond HTTP connections	**266**
Summary	**268**
Chapter 10: Advanced Topics	**269**
Introducing the Global Positioning System	**270**
The LocationProvider class	270
Criteria	271
Three ways to get GPS data	271
Bringing it all together	272
Getting coordinates	273
Time for action – acquiring a location	**274**
Expanding Hansel	285
Time for action – expanding Hansel	**285**
Alternate entry points	**294**
Creating a focus icon	295
Time for action – creating an alternate entry point project	**296**
Time for action – adding a focus icon to Hansel	**298**
Summary	**304**
Chapter 11: Wrapping It All Up	**305**
Using resources for localization	**306**
Time for action – adding a resource file	**306**
Resource bundles	**309**
Time for action – adding a second resource file	**310**
Time for action – populating a resource file and configuring the project	**311**
Time for action – using a resource in your code	**314**
Code signing your application	**317**
Time for action – configuring projects to allow access	**317**
Time for action – installing the code-signing keys	**319**
Time for action – code-signing the application	**320**
Distributing your application through BlackBerry App World	**324**
Licensing models	325
Submitting an application	326
Summary	**326**
Appendix: Pop Quiz Answers	**329**
Chapter 2	**329**
Chapter 3	**329**
Chapter 4	**330**
Pop Quiz 1	330
Pop Quiz 2	330
Pop Quiz 3	330

Chapter 5	**331**
Pop Quiz 1	331
Pop Quiz 2	331
Pop Quiz 3	331
Pop Quiz 4	332
Pop Quiz 5	332
Chapter 6	**332**
Pop Quiz 1	332
Pop Quiz 2	333
Pop Quiz 3	333
Chapter 7	**333**
Pop Quiz 1	333
Pop Quiz 2	334
Pop Quiz 3	334
Chapter 8	**334**
Pop Quiz 1	334
Pop Quiz 2	335
Pop Quiz 3	335
Chapter 9	**335**
Pop Quiz 1	335
Pop Quiz 2	336
Pop Quiz 3	336
Chapter 10	**336**
Pop Quiz 1	336
Pop Quiz 2	337
Chapter 11	**337**
Index	**457**

Preface

The book teaches how to write rich, interactive, and smart BlackBerry applications in Java. It expects the readers to know Java but not Java Mobile or the BlackBerry APIs. This book will cover UI programming, data storage, programming network, and Internet API apps. As we move on, you will learn more about the BlackBerry's device features, such as messaging, GPS, multimedia, contacts and calendar, and so on. This book also helps you build your own applications to illustrate the platform and the various capabilities that developers can use in their programs.

What this book covers

Chapter 1, Introducing BlackBerry Application Development gets you started by talking about the capabilities of a BlackBerry smartphone and what kind of things can be done with these capabilities with a custom application. It talks about the other tools which are available and why writing native Java applications by using the BlackBerry SDK is the most powerful and practical approach to developing applications. Finally, it covers how to select which version of the SDK to use and when you might want to use an older version of the SDK instead of the latest.

Chapter 2, Installing the development Environment steps you through the process of installing the proper versions of Java and Eclipse. This chapter talks about when to install additional versions of the SDK and how to do so through the Eclipse over-the-air update tool as well as how to install them manually.

Chapter 3, Getting Familiar with the Development Environment starts off the learning process by importing an existing sample application—the standard "Hello World" application. After importing the project, the chapter will go over this simple application line-by-line. Afterwards, you will run the application in the simulator and then introduce a bug into the application so that you can debug it as well.

Chapter 4, *Creating your first BlackBerry Project* is where you create a new project from scratch. This chapter demonstrates how you accomplish this using Eclipse and the various wizards that are available within it. It also demonstrates how you can create a simple, but complete application quickly using the User Interface (UI) elements provided by the framework.

Chapter 5, *Learning the Basics about the UI* creates an application to demonstrate each of the UI elements that are available to you when using the BlackBerry SDK. This sample application demonstrates how to set and retrieve data from each field and discusses when each field should be used according to the BlackBerry development guidelines. By demonstrating each field, you will get a complete understanding of the capabilities of each field.

Chapter 6, *Going Deeper into the UI* picks up where the previous chapter leaves off by demonstrating how to use some of the advanced fields, such as lists and trees. It also covers navigation between screens, displaying dialogs, and common patterns used in the BlackBerry SDK. By the time you are done with this chapter, you will be well equipped to create the entire UI for an application.

Chapter 7, *Storing Data* jumps right into how to use the data storage tools of the SDK and when it is appropriate to use each one. This covers the Java standard RMS, the BlackBerry-specific *PersistentStore*, and even how to access the removable media cards that are available on some devices.

Chapter 8, *Interfacing with Applications* shows you how to take advantage of one of most powerful features available to a BlackBerry application. Each BlackBerry device comes with standard applications that you can interface with. These include the address book, calendar, and even the messaging applications. Being able to tightly integrate an application with these can make it even more valuable and useful to the end user.

Chapter 9, *Networking* wades into the complex, but an important area of how to make an application networking aware. Here, you will discover what transports are available, how to open connections , and how to send data through them. The sample also demonstrates how to communicate with a simple web service and parse the resulting XML data.

Chapter 10, *Advanced Topics* covers two distinct, but powerful topics. The first topic is how to utilize the built-in GPS receiver that is built in to some smartphones in order to get location information. You will learn about the various methods that can be used to get location information and how to do some common calculations using these coordinates. The other topic covered in this chapter covers how to use alternate entry points so that a single project can be used to launch multiple applications. Because these applications share a common project, they can share code and even memory.

Chapter 11, Wrapping It All Up finishes the book with tasks that commonly are done last, such as localization with language resource files and code-signing your application so that it can be installed on real devices. You will also learn what it takes to distribute your new application through the BlackBerry App World marketplace.

What you need for this book

In order to get started you don't need anything at all except some starter code, which is available with the code bundle of this book. Everything else that you will need will be downloaded and installed through the course of this book, mostly in Chapter 2. In this chapter, we will install the Java 2 JRE (Java Runtime Environment) and JDE (Java Development Environment), which are both needed to run Eclipse, the development environment, and to compile the applications you will be making. Eclipse comes in several versions from www.eclipse.org, but we will be using a version from RIM, which has been pre-bundled with the BlackBerry SDK.

Beyond the software needs you will also need experience with an object-oriented development language such a Java, C#, or even C++. You should be familiar with common object-oriented terms such as classes, members, inheritance, and even interfaces. Furthermore, you should understand common concepts such as threading and serialization.

Who this book is for

If you are a Java programmer who wants to build BlackBerry applications with Java, this book is for you.

Conventions

In this book, you will find several headings appearing frequently.

To give clear instructions of how to complete a procedure or task, we use:

Time for action – heading

1. Action 1
2. Action 2
3. Action 3

Instructions often need some extra explanation so that they make sense, so they are followed with:

What just happened?

This heading explains the working of tasks or instructions that you have just completed.

You will also find some other learning aids in the book, including:

Pop quiz – heading

These are short multiple choice questions intended to help you test your own understanding.

Have a go hero – heading

These set practical challenges and give you ideas for experimenting with what you have learned.

You will also find a number of styles of text that distinguish between different kinds of information. Here are some examples of these styles, and an explanation of their meaning.

Code words in text are shown as follows: "Next, you need to find the `HelloWorldDemo` application."

A block of code is set as follows:

```
public class TipCalcApplication extends UiApplication {
    /**
     * @param args
     */
    public static void main(String[] args) {
        // TODO Auto-generated method stub
    }
}
```

Any command-line input or output is written as follows:

```
Feb 21, 2010 3:45:50 PM org.apache.coyote.http11.Http11BaseProtocol init
SEVERE: Error initializing endpoint

java.net.BindException: Address already in use: JVM_Bind:8080
```

New terms and **important words** are shown in bold. Words that you see on the screen, in menus or dialog boxes for example, appear in the text like this: " Either go to **File | Exit** or simply close the simulator window".

> Warnings or important notes appear in a box like this.

> Tips and tricks appear like this.

Reader feedback

Feedback from our readers is always welcome. Let us know what you think about this book—what you liked or may have disliked. Reader feedback is important for us to develop titles that you really get the most out of.

To send us general feedback, simply send an e-mail to feedback@packtpub.com, and mention the book title via the subject of your message.

If there is a book that you need and would like to see us publish, please send us a note in the **SUGGEST A TITLE** form on www.packtpub.com or e-mail suggest@packtpub.com.

If there is a topic that you have expertise in and you are interested in either writing or contributing to a book on, see our author guide on www.packtpub.com/authors.

Customer support

Now that you are the proud owner of a Packt book, we have a number of things to help you to get the most from your purchase.

> **Downloading the example code for this book**
>
> You can download the example code files for all Packt books you have purchased from your account at http://www.PacktPub.com. If you purchased this book elsewhere, you can visit http://www.PacktPub.com/support and register to have the files e-mailed directly to you.

Errata

Although we have taken every care to ensure the accuracy of our content, mistakes do happen. If you find a mistake in one of our books—maybe a mistake in the text or the code—we would be grateful if you would report this to us. By doing so, you can save other readers from frustration and help us improve subsequent versions of this book. If you find any errata, please report them by visiting http://www.packtpub.com/support, selecting your book, clicking on the **let us know** link, and entering the details of your errata. Once your errata are verified, your submission will be accepted and the errata will be uploaded on our website, or added to any list of existing errata, under the Errata section of that title. Any existing errata can be viewed by selecting your title from http://www.packtpub.com/support.

Piracy

Piracy of copyright material on the Internet is an ongoing problem across all media. At Packt, we take the protection of our copyright and licenses very seriously. If you come across any illegal copies of our works, in any form, on the Internet, please provide us with the location address or website name immediately so that we can pursue a remedy.

Please contact us at copyright@packtpub.com with a link to the suspected pirated material.

We appreciate your help in protecting our authors, and our ability to bring you valuable content.

Questions

You can contact us at questions@packtpub.com if you are having a problem with any aspect of the book, and we will do our best to address it.

Introducing BlackBerry Application Development

The BlackBerry family of devices has long been the undisputed king of e-mail for business professionals. In recent years, the company that makes BlackBerry handhelds, **Research In Motion (RIM)**, has been making devices targeted more towards consumers with devices such as the Storm and Pearl. Because of this shift the demand for quality applications has exploded in recent years. The creation of the BlackBerry App World has only fueled this growth and the size of the opportunity. According to recent statistics, the BlackBerry App World has the fewest number of titles and the highest average cost, all of which means there is a big opportunity here!

Now, with more than 28 million subscribers and 60 million devices manufactured, it is hard to go anywhere and not see someone using a BlackBerry. Maybe you see these numbers as a fertile market for your application, or maybe your company has long ago standardized on BlackBerry handhelds and you want to leverage that existing investment. Either way, you will learn how to tap into that potential and create custom applications for BlackBerry handhelds by using the object-oriented development experience you already have.

In this chapter, we shall:

- Learn about the two approaches to application development
- Learn generally what features can be used by an application
- Understand how the SDK version relates to target devices
- Learn about the BlackBerry Developer Zone

So let's get on with it...

Expectations of this book

This book is part of the Basic series which means we will start at the very beginning of the learning curve. We start with the simplest task of getting the right tools downloaded and installed. We then take you through to the final stages of putting the last finishing touches on your application and then submitting it to the BlackBerry App World so that the world can use it. Along the way, we will cover each of the major areas of application development: user interface, storage, connectivity, and interfacing with other applications in ways that are clear and useful.

There are a few things that we assume and that you should be familiar with before starting down this road. The first is an understanding of an object-oriented programming language. BlackBerry development is done using Java, but you don't need to be a Java expert to get started. Experience in C#, C++, or some other object-oriented language is enough to get started.

Most of what we do will use the BlackBerry-specific APIs, but there are times when an understanding of basic Java framework is important, such as when we need to use threads. For this I recommend having a Java book available as well.

The second is an understanding of general operating system concepts such as a file system, messaging, events, processes, and threading. The BlackBerry APIs actually do a very good job of hiding many of these details, but they are there and understanding them will help to understand the big picture.

General device capabilities

BlackBerry handhelds, like many smartphones today, are very powerful in spite of their small size. The processing power and capabilities of these handhelds could accurately be described as smaller versions of our desktops or laptops. They have many strong capabilities yet have a small size that makes them convenient to carry around. This combination makes smartphones in general, and BlackBerry handhelds in particular, well suited for on-the-go applications.

But just what can they do? There are so many possibilities! Let's take a look at the general capabilities of BlackBerry handhelds.

- Every handheld has a keyboard designed for typing on it. BlackBerry handhelds have always been specifically designed to send and receive e-mail, and as a result, the keyboards are well-suited for entering free-form data. The BlackBerry SDK offers no less than ten different kinds of text fields that can be used in nearly any kind of application. Plus, if you need something special, you can always create your own!

- Another area that BlackBerry handhelds excel at is network connectivity. Again, this is by design in order to provide excellent e-mail service. This connectivity includes fully encrypted TCP/IP communication, and the ability to receive as well as send raw data. Whether it be HTTP or UDP, the BlackBerry SDK supports all of the major networking protocols and can handle receiving as well as sending data. Furthermore, you can leverage the same secure protocols that are used to deliver e-mail.

- Most applications will need to store data on the local device. Applications can, of course, store data on the device in their own private stores, but they can also access and interface with other applications on the handheld. These include the pre-installed applications such as messages, address book, and calendar that come with the handheld.

- Cameras are nearly ubiquitous on smartphones and can be accessed by an application as well.

- Many newer devices include removable memory card slots for storage of large media files. Applications can access this storage as well to give applications with large storage needs the room to work.

- Another feature that is extremely common on handhelds is a GPS receiver that enables **location-based service** (**LBS**). This is one area that many in the smartphone industry will say holds the most promise for the future.

Two different approaches to application development

If you've visited the BlackBerry Developer website you may have noticed that there are two recommended approaches to developing applications for BlackBerry handhelds—Java Application Development and BlackBerry Web Development. This book is focused on the Java Application Development approach, which is the more versatile of the two, but the other can be very useful in the right situation.

- **Java Application Development approach**: This is the most powerful approach and it creates applications written in Java that are loaded onto and executed on a BlackBerry handheld. They will be the focus of this book and are one of the most common ways to deploy an application. Two different tools exist to support this approach—the BlackBerry **Java Development Environment (JDE)** and the BlackBerry JDE Component Plug-in for Eclipse. Both offer the ability to create full custom applications. The BlackBerry JDE is a custom application written in Java that can be used to develop applications. The latter leverages the Eclipse **Integrated Development Environment (IDE)**, which is a common platform for Java developers.

- **BlackBerry Web Development approach:** It is the other approach that runs completely within the BlackBerry Browser application and can use various standards such as HTML and AJAX. Applications created using the BlackBerry Web Development approach are similar to more common web applications and generally require network connectivity to work. More powerful features, including native API calls, aren't allowed natively but can be made using BlackBerry Widgets. **BlackBerry Widgets** is a separate SDK for creating small applets that can be leveraged by web applications. Overall, this approach can be powerful but it requires network connectivity, which potentially means data charges and/or delays for network communication.

Choosing an SDK version

Before we dive into developing an application we must choose the SDK version to work with. In most environments, this choice is very simple—just choose the most recent version and use that one. Unfortunately, things are not as simple for BlackBerry handhelds. In fact, it's the opposite.

There is a correlation between the handheld **Operating System (OS)** version and the SDK version. Each time a new version of the device OS is released, a new version of the SDK is released to go along with it. As new devices are released and more capabilities are added to them, the OS must grow to take advantage of the new capabilities. Similarly, the SDK must also grow. It makes sense that SDK version 4.2 won't be able to utilize features added in OS version 4.5. The downside to this is that applications written using version 4.5 of the SDK won't run on handhelds with a version 4.2 OS, but the opposite is true. Applications written using 4.2 will run just fine on a handheld running version 4.5 of the OS.

Therefore, choosing the SDK version to work with becomes a matter of choosing the lowest common OS version for the devices you want to support or, more commonly, the features that they support.

While it is possible for a handheld to upgrade the OS from one version to the other it is rarely done and should never be assumed. Also, unfortunately, this can mean multiple code bases if you wish to support each device in a way that is specific to that device. It all depends on the application you want to write.

For the majority of the applications that we will make we will be using SDK version 4.5 simply because this is the version that comes bundled with Eclipse.

The following table lists devices, the OS version they were released with, and what important features are new to that version:

Device released	SDK version	Features supported
		Initial release
BlackBerry 5810		MIDP 1.0
BlackBerry 5820	3.3	CLDC 1.0
BlackBerry 6200 series		
BlackBerry 6500 series		PIM API
BlackBerry 6700 series	3.6	Mail API
BlackBerry 7200 series		
BlackBerry 7700 series	3.7	Color support
		MIDP 2.0
BlackBerry 7100		CLDC 1.1
BlackBerry 7290	4.0	Invoke
BlackBerry 7510		
BlackBerry 7520	4.0.2	JSR-179 (Location-based services)

Introducing BlackBerry Application Development

Device released	SDK version	Features supported
BlackBerry 8700		
BlackBerry 7130		
BlackBerry 7100i	4.1	Smart Card APIs
		Multimedia Focus
BlackBerry Pearl	4.2	JSR-75 (File APIs)
BlackBerry 8800 series	4.2.1	JSR-82 (Bluetooth)
		JSR-172 (Web services)
BlackBerry Pearl 8110		JSR-205 (Multimedia SMS)
BlackBerry Pearl 8120		JSR-211 (Content Handler API)
BlackBerry Pearl 8130	4.3	JSR-238 (Internationalization)
		Map Field
		Spellcheck
	4.5	HTML e-mail
BlackBerry Curve 8900		
BlackBerry Bold	4.6	JSR-226 (SVG Support)
	4.6.1	Accessibility API
		Touch Screen
BlackBerry Storm	4.7	Accelerometer
BlackBerry Storm 2		Widgets API
BlackBerry Bold 9700	5.0	MIDP 2.1

What you can expect

This book is structured to take you from beginning to end in terms of application development and touch on all the most important topics along the way. You will learn about each aspect of application development from the very basics of simply installing the tools that you will need to the last steps of submitting your application to BlackBerry App World.

We do assume that you are familiar with an object-oriented programming language already. Syntactically and conceptually, Java is very similar to C# and even C++, so someone experienced in either of these languages should be able to make the transition to Java quickly.

This book starts at the very beginning with downloading and installing the tools necessary to start creating an application. This isn't quite as simple as performing a single install, but it's not too complex either.

In the next few chapters, we'll dive right in by loading and compiling one of the demo applications that comes with the tools. This gives you an opportunity to get more familiar with the development environment and by examining the typical "Hello World!" application in detail.

Then we start from scratch with a brand new empty project and create an application. This simple application is both very functional and very polished, which demonstrates how you can create applications quickly by leveraging the framework provided in the SDK.

We will look at this framework in detail by thoroughly examining all of the screen components available to you and by covering when each screen element is best employed. Many of these screen elements are common among all development languages and platforms, but many have behavior that is unique to BlackBerry and warrant the extra attention.

Once we have the screen elements well understood, it's time to branch out into other areas of the system and data storage is one of the most important areas to understand. One of the chapters focuses exclusively on data storage using each of the methods that are available for storing data on a handheld.

One thing that really makes developing for BlackBerry exciting is the ability to integrate with and leverage the existing applications that are present on every BlackBerry handheld. We will look at how to do this more closely, but this is an area so large that one chapter just isn't enough to do it justice. You will be well on your way by the end of it though!

Probably the most complicated and difficult area of the BlackBerry SDK is networking. We will tackle this topic head-on, giving both practical advice and examples for how to create networked applications.

We will also focus on a couple of areas that are interesting, but which aren't as applicable to some applications. The GPS receiver that is included in many new models of BlackBerry devices is one such area. Although both neat and powerful, not all applications can utilize this feature. The other area covered is truly an advanced topic called **alternate entry point applications**. These have many powerful uses though, one of which is demonstrated for a trivial but common effect that makes your application feel polished and professional.

Our next focus will be on getting your application ready for deployment by covering a number of topics such as localizing and code signing your application. As a final word, we look at what is needed to submit your application to the BlackBerry App World so that it can easily be used by the millions of BlackBerry users world-wide!

Introducing BlackBerry Application Development

Summary

In this chapter, we covered some introductory topics about creating applications for BlackBerry handhelds in general. These will be the foundation as we move deeper into the topic on creating applications.

Specifically, we covered:

- Even though there are multiple tools available, this book will focus on using Eclipse, which is both the most popular and the most powerful of the available tools.
- You must choose the development environment and SDK to use based on the capabilities you need and the devices you want to support.
- How this book is organized in steps that mimic the steps you will take when creating applications. You can follow these steps from the most basic of setting up the tools in Chapter 2 to the final steps before releasing an application in Chapter 11.

Now that we've covered some introductory topics, let's get started with installing the tools we need to use. The next chapter covers installing the tools and making sure they are configured correctly.

2
Installing the Development Environment

Every development task begins with setting up an environment with the right tools for creating applications. As we discussed in the previous chapter, this book will focus on the Java Development approach and this chapter will help you to get that environment set up.

In this chapter, we shall:

- Reveal that there are two different development environments, both of which can be used to create BlackBerry applications
- Install the Java SDK (which is the foundation) for using the development environment
- Install Eclipse with the BlackBerry Component Package
- Configure Eclipse with other Component Package versions

I can tell that you are ready to get on with it, so let's go!

System requirements

Even though most of the tools we will be using are written in Java, and the language we are using is Java, the system requirements still say that a Windows system is needed. This is because not ALL of the tools are written in Java and are therefore not portable. Specifically, the **Simulators**, which are an integral part of developing an application, are not portable and are Windows specific. We require:

- Windows 2000 SP1, Windows XP, or Windows Vista
- 512MB of RAM
- 500MB of disk space
- Java v6 update 16 (32-bit) (older versions of the JDE may work with older JDK versions, but it is best to get the latest version)

Development Environments

The title of this chapter is a little misleading because there isn't just one **Integrated Development Environment (IDE)**, there are in fact two. They are both fully functional and either one can be used to create applications.

The first and original option is called the BlackBerry Java Development Environment or JDE for short. The JDE is a custom development environment created by RIM for the sole purpose of developing applications in Java for BlackBerry handhelds. This customized nature is both good and bad. On the one hand, you have an environment where you can do everything you need to do, and nothing more, which can lead to a concise and simple environment. On the other hand, simplicity also means lack of power, and some users may find this to be frustrating.

The second option is to use the BlackBerry Eclipse plugin. **Eclipse** is an open source IDE that has become the de facto industry standard for Java development. There is a large maintenance team and new features are added to it regularly. The open source nature of it means that the program is largely stable and bug free. However, because it can be used for a wide variety of projects, there are tools and other capabilities that won't be used when working on BlackBerry projects, and this can lead to confusion.

For this book though, we will focus on developing applications using the BlackBerry Eclipse plugin. Because Eclipse is a more common platform, getting help and support should be easier if there are problems. Eclipse is faster, more responsive, and offers more features. Developers with Java experience are more likely to have already used it and this helps to get started quickly.

Downloading and installing Java

Java is required to run both Eclipse and the JDE because they are written using Java. This is handled by the **Java Runtime Environment (JRE)**, but we also need another important component. Compiling the applications that we will be making is handled by the **Java Development Kit (JDK)**, so we also need to make sure that this is installed. Fortunately, we don't have to install two separate packages; the JDK installer also includes the JRE, which makes things a little bit easier.

As you can see, the first order of business is to download and install the latest Java JDK, if it isn't already installed.

> The latest BlackBerry SDK only requires Java 6 Update 16. However, it is always best to install the latest version. All updates in the Java 6 family should be backward compatible.

Time for action – downloading the Java Development Kit

1. There are many versions of Java, and if you are unfamiliar with the various flavors, this can be confusing. To be more specific, you need to download and install the Java SE SDK without any other bundles. You will need version 6 Update 20, which is the latest version at the time of this writing. The latest versions can be found at http://java.sun.com/javase/downloads/.

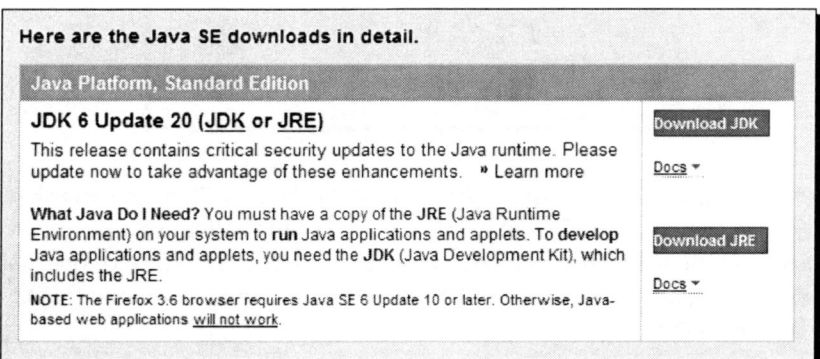

2. The next step is to select which version of the JDK is to be downloaded. The drop list offers choices for many common systems and environments. You want to make sure to select the "Windows" version. You must also check the **I agree** checkbox before continuing.

Installing the Development Environment

 You may be tempted to select the **Windows x64** option if you are running Windows Vista x64 or Windows 7 x64. The BlackBerry SDK does not support 64-bit operating systems, so even if you have a 64-bit operating system, select the standard Windows 32-bit version. You can do development on 64-bit versions of Windows, but the SDK will operate in 32-bit compatibility mode.

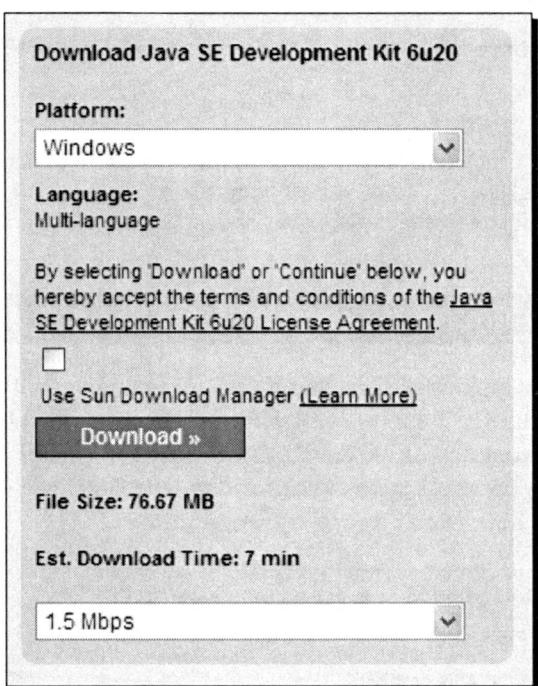

3. Upon clicking the **Download** button, a browser dialog will be shown asking you to log into a Sun Online Account. This step isn't required and even though it says **Optional** in the title bar, the **>>Skip this Step** link at the bottom of the dialog is easy to miss. You can create an account if you like, but there are no drawbacks to skipping the process either.

Chapter 2

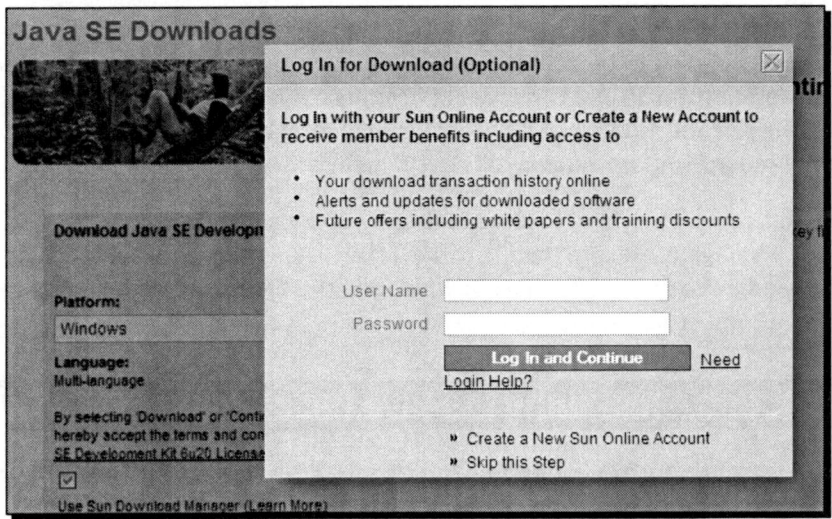

4. The next page gives you the actual download links to begin the download process. You can click on the link `jdk-6u20-windows-i586.exe` and download it directly using your browser, or you can check the checkbox and click on the red **Download Selected with Sun Download Manager** button. Using the download manager will allow you to pause and resume a download in process.

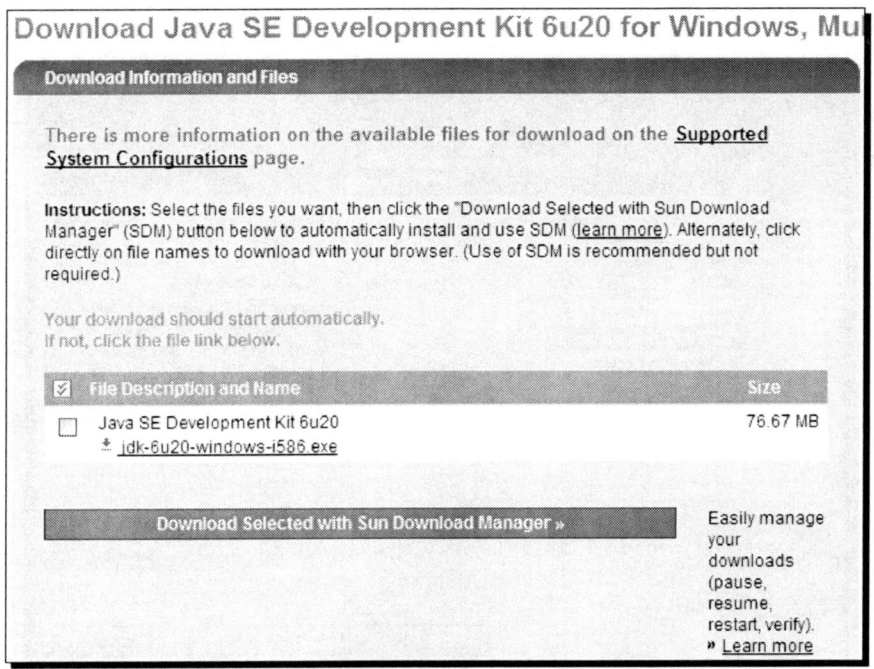

Installing the Development Environment

What just happened?

Obviously, if you are going to be doing Java development, then you need the proper software installed to compile and run Java applications. This process can be surprisingly confusing because of the number of different install packages that are available. You need the basic (or Standard Edition) version of the JDK in order to accomplish your goals.

Once the file has completed downloading (either by doing a standard download or using the Sun Download Manager), execute the file to start the installation. In either case, navigate a File Explorer window to the location you downloaded the file to and double-click on the file `jdk-6u20-windows-i586.exe`.

Time for action – installing the Java Development Kit (JDK)

1. The installation starts off with the End User License Agreement for the Java Development Kit. If you enjoy reading legalese, feel free to read through it, but if you are like most people, just click on the **Accept** button and go on.

2. The next screen shows several components that could be installed. All of the components are enabled by default, but you really need only the public JRE and the **Development Tools**. The **Source Code** can help with debugging at times, but in all honesty you probably won't ever use it. **Demos** and **Samples** can be helpful for understanding Java in general, but won't have any of the BlackBerry-specific topics in it. The **Java DB** definitely won't be used on any BlackBerry applications.

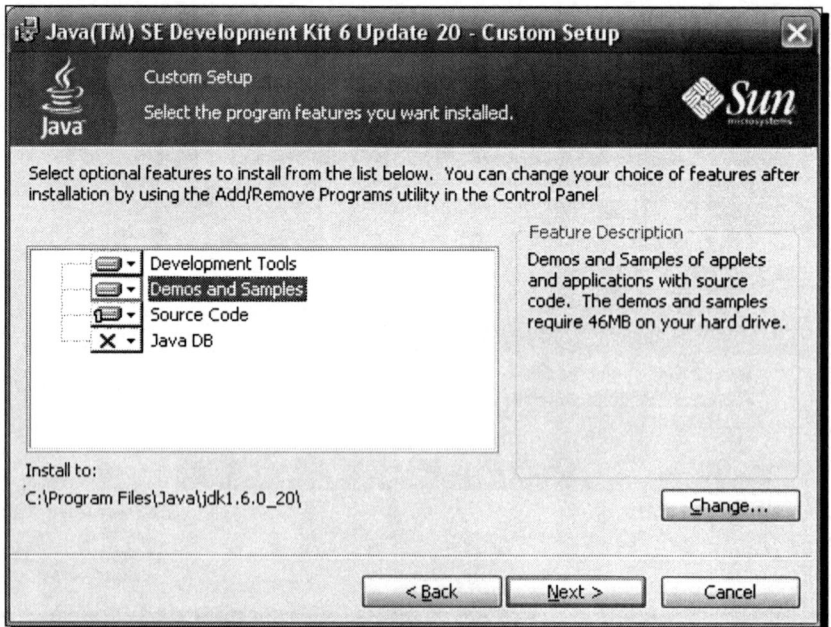

3. After this, the setup program does a lot of work before stopping at another screen asking where to put the install files. I recommend accepting the defaults.

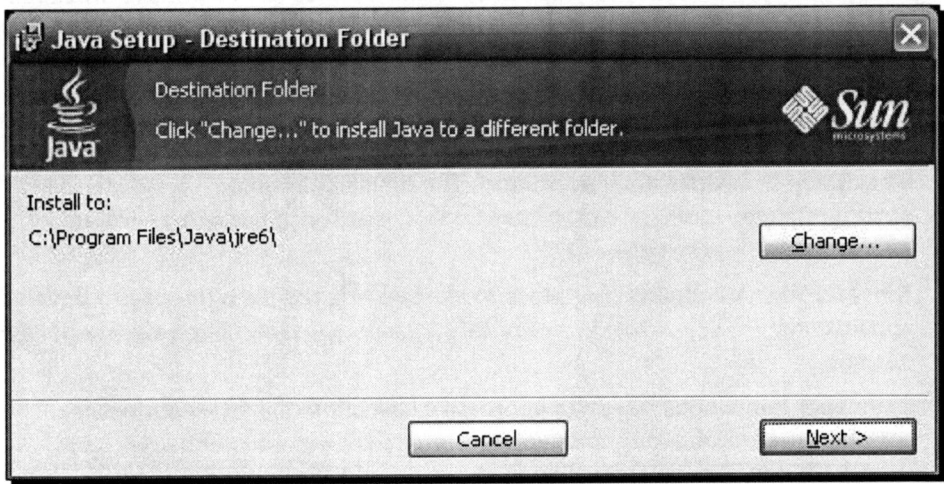

4. This package is also installing the JRE, which does integrate with browsers, so you might get a warning screen if you have the browser window still open from where you downloaded the JDK. If this is the case, exit this, or any other applications listed, and continue with the setup. If you check the checkbox, the setup program will shut the applications down for you.

5. From this point on, the installer does its thing and finishes the install. Look Microsoft, no reboot required!

What just happened?

In this step we installed the **Java Development Kit** (**JDK**). The JDK is used for all Java development, but an essential part of the BlackBerry development environment includes the Java compiler. This particular package that we picked will also install the **Java Runtime Edition (JRE)**. The JRE is required to run any Java application and includes the **Java Virtual Machine (JVM)**, or runtime engine.

Introducing the BlackBerry Developer Zone

Before getting focused on creating applications, I think it's wise to present the official source for information, support, downloads, and forums for BlackBerry—the BlackBerry Developer Zone at http://www.blackberrydeveloper.com. Here you can find the official documentation, a knowledge base full of great articles, support forums, and much more. Specifically, here are some great resources to go for more information in the future:

- **BlackBerry developer documentation**: The official source for documentation—http://na.blackberry.com/eng/support/docs/developers/?userType=21.

- **Tool and SDK downloads**: The place to start getting the tools needed to develop applications—http://na.blackberry.com/eng/developers/resources/devtools.jsp.

- **Developer knowledge base**: An impressive collection of articles addressing specific issues, problems and situations—http://www.blackberry.com/knowledgecenterpublic/livelink.exe/fetch/2000/348583/customview.html?func=ll&objId=348583.

- **Developer forums**: Can't find an answer anywhere else? Ask the question here—http://supportforums.blackberry.com/rim/?category.id=BlackBerryDevelopment.

You will need to register for the BlackBerry Developer Community in order to download any of the tools, SDK, simulators, or in some cases, documentation. So, let's head over to https://www.blackberry.com/CorpDevZone/register.do and get that done. Registration is free.

Register for access to the BlackBerry Developer Community

Please enter your information below to register for the BlackBerry Developer Community.

The information you provide may be used by Research In Motion Limited (RIM) and/or RIM's authorized business partners to send you relevant information related to BlackBerry and/or RIM. Research in Motion is committed to maintaining your privacy. For more information please see our Privacy Policy.

✣ indicates a required field.

- ✣ First Name:
- ✣ Last Name:
- ✣ Company:
- ✣ City:
- ✣ State/Province:
- ✣ Country: Select an option
- ✣ Email Address:
- ✣ Password:
- ✣ Re-enter Password:
- ✣ Would you like to sign up for the Developer Newsletter?
  ○ Yes ● No

[Register]

The registration process is typical and straightforward. The e-mail address you give on this page will serve as your login ID at the website from this point forward. After supplying the information on the registration page, the system will send an e-mail to the e-mail address given with a link that you must click on to activate your account.

The e-mail should arrive quickly, and once you click on the link to activate your account you're ready to actually download the files and get started!

Downloading and installing Eclipse

Now that you've got Java installed, let's start installing Eclipse! There are two different ways to install the software. You can download Eclipse directly from the Eclipse website at `http://www.eclipse.org/downloads/packages/release/ganymede/sr2` or you can download a version from the BlackBerry Developer Zone, which is already pre-bundled with the BlackBerry JDE component plugin. You can download it from `http://na.blackberry.com/eng/developers/javaappdev/javaeclipseplug.jsp`.

Installing the Development Environment

I recommend using the pre-bundled version of Eclipse. This pre-bundled version includes version 4.5 of the SDK, but more importantly it is much easier to install than installing Eclipse and the component pack separately.

Time for action – downloading Eclipse with the JDE plugin

1. On the BlackBerry website the pre-bundled version is called the **Full Installer** and has a large **Download Now** button, as shown in the following screenshot. Click on the **Download Now** button to get started.

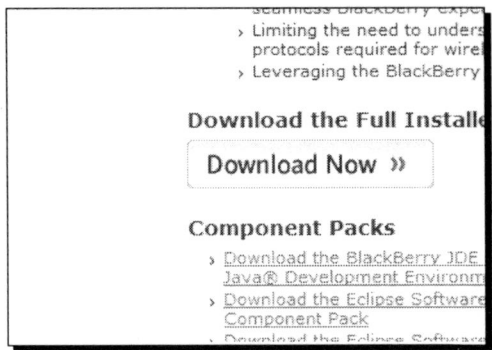

2. When you click on the **Download Now** button, you will be shown another registration page. I know you already filled out all of that information, but you have to do it again, and again, and again. It's rather annoying really. Be sure to change the radio button at the bottom confirming that you are not lying to them because it defaults to **No** and won't proceed until changed to **Yes**.

[Screenshot of a registration form with fields: First Name: Bill, Last Name: Foust, Job Title, Company, Address 1, Address 2, City, Country: United States of America, State/Prov: Select an option, Email: BillFoust@rimdev.com, Update my profile checkbox, confirmation (No selected), marketing preferences (No), and BlackBerry Connection Newsletter signup (No).]

3. Next, you will find one or two license agreements that you must accept (depends on which version you download). After all that, you can finally download the setup file.

What just happened?

The Eclipse Full Installer includes both the BlackBerry 4.5 components as well as the Eclipse installation already integrated together. We chose to install the Full Installer.

Notice that you can download just the individual component package for each version of the BlackBerry SDK from here as well. You don't need to install Eclipse over and over for each different version of the SDK. Instead, you can download just the component pack for only that version and add the component pack to your Eclipse installation.

Installing the Development Environment

There is a way to download and install the component packs directly within Eclipse (which I think is easier), but we will do that later.

Time for action – installing the JDE plugin for Eclipse Full installer

1. Once the download is complete, begin the installation by running the setup program. As is typical with install programs, the first dialog in the setup program is a simple welcome screen reminding you what you are about to install. It is worth noting that this screen reminds you that you will need administrator privileges in order to install it. Click on the **Next** button to get started.

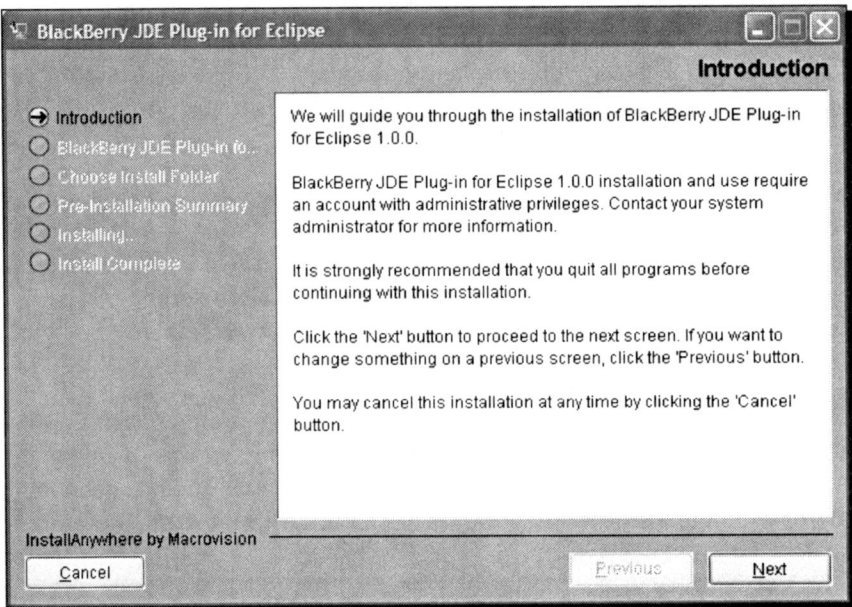

2. The next screen is the license agreement that you must accept. Like everyone else in the world, just accept the terms and move on. Click on the **Next** button after selecting the **Accept** radio button.

3. Following the "License Agreement" dialog is an "Install Location" dialog. I recommend using the defaults, but there will always be one person in the crowd who wants to do things differently. That's OK. That's what this page is for. You will need to come back to this location though, so be sure to remember it. Click on the **Next** button when you are done.

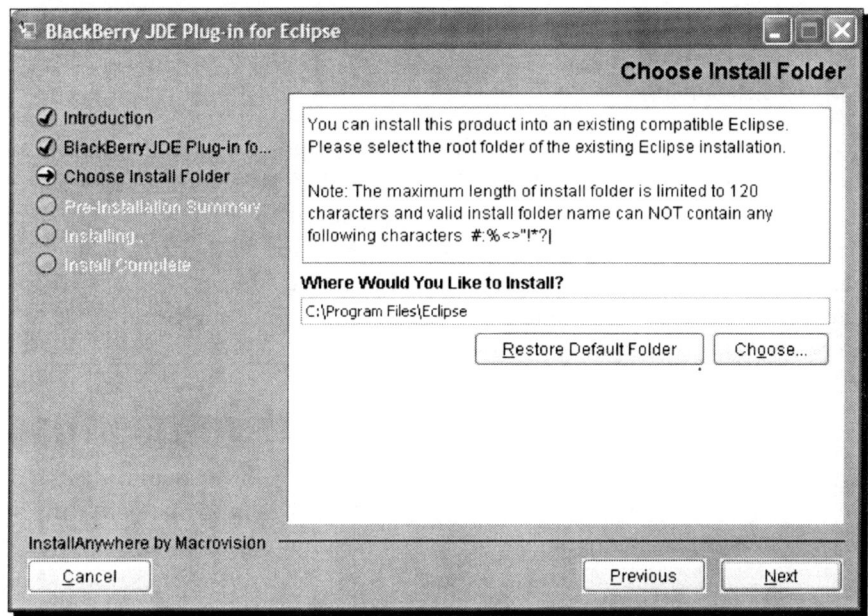

4. Proceed to the next screen that shows the "Confirmation" dialog. Check it over and make sure you didn't make a mistake somewhere along the way before clicking on **Next** to begin the installation.

5. At this point, the setup program will install Eclipse into the directory you provided. When it is done, a final "Confirmation" dialog is shown. Click on **Finish** to dismiss it.

What just happened?

Installing Eclipse with the JDE plugin is easier than installing Eclipse directly and then installing the proper component pack and so is the best way to get started quickly. You will need to install other component packs with other versions of the SDK at some point in the future, but for now we will focus on using version 4.5.

Installing other JDE component package versions

Now that you have Eclipse installed you may want to install other JDE Component packages as well. Remember, the full-package installer contains the JDE Component Package version 4.5, but also remember that you need to choose the version of the SDK based on the devices that you want to support, and version 4.5 might not be the one you need.

With the JDE there is no choice; you must install another JDE instance for each version of the SDK. The majority of the JDE is unchanged between versions, but the JDE itself is tightly coupled with the SDK version.

Eclipse is not this way. You can have one installation of Eclipse and install several BlackBerry JDE component packages—one for each version of the BlackBerry SDK. A workspace can use only one component package at a time, but switching between them is not very hard. The nice thing is that you can download them to install later or install them using an on-the-fly download and install. The following screenshot shows that there are several component packs available for download on the BlackBerry Developer Zone website.

Component Packs

- Download the BlackBerry JDE Plug-in for Eclipse v1.0 with the BlackBerry® Java® Development Environment (BlackBerry JDE) v4.5 Component Pack
- Download the Eclipse Software Update for the BlackBerry JDE v4.2.1 Component Pack
- Download the Eclipse Software Update for the BlackBerry JDE v4.3 Component Pack
- Download the Eclipse Software Update for the BlackBerry JDE v4.5 Component Pack
- Download the Eclipse Software Update for the BlackBerry JDE v4.6 Component Pack
- Download the Eclipse Software Update for the BlackBerry JDE v4.6.1 Component Pack
- Download the Eclipse Software Update for the BlackBerry JDE v4.7 Component Pack

Time for action – installing other JDE component packages over-the-air

1. Whether you want to install from a pre-downloaded package or use the over-the-air installer, you must use a wizard in Eclipse to do it. So to get started, launch Eclipse and navigate to **Help | Software Updates...**.

Chapter 2

2. The first tab of this dialog shows all of the component packages that are installed in Eclipse currently. The second tab, the **Available Software** tab, is where you go to add new component packages.

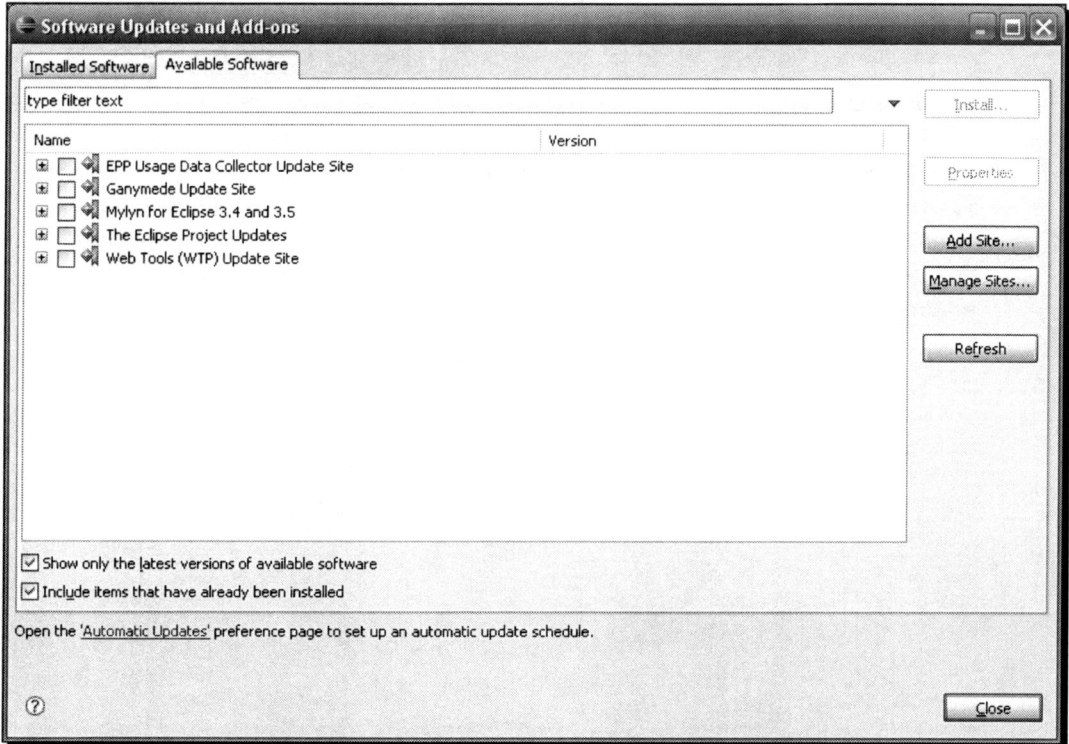

Installing the Development Environment

3. The provided list has a few packages that they think you might be interested in, but BlackBerry is not part of that list. Click on the **Add Site** button to add the site for BlackBerry updates manually. If you would like to use the on-the-fly installer enter the URL `http://www.blackberry.com/go/eclipseUpdate` into the **Location** field in the dialog. Note the **capitalized U** in **Update!** Using this site you can download all versions of the Eclipse plugin component packages, which can be very handy. Click on **OK** to return to the **Software Updates** dialog.

>  Note: The `BlackBerry.com` documentation indicates that this download link works only in North America. I don't know if this is true or not, so be warned that your mileage may vary.

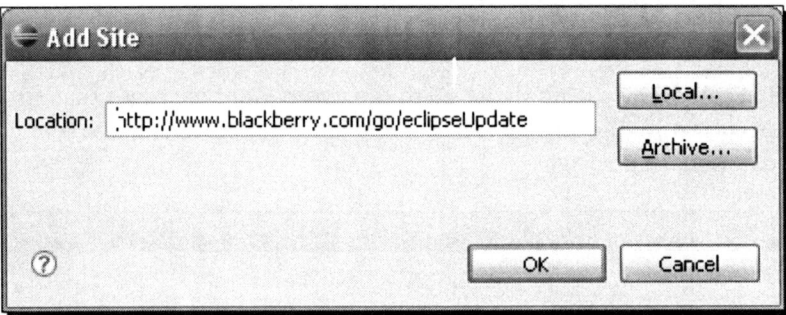

4. Now you can see that BlackBerry is in the list of **Available Software**. Also note that even though version 4.5 of the component package is already installed, it is still available in the list. To hide the components that are already installed, uncheck the checkbox at the bottom of the dialog labeled **Include items that have already been installed**.

Chapter 2

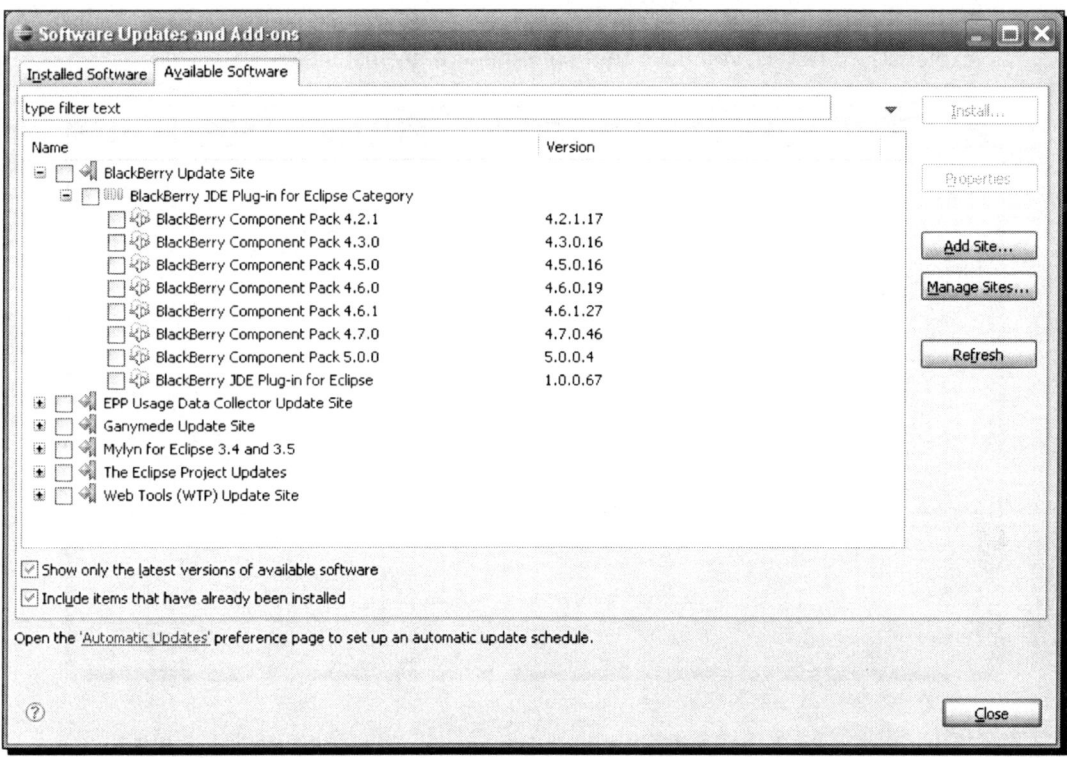

5. If you do happen to select a package that is already installed, it will show this "Confusing" dialog.

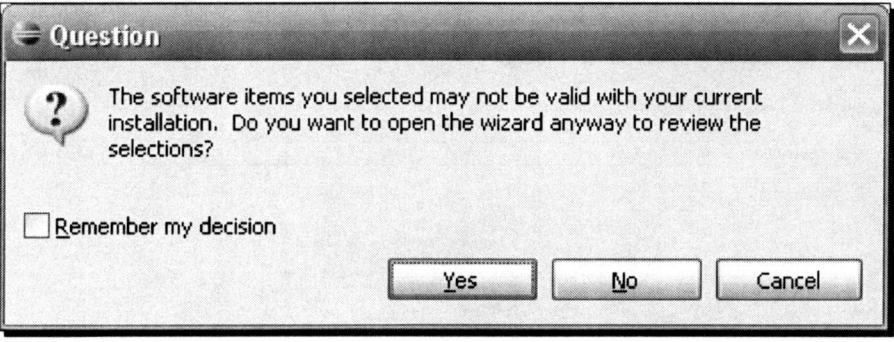

Installing the Development Environment

6. But, after clicking on the **Yes** button, you get another dialog with a better explanation. That is, you have that package already installed.

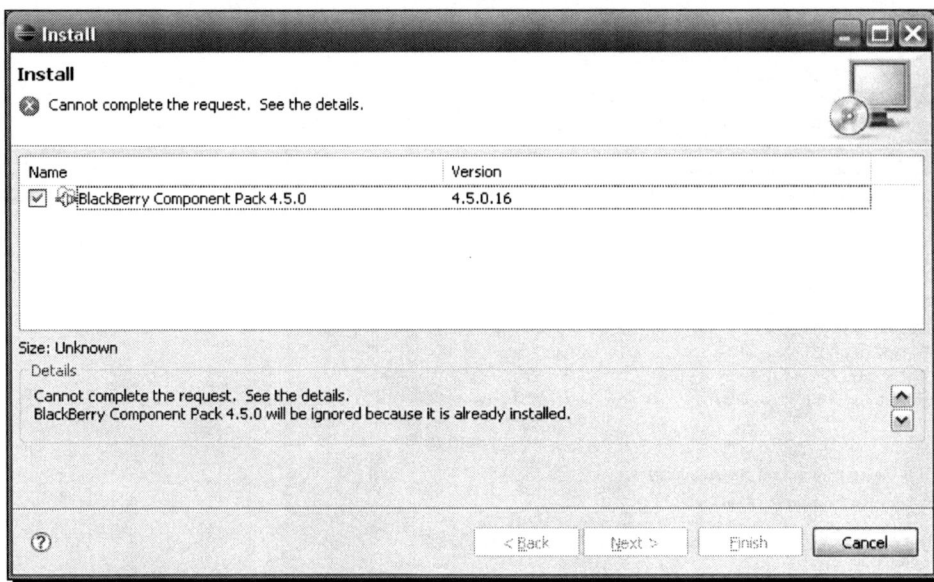

7. If the package is not already installed, Eclipse will do some thinking about the size and space requirements and then present a "Confirmation" dialog before continuing with the installation.

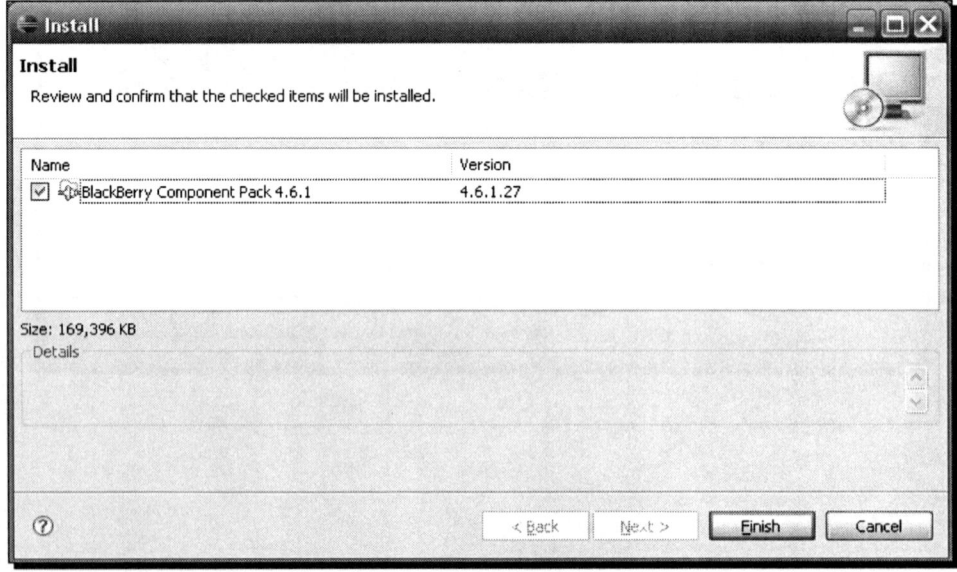

Chapter 2

8. In order to download the component package directly from the website, you must be registered with the BlackBerry Developer Zone. Downloading the software through Eclipse is no different. You must log in using your Developer Zone ID and password.

9. Once this is successful, the installation will continue without bugging you anymore. You can click on **<<Details** to see the progress or click on the **Run in Background** button to hide the dialog entirely and finish the installation in the background.

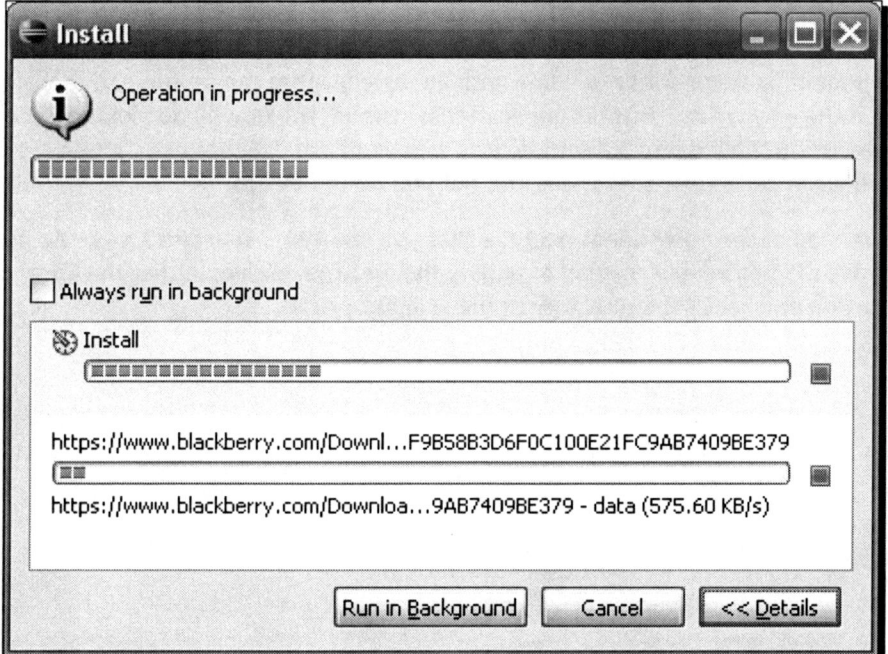

Installing the Development Environment

10. When the installation is completed, a dialog is shown advising you that Eclipse should be restarted for the changes to take effect.

What just happened?

We demonstrated installing other component packages using the over-the-air install approach. Using this approach, there is no need to download the files and run a setup program in two different steps. Of course, you can install the JDE component packs that way if you want to, but we won't cover how to do it at this time.

Installing over the air is the cleanest way to install new SDK versions, but there can be problems that may be simplified by installing the package separately. For instance, there is a network connection involved that could pose problems. Also, the login dialog doesn't give any feedback about whether there are problems or not, so it is easy to be unsure whether you entered the login correctly or if there are other networking issues going on.

I'd like to say that I've never had problems using this feature, but I can't. I find it best to log into the BlackBerry Developer zone in a separate browser window just so that I have my login and password fresh in my mind.

If you do decide to download and install the JDE Component package rather than use the over-the-air installer, you follow many of the same steps we did for installing it over-the-air.

Each component package does not come with an installer that can be run and therefore can't be installed the way we do for most applications. Instead, the download yields a ZIP archive file. You can unzip the file into a directory (say as part of the `C:\Program Files\Eclipse` tree where we installed everything before), but you don't have to.

For each version of the component package that you want to install add a new site in the same way we did before, but instead of adding the website, click on either the **Local** or the **Archive** button and select the directory or file as appropriate.

If you unzipped the file into a directory, click on the **Local** button and select that directory. If you want to use the archive directly, click on the **Archive** button and select the .zip file that was downloaded.

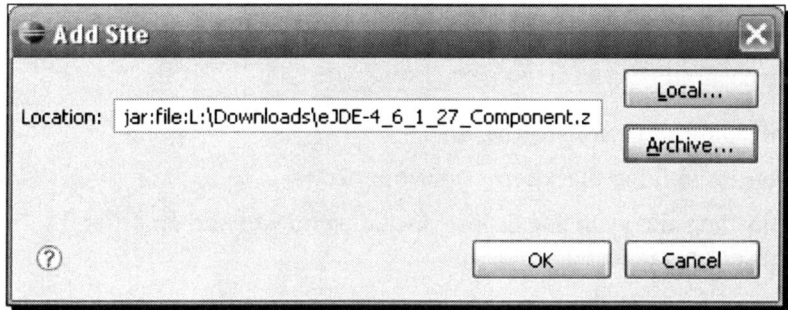

From this point, the installation steps are the same with one exception. A login is no longer required because you have already done a login in order to download the file.

This process is also quicker because there are no delays, as all of the files are already on the local drive and don't need to be downloaded.

Have a go hero – installing other versions of the SDK

We've just covered how to install another version of the SDK, but you can use these same steps to install any version. It can't hurt to have many different versions installed so why not take this opportunity to install other versions of the SDK. We will need version 4.2.1 in Chapter 4, so go ahead and install that version now.

Pop quiz

1. The Java package we installed really installed two different packages, both of which are needed. What are they?
    a. Java SE and Java EE
    b. JDK and JRE
    c. JVM and JRE
    d. Java ME and Java SE

2. We've been working with Eclipse so far, but there is another development environment available. What is it?
    a. Visual Studio
    b. Java Development Environment (JDE)
    c. BlackBerry IDE

Summary

This chapter was devoted to learning how to set up and install the development environment used in creating BlackBerry applications. Even though there is more than one available, we've focused on using Eclipse as the tool of choice for this book.

Specifically, we covered:

- Downloading and installing the JDK
- Registering with the BlackBerry Developer Zone
- Downloading and installing Eclipse, including how to add on other component packages

Now that we've gotten the necessary software installed, we can get started with looking at some code and getting familiar with using Eclipse. The first part of the next chapter covers the basics of using Eclipse and then dives right into an actual application by importing, compiling, and debugging one of the sample applications that comes with the SDK. This simple "Hello World" application is then dissected and explained practically line-by-line.

3
Getting Familiar with the Development Environment

Now that you've gotten the development environment installed, jump right in and run one of the samples. When you are done you should be able to start up the development environment, open a project, and compile it.

In this chapter, we shall:

- Launch the development environment
- Import the existing `HelloWorldDemo` supplied with the software
- Compile and debug the `HelloWorldDemo` application
- Discuss many of the windows and buttons in the environment and outline what their uses are

Starting the Eclipse IDE

Starting Eclipse isn't like starting most other Windows programs. Even though we used the full installer to install Eclipse, the installer didn't create any program groups or icons on the Windows **Start** menu, so you can't launch it from there like a typical application. Instead, you need to open a Windows Explorer and browse to the installed directory (the default in the setup program was `C:\Program Files\Eclipse`). Once there, double-click the Eclipse program and it will start up.

Getting Familiar with the Development Environment

 Your Explorer preferences may be set up slightly differently than in the following screenshot. The important thing to look for here is the file with the purple globe icon in it. The name may be `Eclipse` or `Eclipse.exe`, again depending on your preferences.

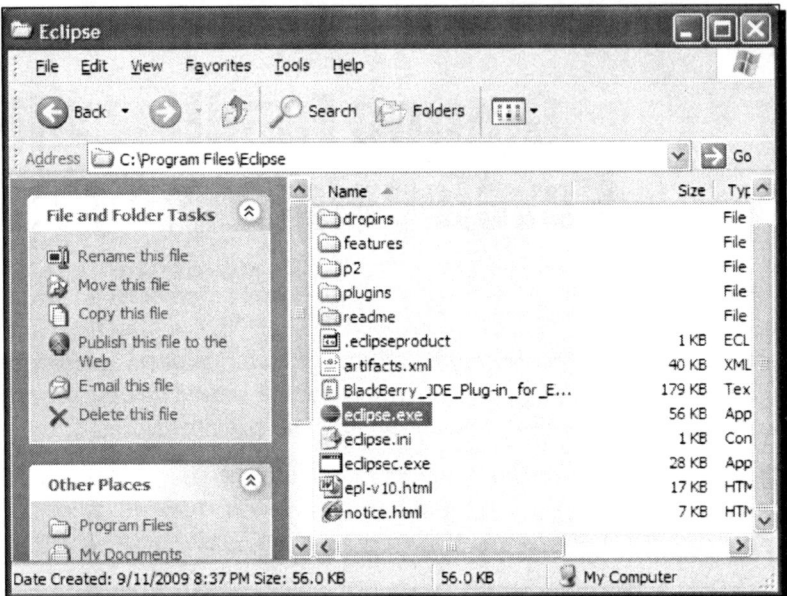

Now, even though you can do this each time, it is somewhat of a pain to do. There are a couple of different approaches that you can take to make this easier. You could make a program group on the **Start** menu and place a shortcut to Eclipse in that group; however, it is a more advanced option. A simpler option is to place a shortcut to Eclipse on the desktop so that next time launching the program is a lot easier.

Like a lot of programs available today, Eclipse has a number of steps that you have to follow the first time you start the application.

Time for action – launching Eclipse for the first time

1. Double-click the Eclipse icon or shortcut.
2. If you installed Eclipse to a location other than the default, or you installed Eclipse by simply downloading it directly, you may get a warning from Windows when running the application. If this happens, click on the **Run** button to continue.

Chapter 3

3. Place a check in the **Use this as the default and do not ask again** checkbox and then click on the **OK** button to accept the default workspace location.

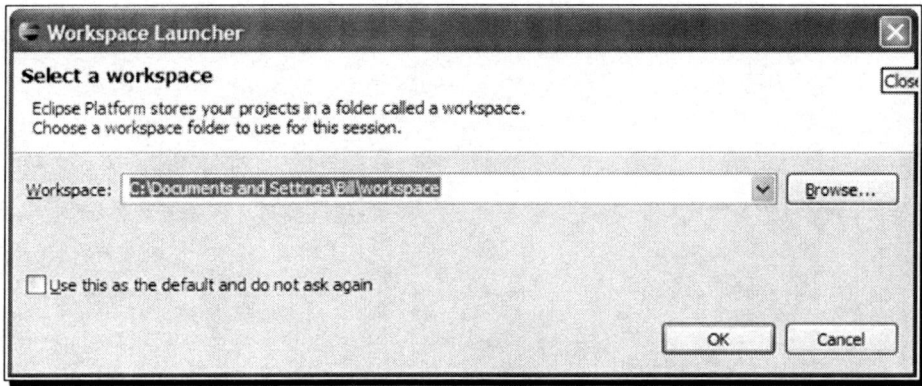

4. The next screen to be shown is a stylish, but not a very useful, welcome screen. The important part of the welcome screen is the workbench icon, shown as a curved arrow icon, located on the right side of the screen. The **workbench** is where you will do all the real work in developing an application. Click on the workbench icon now.

Getting Familiar with the Development Environment

What just happened?

When Eclipse is started for the first time, the "Workspace Launcher" dialog is shown asking what location to use for saving workspace and project files. It suggests a location in your user directory, but you can change this to any directory you wish. There are situations where multiple workspace folders are helpful, but we won't need them for work in this book. The suggested default location is just fine for our purposes.

At the bottom of the dialog is a checkbox allowing you to skip the dialog next time Eclipse is launched and it is a good idea to check that checkbox. You can always open a different workspace later through a menu item.

After getting past the "Workspace Launcher" dialog, you are shown a stylish welcome page. From here you can peruse general help, links, and samples that are pre-installed with Eclipse. Each bubble on the welcome screen represents a different topic. These can be useful for general Java programming, but they are not specific to BlackBerry, so we won't be using any of them.

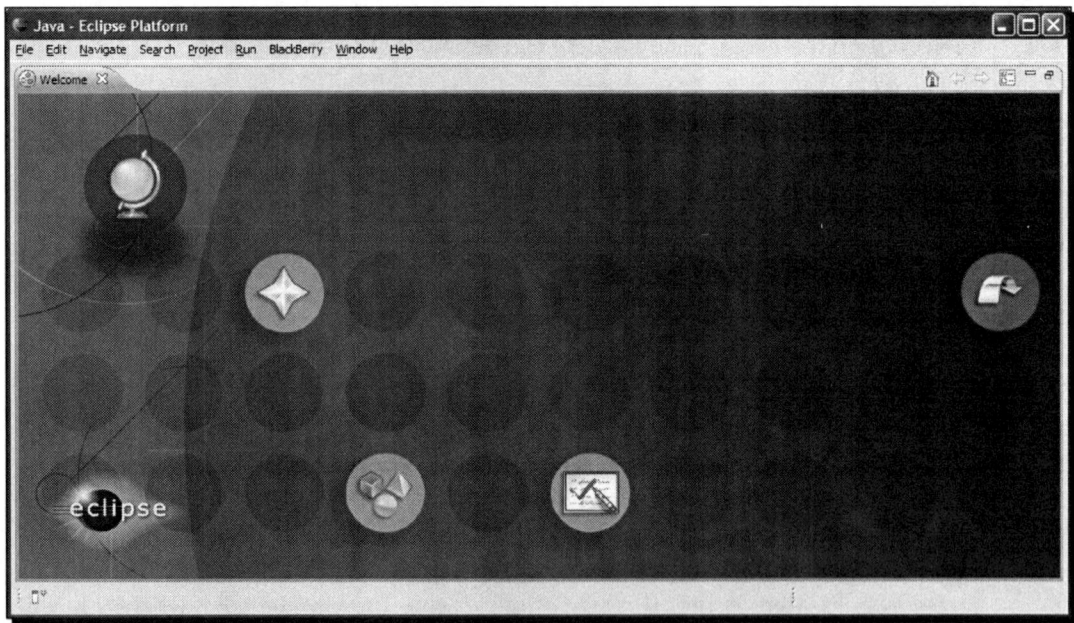

Next time you launch Eclipse, you won't start at this screen, but there are some things that could be useful later, especially if you will be doing Java application development for other platforms. If you want to come back to this screen once you navigate away from it, you can do so by using the 'home' icon in the upper-right portion of the screen.

Once you get past the welcome screen you will see the Eclipse workbench. The workbench should look familiar if you have used other IDEs before—it's filled with lots of toolbars, windows, and other tools that you will use when developing an application.

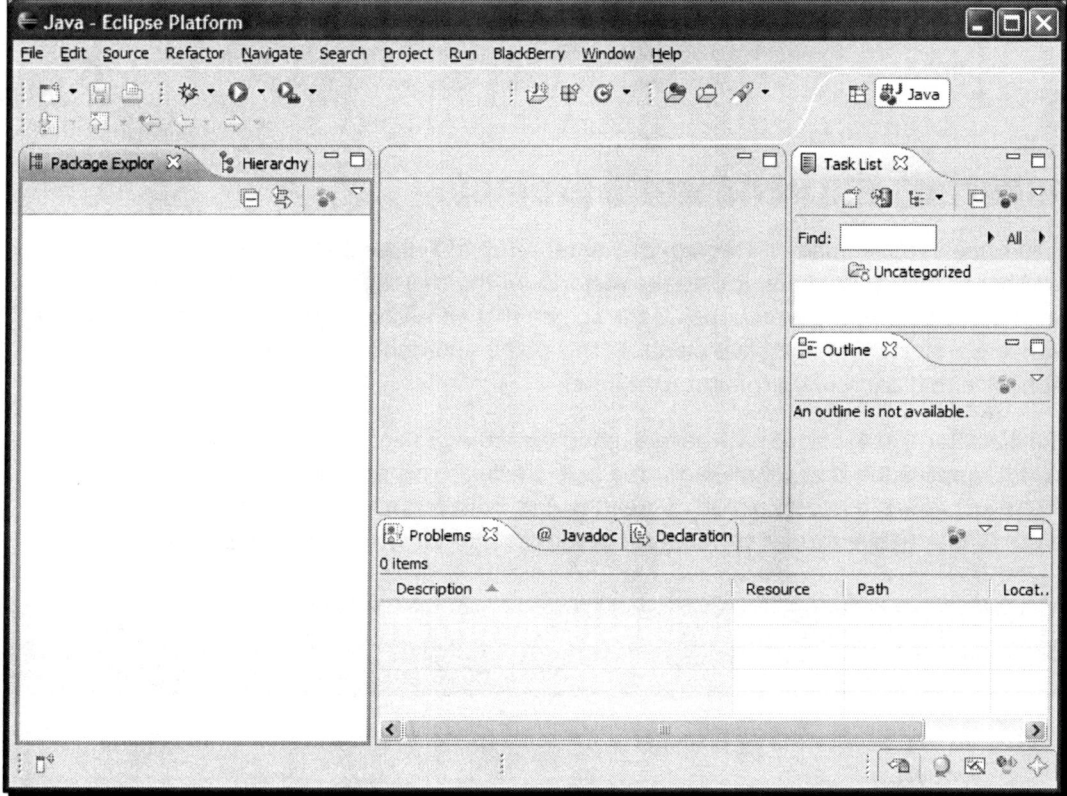

> **A note about workspaces**
>
>
>
> Eclipse uses the concept of a workspace as a way to collect several projects so that they can be worked on together. In a nutshell, a workspace is a container for projects. Many common IDEs also use workspaces or similar concepts. In Microsoft Visual Studio, a solution is a concept equivalent to an Eclipse workspace.
>
> A project is the next level of container. A project contains source files and generates a single compiled output, usually an application. Generally, one workspace is used to hold all of the projects for an organization, even if the projects are not necessarily related.
>
> In Eclipse the workspace is tied to a directory, but in the JDE a workspace is a specific file. Obviously, these two formats are not compatible. Fortunately, there is a tool to import a JDE workspace into an Eclipse workspace, which is what we will do shortly.

Importing the hello world project

At this point you've made it through the initial setup of Eclipse and are looking at the workbench, which is where you do the majority of the real work. When you start Eclipse again in the future, the workbench is the screen that should be shown automatically, along with any projects that you have made. At this point, you don't have any projects open, so let's solve that particular problem right now!

The BlackBerry SDK comes with several good example projects, including the standard "hello world!" application that we all know and love. Because this simple project already exists, you're just going to use it instead of creating one from scratch. These sample projects aren't in the Eclipse native format so you have to import them in by using an **Import wizard**.

Time for action – importing the HelloWorldDemo sample application

1. To import an existing BlackBerry JDE workspace, the first step is to select **File | Import...**.

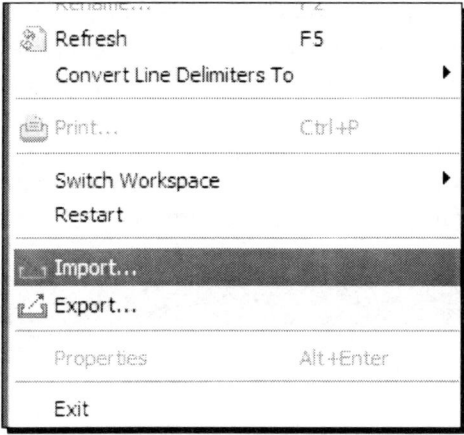

2. This displays the "Import" dialog that displays a collapsed tree with the many different kinds of projects that can be imported, as shown in the next screenshot. Notice the node labeled **BlackBerry** in that tree. Click on the small plus (**+**) sign next to that node and select **Existing BlackBerry Projects into Workspace** and then click on the **Next** button.

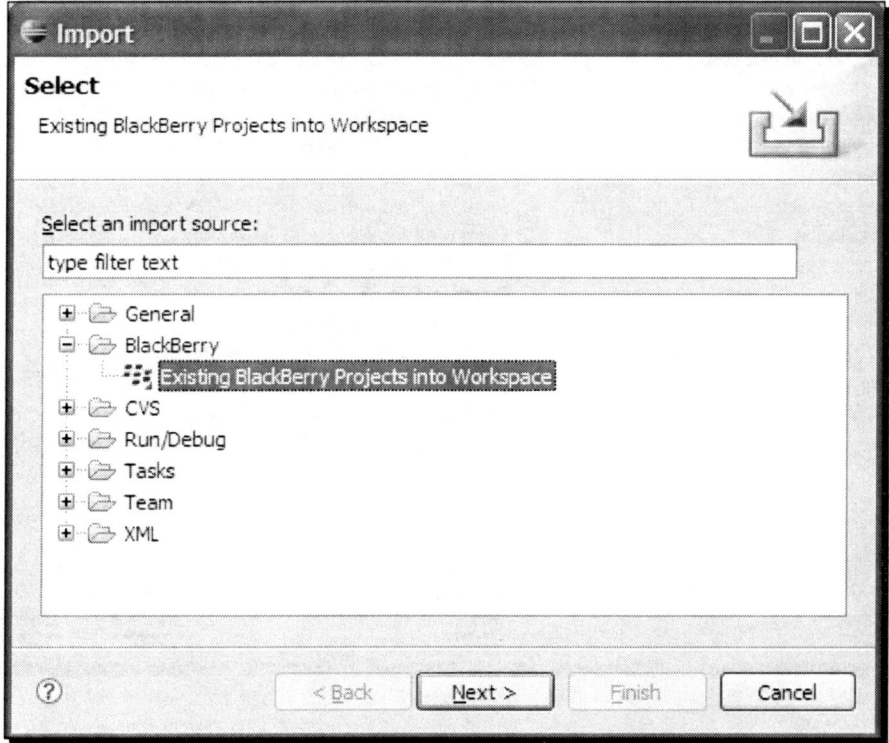

Getting Familiar with the Development Environment

3. The next step is to select the projects to be imported. The dialog is empty initially, but is populated by clicking on the **Browse** button and navigating to the proper directory. If you accepted the defaults when installing Eclipse, the path should be `C:\Program Files\Eclipse\plugins\net.rim.eide.componentpack4.5.0_4.5.0.16\components\samples`. **Navigate there,** click on the **Browse** button, navigate to the `samples` directory, and select `Samples.jdw`. Then, click on the **Open** button.

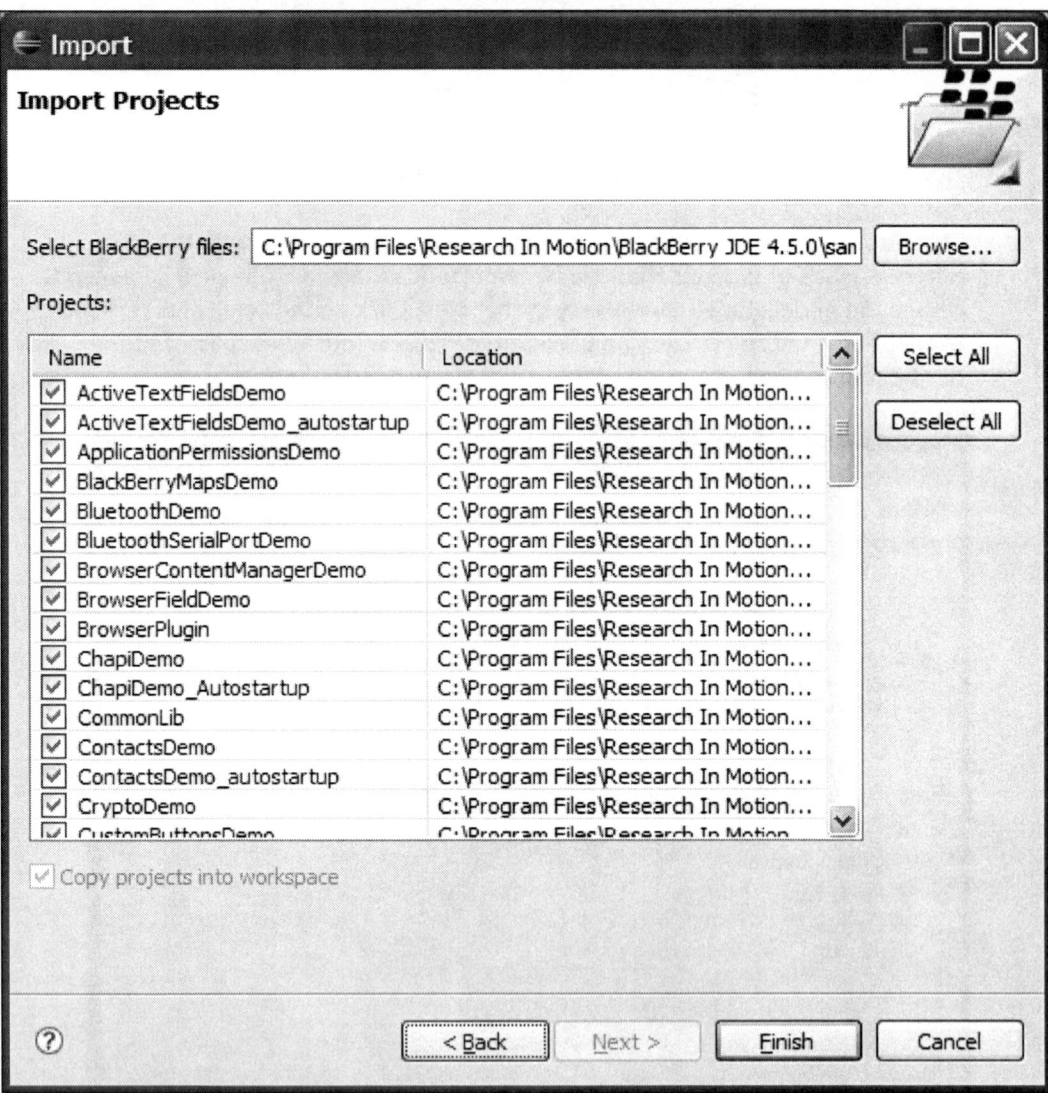

> If an Eclipse project happens to be opened already, a dialog will be shown warning you that the current project will be overwritten.
>
>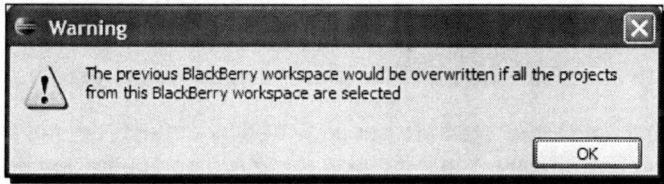

4. As soon as you select **Open** in the browse window the import tool will load the workspace file and all of the projects in that workspace will be shown in the list. By default, all of the projects are selected, but the projects' list allows you to selectively choose which projects to import. The fastest way to select just one project is to click on the **Deselect All** button, scroll to `HelloWorldDemo`, and check the checkbox next to it. Now that you're done with this step, click on the **Finish** button.

5. Whether by design or not, imported projects are not activated automatically. To activate the project, open the **Package Explorer** (if it is not already open) and right-click the `HelloWorldDemo` project. Then, click on the **Activate for BlackBerry** menu item.

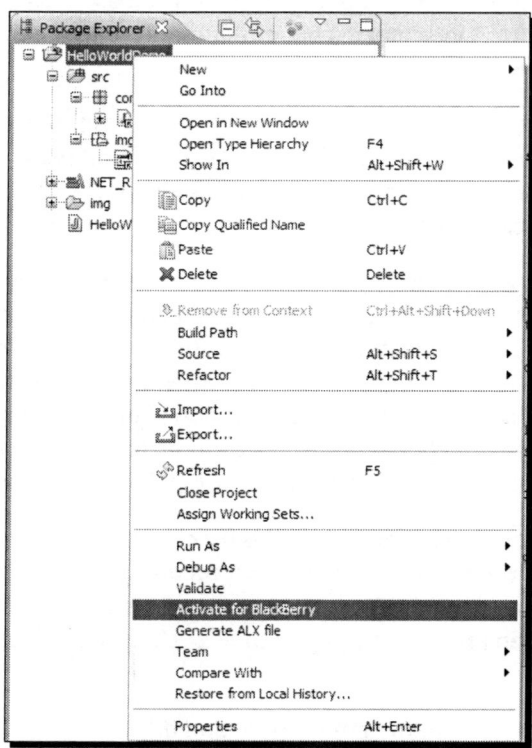

What just happened?

Well, that was exciting wasn't it? At this point you've started up Eclipse and loaded up the `HelloWorldDemo` sample application into Eclipse. To do this you had to import the sample from the JDE-formatted workspace file. Most of the time you won't be importing a project, but working with one of the supplied samples is a good way to get started!

Projects that have been imported are not activated by default. I'm not sure if this is by design or a bug, but the bottom line is that if you want to run an application after importing it you must activate it. If it is not done, the project will not be loaded into the simulator and you will be wondering why your application isn't showing up in the simulator.

If you create a new BlackBerry project instead of importing one, this step is already done for you! However, because we imported the project, we need to activate it before we can use it.

Running the application

Now that you have the project imported, it's time to fire it up and run it in the simulator. The simulator is there to provide a test environment that is pretty close to a real device. Of course, it isn't a real device, but for most applications and most situations it works just fine. The most important feature of the simulator is that you can use it to do debugging line-by-line (if you need to). We'll get into that aspect of it a bit more later on, but for now let's just get the application running.

Working with the simulator is straightforward and is easy to use. Most of the time you will just need to use the keyboard to simulate keystrokes, but if you really want to, you can click on any button on the screen. You can even click and drag the trackball to move it around, but this isn't very efficient most of the time.

Each key on the BlackBerry simulator is mapped to a key on your PC keyboard. Most of those mappings are direct, that is, the *a* key on your PC maps to the *a* key in the simulator (or whatever key the *a* is on, if simulating a SureType style device). Some of the key mappings make sense, such as using the *End* key on your PC to simulate pressing the *Call-end* key. Others have no correlation at all, such as using the *Insert* key on your PC to simulate pressing the *Menu* key on the simulated BlackBerry. While you cannot change these mappings, you can find the mapping for a simulator key by placing your mouse pointer over the key in the simulator.

The BlackBerry simulator is quite thorough in the functionality it provides for simulating a device. A quick view of the menu shows that the simulator has the ability to simulate a phone call, network connectivity, SD cards, as well as holster and battery conditions. In addition, the simulator can provide debugging tools such as displaying the event log and taking screenshots.

Enough overview though, let's jump right in there and do it!

Chapter 3

Time for action – running an application in the simulator

1. The best way to start the simulator and run the application is to click on the **Run** button on the toolbar. This button looks like the standard **Play** button that is commonly used in many IDEs. Of course, you can also use the **Run** menu item, which is found under the **Run** menu. Finally, like all good IDEs, there is a hotkey as well. In this case, pressing *Ctrl + F11* will start the simulator to running.

At this point the BlackBerry simulator is starting up. This should be pretty quick and when it is done you should see a window with the picture of a BlackBerry Curve in it. You can change the device being simulated, but because we are using the BlackBerry 4.5 component pack, the curve simulator is shown by default.

Getting Familiar with the Development Environment

2. Next, you need to find the `HelloWorldDemo` application. Click on the **Menu** button (or press the *Insert* key to simulate that) and use the arrow keys to simulate scrolling the trackball to select the `HelloWorldDemo` icon.

3. Next, press F9 to simulate clicking the trackball to start the application. Pressing the *Enter* key will also start the application, but not because pressing *Enter* simulates clicking the trackball. On a real handheld pressing the *Enter* key will start the selected application because that is specifically handled on the Home Screen. Therefore, in the simulator, pressing *Enter* also works to start the application.

It shouldn't take long for the application to start. When it does, you should see the following screenshot.

4. The `HelloWorldDemo` application has already done all it is intended to do. That task is to display the string **Hello World!**. As there isn't anything more to be done, let's just quit the application. Open the menu (by pressing the *Insert* key or by clicking on the **Menu** button) and select the **Close** menu item by pressing F9, or *Enter*. Now, press *F9* or *Enter* again to dismiss the dialog that is shown.

5. Now, the simulator should be back at the Home Screen just like it was when we started. The last thing to do now is to quit the whole simulator session. Either go to **File | Exit** or simply close the simulator window.

What just happened?

As you can see, using the simulator is both an easy and effective way to see what your application will look like on a device. The keyboard mappings are generally intuitive, but if you forget the ones that aren't, you can always use the mouse to click on the screen and simulate key presses. The simulator can do so much more than just display the application for you.

Many of the features of the device can be controlled using the various menu items that are available at the top of the simulator application. For instance, navigating to **Simulate | Incoming Voice Call** will display a small dialog where you can set information about the incoming call and then actually initiate an incoming call in the simulator. Of course, there is no way to communicate on the call, but this can be used to test how your application might handle being interrupted by an incoming phone call.

Another clever simulation feature is the ability to set the image that the camera will get when a picture is taken. Using **Simulate | Camera Image**, you can browse to and select an image file. Later, when you use the camera within the simulator and press the track wheel to take a picture, the selected image will be displayed.

These are just a couple of the interesting tools that are available for simulating a real device as closely as possible.

Debugging the application

In the last section, we simply ran the application in the simulator and the debugger wasn't involved. Debugging an application is an essential part of the development process in order to find and fix bugs that are an inevitable part of the application development process. Eclipse provides a robust debugging environment with many tools to make it as easy as possible. You've already seen the simulator, which is also integrated into the debug process of Eclipse. With Eclipse and the BlackBerry simulator, you can simulate and debug your application very effectively.

So now, let's see these tools in action. What better way than to actually see a bug in the application. However, as this application is one of the samples and has already been debugged, you will have to introduce a bug to use.

Getting Familiar with the Development Environment

Time for action – starting the debugger

1. As we said before, the first step is to actually introduce a bug. This application is so simple that it was actually hard to decide how best to do this! Simple is always best though, so for this exercise let's add something that is obviously a bug. Passing a null value to the add method will work nicely for this purpose. Add the following code into the constructor of HelloWorldScreen at the end of the method, add(null);

   When you are done, it should look like this:

   ```
   add(new RichTextField("Hello World!" ,Field.NON_FOCUSABLE));
   add(null);
   ```

2. The next step is to start debugging the application. On the toolbar is an icon with a bug-like image on it. You can also start debugging the application by clicking on the **Run** menu item on the **Debug** menu. Click on the **Debug toolbar** button to start debugging the application.

3. When you use Eclipse to debug for the first time, you will see a dialog like the next one asking how you want to debug the application. This dialog is shown only the first time you start the debugger, but you can change it later if need be. We want to use the simulator, so select **BlackBerry Simulator** from the list and click on **OK**.

   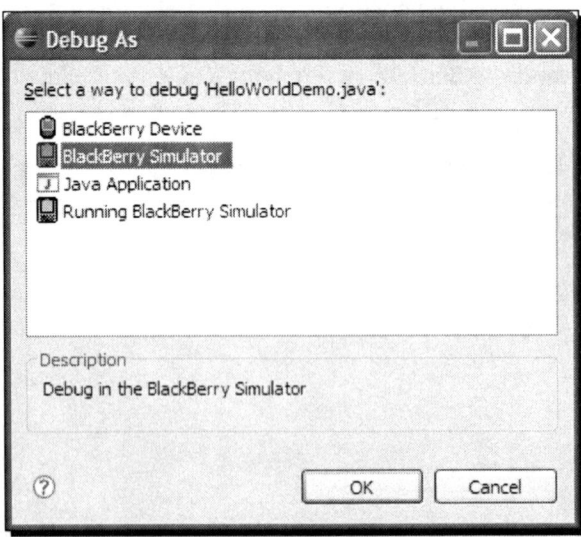

Chapter 3

4. At this point, the debug server is starting and the simulator is getting set up. This process takes a lot more time than just running the simulator by itself. It can take more than a minute to get all set. During this time, the simulator will display a wait screen like the one shown in the following screenshot and will not be usable.

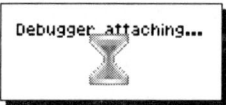

5. Once it is all set up, the simulator will be shown and look the same as it did before.

What just happened?

OK, so now we have the simulator actually running and debugging the `HelloWorldDemo` sample application. To get here we only had to do a couple of things.

After setting things up, we actually launched the simulator and debugger by clicking on the debug icon on the toolbar. You may have noticed that the toolbar icon has a small down arrow next to it. If you click on the arrow, a small menu will be displayed with additional debugging options such as those we also saw in the "Debug As" dialog. We aren't going to use them, so if you accidently click on the arrow, just click on the bug icon or click away to close the menu up.

Before an application can be debugged it must be compiled and built. Like most common IDEs, starting the debugger will automatically build the application if it needs to be done. We did change the code by introducing the bug, but otherwise there shouldn't be any errors so that this build should be quick and event free.

Introducing Eclipse perspectives

Eclipse uses the term **perspective** to mean a saved configuration of views and their placement on the workbench. So far, you've seen only the "Java" perspective that is used when developing applications. This perspective contains things such as a task list, console output, and documentation views, but there is another important perspective that we will encounter next—the **Debug perspective**.

The views in the Java perspective aren't particularly useful when you are debugging an application, so they are hidden and an all new set of windows is displayed once you switch to the Debug perspective. These views include the call stack, variables, and watch windows that are more useful when trying to look at the current state of the running application. Let's take a look at that right now by going back to the simulator and finding that bug we made.

Time for action – changing the perspective

1. After starting the application under the debugger you left the simulator still running and waiting to be used. Go back to the simulator and find the `HelloWorldDemo` application and activate it by pressing the *F9* or *Enter* key.

2. Unlike before, this time you see a new dialog being displayed right away. Generally, you don't want to see this dialog each time so check the **Remember my decision** checkbox and then click on the **Yes** button.

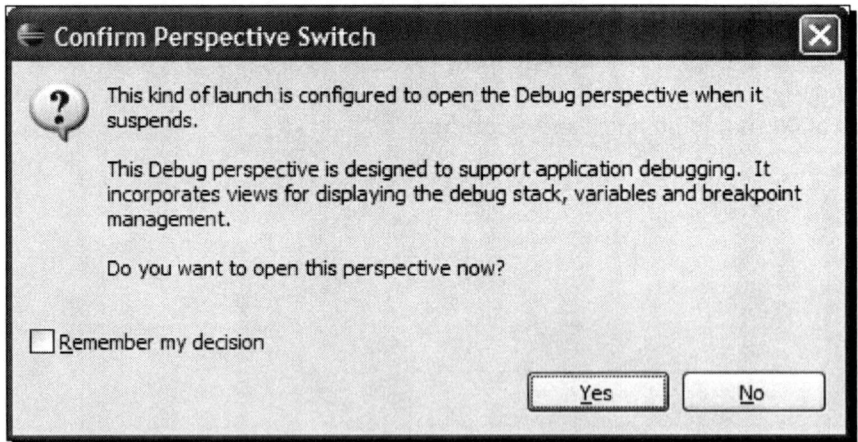

Chapter 3

3. Now, Eclipse looks very different than it did just a moment ago. Eclipse has been brought to the foreground and is now showing the Debug perspective. The code view isn't showing any of the `HelloWorldDemo` application though because the actual error occurred deep inside the framework.

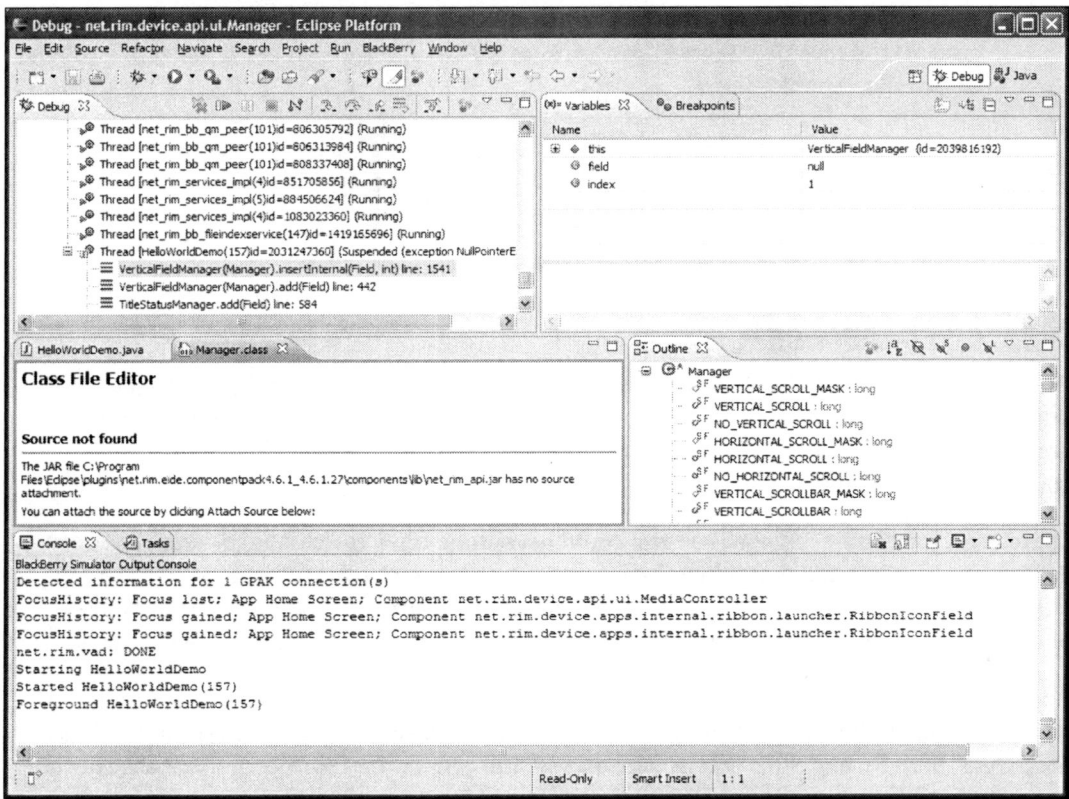

4. Because the actual bug happened deep inside a framework method, the source code for that method can't be shown. Instead, you need to look at the call stack and find the last point where the code in the application was executed. Click on the item labeled **HelloWorldScreen.<init>() line:79**; this should display the source code for `HelloWorldDemo.java` in the code view. Now, place the cursor on your bug at line 79.

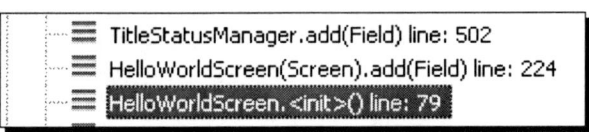

5. As we know where the problem is, it's time to go and fix it. There are some tricks to keep on debugging the application, but for now let's just stop debugging the application. Do this by simply closing the simulator by using the standard methods.

6. Now that the debugging session is over I bet you expected Eclipse to change the screen back to normal. I did too, but this is not the case. To change the perspective back to the Java perspective, just click on the **Java** button on the perspective toolbar above the variables view.

What just happened?

How's that for some fun? In this section, you did some basic debugging by creating a bug in the source and then running the application in the simulator. You saw how the debugger stopped when the bug was encountered and used the call stack to find the source of the problem.

There are a lot of other things that you could have done once the debugger was active. Eclipse has a lot of tools that make the interactive debugger powerful and useful. The call stack is just one of the many windows available on the Debug perspective. The variables and watches allow you to see the current state of variables at each step in the call stack.

Additionally, above the call stack as part of the Debug window you will find the **Run** menu that gives you all the normal run operations. There are buttons for each operation such as **Step Over**, **Step In**, and **Step Out** as well as **Run** and others. Furthermore, there are special actions available on the right-click menu such as **Set Next Statement** or **Run to line**, which can be very helpful in some situations.

One of the surprises is the discovery of the Debug perspective and how it changes the way Eclipse looks and what windows are displayed. This change is a little startling if you aren't already familiar with it and having to change it back can also be confusing when getting started with Eclipse. Perspectives are an integral part of the debugging process though, and it won't be unusual for long.

Getting some help!

The last thing to do here is point you to the help documents. A book like this is an excellent way to get started, but we can't cover everything. Eventually, you will have to look at the documentation directly for something.

The BlackBerry SDK help is written using the Javadoc format that is viewable through any standard browser. In Eclipse those docs are also embedded into the Eclipse help viewer so that they can be searched and browsed with the other documentation. Let's look at that help now.

Time for action – displaying the Help

1. To show the Eclipse help, go to **Help | Help Contents** at the top of the application.

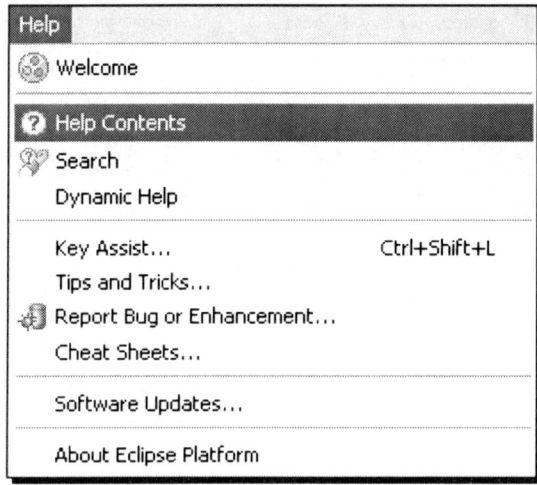

Getting Familiar with the Development Environment

2. The Eclipse "Help" dialog provides a central place for help from all of the plugins to be merged into one place. The list of help topics that are available is on the left side of the screen and there you will see one topic labeled **BlackBerry JDE Plug-in for Eclipse Guide**. Expanding that node shows a more detailed list of help topics and at the bottom of that list is the **API Reference**. Click on that item.

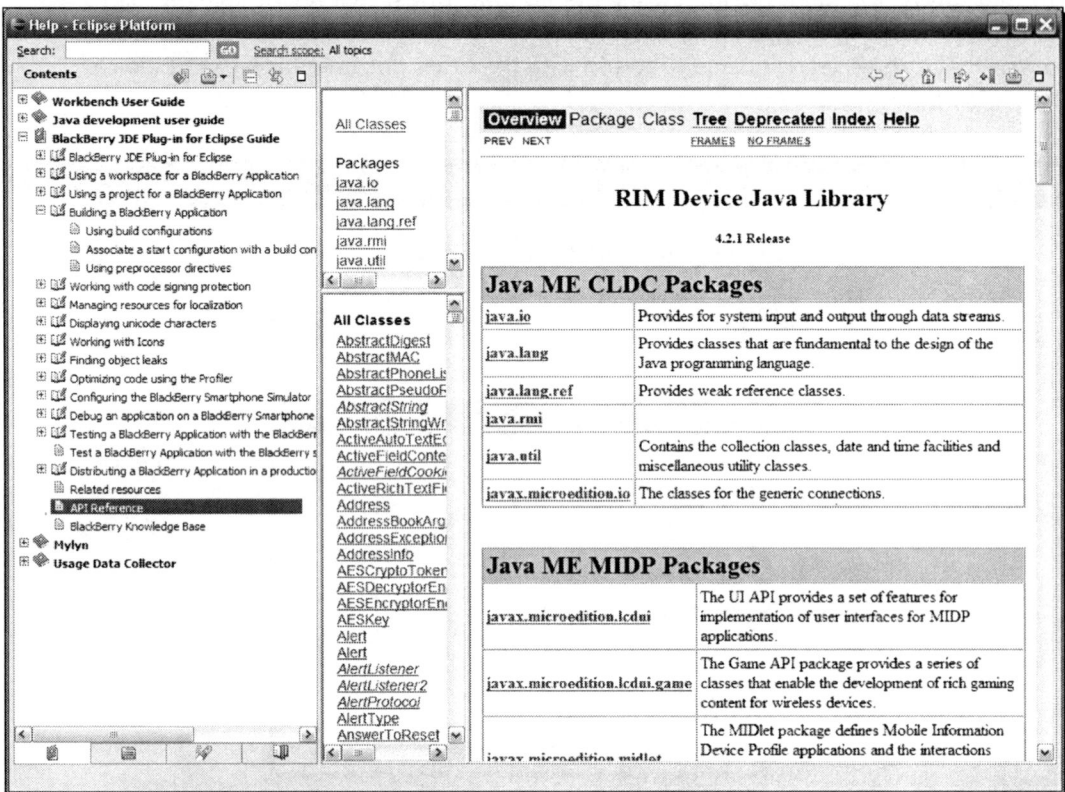

What just happened?

This simple exercise simply demonstrated how to show the documentation about the SDK that comes with the environment. There are a number of topics available for Eclipse, BlackBerry, and even a few other things. The API reference is the most useful source of information though.

The BlackBerry documentation is formatted using Javadoc and is shown in the pane to the right of the contents tree. You can find the class that you are interested in by selecting it from the "All Classes" list or by following the package hierarchy if you know it. For me, the "All Classes" list is the best way to jump from help on one class to help on another if there is no other direct link. The documentation should have links to any classes referenced, derived from or a parent of the selected class, so you probably don't need to select classes from the "All Classes" list often.

You can also access the help directly from the `BlackBerry.com` website through the documentation portal at `http://docs.blackberry.com/en/developers/?userType=21` or directly at `http://www.blackberry.com/developers/docs/4.5.0api/index.html`.

Pop quiz

1. What is the extra step that must be taken when importing a project in order to be able to run it?
    a. The project must be activated
    b. There are no extra steps needed
    c. The project settings must be changed to use Eclipse

2. What is the name for a collection of windows and views in Eclipse?
    a. View Collection
    b. Snapshot
    c. Perspective

3. BlackBerry documentation is written using what common format?
    a. First person
    b. Javadoc
    c. Microsoft Word

Have a go hero – advanced debugging tools

As we mentioned earlier, there are many other tools that can be used for more advanced debugging. Run the application again and try a few of these out to get more familiar with them. Set a breakpoint before the bug that you've added, and use the **Step Over** tool to step the execution of the application, one line at a time. Then, when the bug is encountered, use the **Set Next Statement** menu to skip over the bug that we added, so that you can continue running the application without stopping the simulator.

Summary

In this chapter, we covered the basics of how to use each development environment. Additionally, we demonstrated how to run and debug an application using the simulator.

Specifically, we learned how to:

- Launch Eclipse after installing it
- Run an application using the simulator
- Use the simulator
- Debug an application using the simulator
- How to switch between perspectives and their purposes
- Get to the help documentation

At this point, you should be able to get started with developing an application using Eclipse and this is what we will be doing in the next chapter by creating a new application from scratch. You will be ready to create your own real application in no time!

4
Creating your First BlackBerry Project

Ah, here we are-finally to the real meat of the topic. In this chapter, you will create a simple standalone application to calculate the tip of a bill at a restaurant. The initial application will be very simple and will be like the first step on a project. As you progress through the rest of this chapter the application will grow and become more robust.

Specifically, we will look at:

- How to create a BlackBerry project using Eclipse
- How to add the essential classes—an `Application` and a `Screen`
- Setting up a screen with fields
- Creating and using menus

So, without any further words, let's get to work!

Choosing the SDK version

Remember that the first step is to choose the SDK version to use. For this project we want to choose the lowest possible SDK version, which is 4.2.1. This is because this application is so simple that it will not need to use any of the newer features of more recent versions of the SDK.

Creating your First BlackBerry Project

By choosing a lower version, more models of handheld can be used to run this application. Conversely, choosing a higher SDK version means that fewer models of handhelds can run the application. Therefore, you should choose the lowest version of the SDK that still supports the features you require in order to support as many devices as possible. We will go through the steps of actually applying this later on, but for now, the choice is made and we are ready to move on.

Creating a new project

In the last chapter you imported an existing project, but this time you need to create a new one for your new application. The IDE makes it very simple to get started, but because you are creating a BlackBerry project you have to be careful. Let's get started and see what I mean.

Time for action – creating a new project

1. You can create a new project by clicking on **File | New | Project...** option in the menu bar (not the **File | Java Project** menu item).

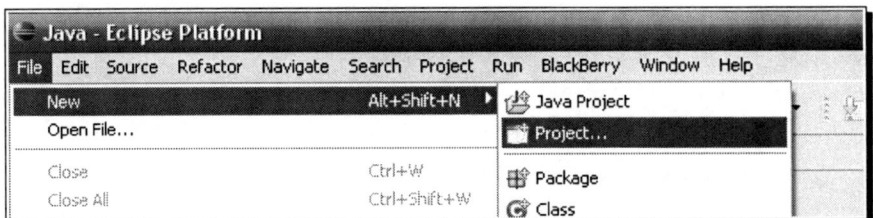

2. The **New Project** dialog gives you many choices for which type of project to create. You want to create a BlackBerry project, of course. Expand the **BlackBerry** folder in the tree and then select the **BlackBerry Project** node. When that is done click on the **Next** button.

Chapter 4

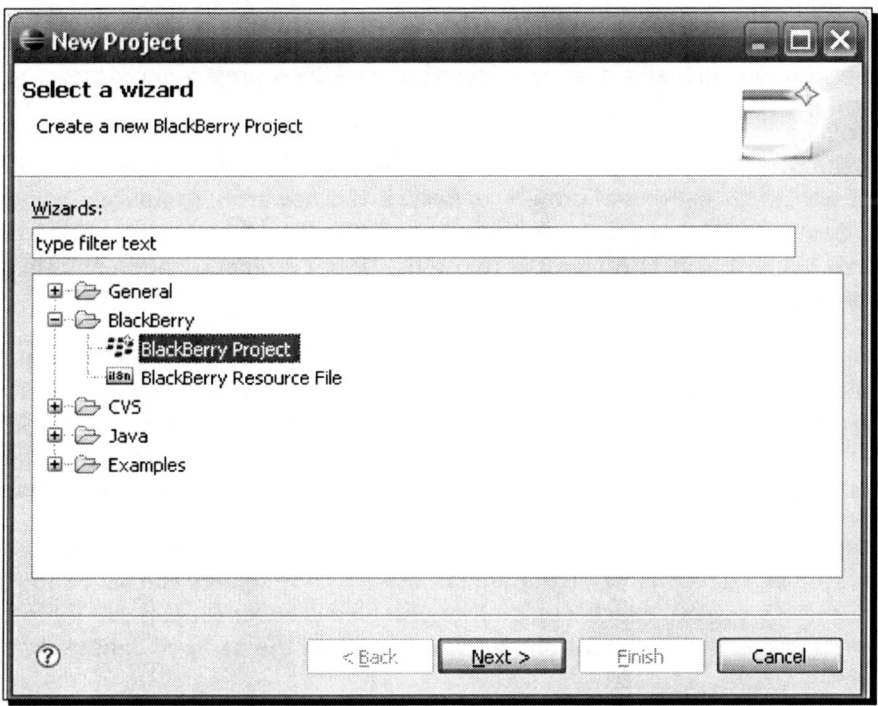

3. Enter **TipCalc** as the name of the application and click on the **Finish** button to create the new project.

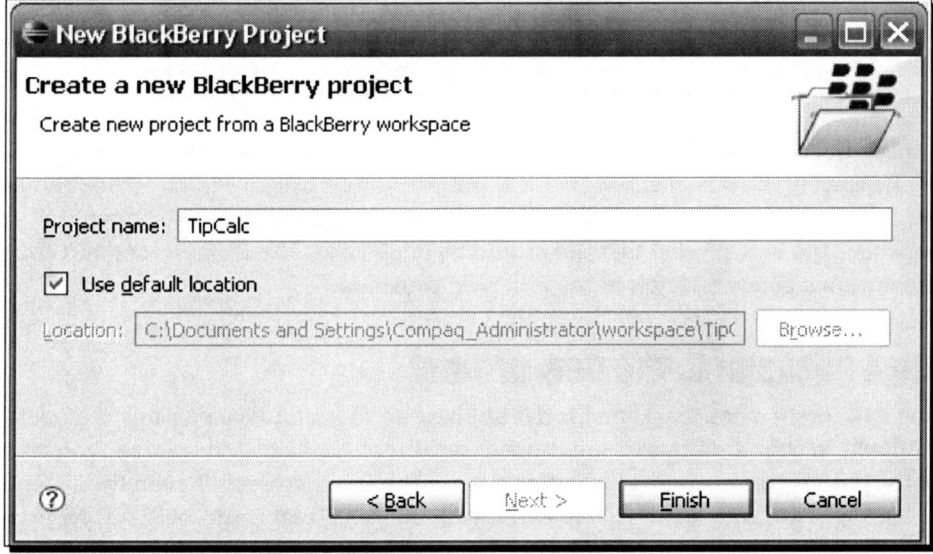

Creating your First BlackBerry Project

What just happened?

These three steps are all that is needed to create a BlackBerry project in Eclipse.

You were told earlier that choosing **New | Java Project** was not the right thing to do. This is because the wizard that you get from choosing this menu item is the Swiss Army Knife wizard that will set up any kind of project for Eclipse. It is powerful, complicated, and not for beginners. Because of this, we just won't use it at all. The **BlackBerry Project** option is much easier to use, you just have to remember to use the **New | Project...** option instead of the **New | Java Project** option.

Once you have chosen the right menu item, the **New Project** dialog is shown. Apparently, it is possible to have so many project types available that finding the one you want can be a challenge. The text field at the top of the dialog will filter the tree below to include only projects whose name matches the filter test. In our case though, the BlackBerry project is right near the top and easily accessible so there really isn't a need for the search feature.

The last step of the wizard prompts you to enter the name of your new application. Project names are used as a directory name but are not used in code so they can have some special characters, such as a space, which would otherwise be invalid for code. If you try to provide a name that is invalid the wizard will show a warning about the name to indicate the name is not valid.

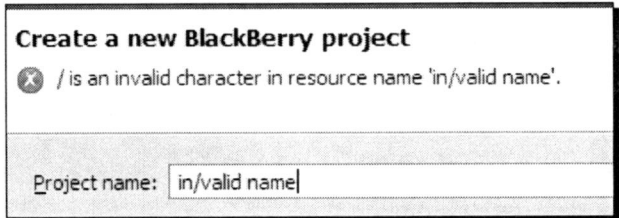

Below the **Project name** text box is a checkbox indicating to use the default workspace location. By leaving the box checked the new project will be placed in a directory named after the project name under the directory set as the workspace. You can change the location where the new project files are stored by unchecking the **Default location** checkbox and then entering a new location in the edit field provided.

Adding a package to the new project

Next, you will create a new package for the application to use. A Java package is a container for the objects in your application and is used to prevent conflicts if the classes you create happen to have the same name as another class in the same project or even the system classes. Packages are equivalent to namespaces in **C#** and **Visual Basic .NET (VB.NET)**.

Chapter 4

Adding a package to the project in this way is a minor housekeeping task, but is also an overall good technique because it forces you to choose your package name up front before creating any code. In Java, the naming convention for a package is to use your Internet domain name in reverse—almost like you were creating a new server. In this case, we will use the package name `com.rimdev.demo.tipcalc`. The package name can be any valid Java name and doesn't have to follow these conventions.

Time for action – creating a new project

1. Add the package by right-clicking on the `src` folder in the **Package Explorer** and then selecting **New | Package**.

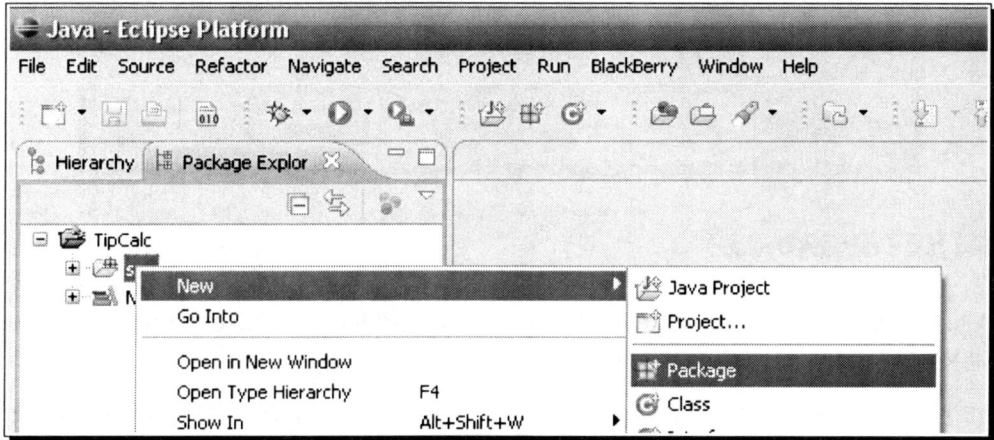

2. After selecting the menu the **New Java Package** wizard is shown. This small wizard is here only to collect the folder where the package files will be and the name of the package itself. Because you selected the `src` folder to begin with, that part is already filled in so you need to specify only the name of the package.

Creating your First BlackBerry Project

3. Enter the package name `com.rimdev.demo.tipcalc` into the **Name** field and then click on **Finish** to create the package.

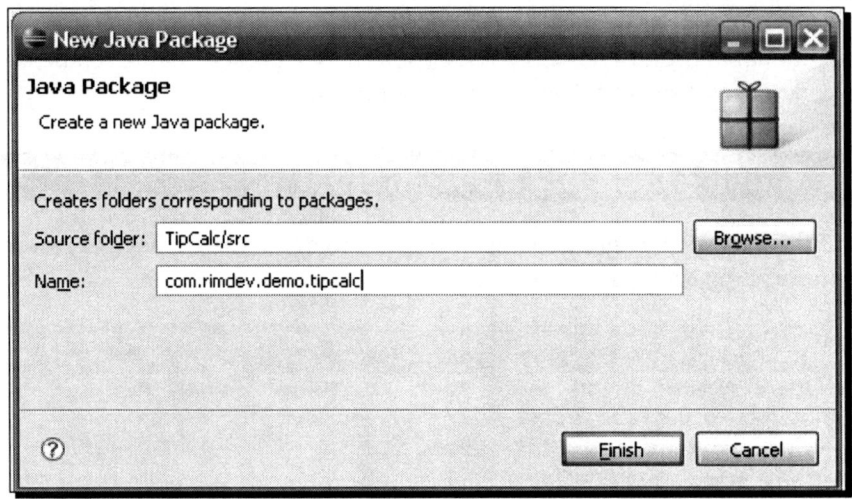

What just happened?

At this point you have an empty project that is ready to start being used. You've taken the BlackBerry application project that you had before and added a package to the `src` directory in preparation for creating the actual source files (which will come next).

The project tree is expanded slightly to include the package you just created under the `src` directory—the directory whose icon looks like a little mail parcel. Creating a package in your project doesn't result in any actual source files being created. Instead, it sets up the project so that when you do create files later on they will be created with package definitions already included in them.

Start at the beginning

Every application must have a starting point, and for BlackBerry applications it is at a method named main. The use of the name main goes all the way back to the C programming language, if not further. At that time, simply making a method named main was enough to be able to run an application. However, because Java is an object-oriented language, you can't just make a method named main. In Java, all methods must be in a class, and this includes the method main as well.

In addition to the main method all BlackBerry applications must contain an object derived from Application as well. As both the Application-derived class and the main method are required, it is standard practice to include the main method in the same class as your Application.

Application and UiApplication

As we just said, every BlackBerry application must contain a class derived from Application. The Application class contains the bare essentials for interacting with the BlackBerry operating system. If an application displays a **User Interface (UI)** then the bare essentials in the Application class are not enough. Instead, you should use UiApplication—the derived class that handles the special processing needed to interact with the user as well as the operating system.

So, the next step is to create a class derived from UiApplication and that contains the main method to serve as the starting point of your BlackBerry application.

Time for action – adding the UiApplication class

1. To create this starting class right-click on the package you just created in the project and select **New | Class**.

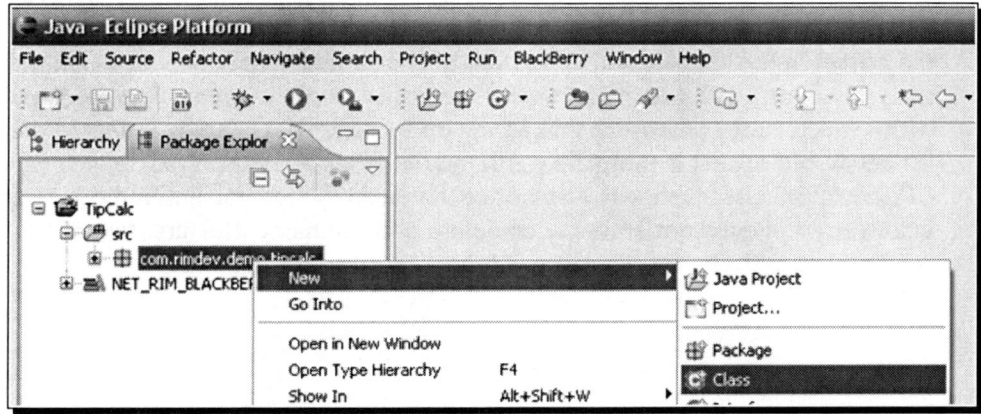

Creating your First BlackBerry Project

2. First, give the class a name; enter **TipCalcApplication** into the **Name** field.

The next step is to set the superclass for your new class. The **superclass** is another name for a base class, or the class from which your new class will be derived. Eclipse offers a strong browser tool to quickly and easily find the class.

3. Click on the **Browse** button next to the **Superclass** field. This dialog is aware of all of the classes in the libraries and allows you to choose the proper one. By default, the class `java.lang.Object` is set as the superclass. Replace `java.lang.Object` with `uiapplication`. Notice that as you do so, other class names appear in the list below, but once it is completely entered only the `net.rim.device.api."ui.UiApplication"` class is shown. Also notice that even though you entered the name in lowercase and did not enter the complete package name, the filter found the correct class with the correct casing. Click on **OK** to select this class.

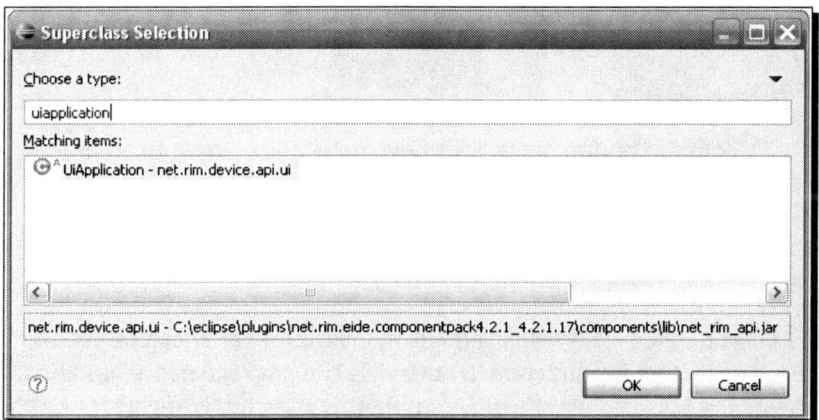

4. Back at the **New Java Class** dialog there is one more setting to make and that is to check the **public static void main(String args[])** option. This creates a stub `main` function that is used to initiate the application. Use this checkbox only when creating `UiApplication` objects; no other classes need them. Check the **public static void main(String[] args)** checkbox so the wizard will generate the `main` function.

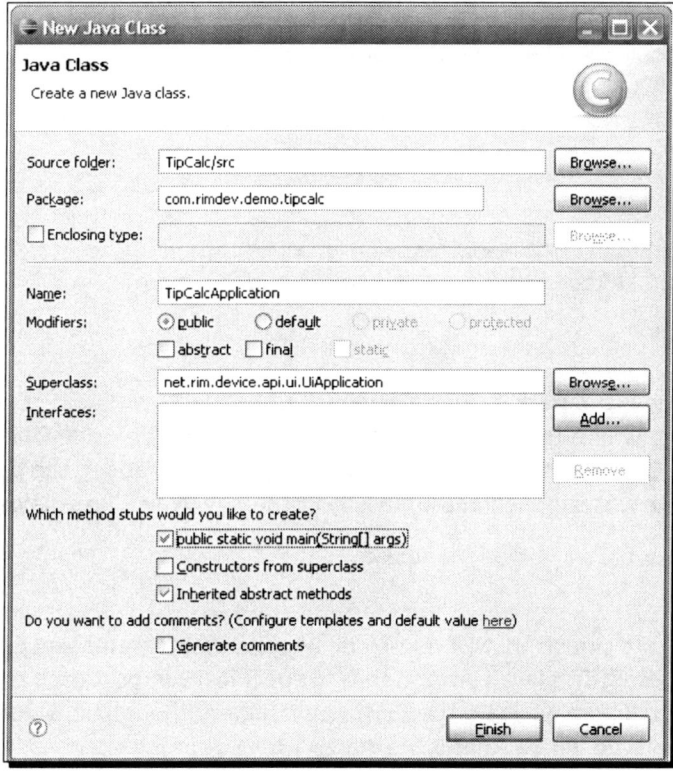

5. Finally, click on **Finish** and see the new class in the project.

What just happened?

You just created the first class for use in your new application! Well, to be more accurate you used Eclipse to set up a new class with some standard elements based on how you filled out the dialog. You could have done the same thing by simply creating a new file and manually adding all of the code by hand, but that's just not as interesting, is it? To be real though, the tools that Eclipse provides are truly helpful and easy to use.

The **New Java Class** dialog that is displayed has many options that can be set and which will cause Eclipse to generate different code. Notice that the package name has already been supplied in the dialog because we started creating this class by right-clicking on the package name in the project. Also, the **Source Folder** is properly set already because you created the package inside the `src` folder previously.

A closer look at the code

Now, let's look at the code that was generated.

```
package com.rimdev.demos.tipcalc;

import net.rim.device.api.ui.UiApplication;

public class TipCalcApplication extends UiApplication {
    /**
     * @param args
     */
    public static void main(String[] args) {
        // TODO Auto-generated method stub
    }
}
```

The first line of code is the package declaration for `com.rimdev.demos.tipcalc`. This line defines the package where the `TipCalcApplication` class will reside. The package can be specified in the **New Class** dialog but because we previously added the package to the project, the package was supplied automatically to the new **New Class** dialog.

```
package com.rimdev.demos.tipcalc;
```

The next line is an `import` statement for `net.rim.device.api.ui.UiApplication`. Import statements are similar to .NET `using` or `imports` statements and declare which libraries are being used. The Java convention is to specifically import each class being referenced. It is possible to wildcard the `import` statement though, in which case the class name would be replaced with `*`, that is, `net.rim.device.api.ui.*`.

When doing this all of the classes in that package will be imported into your application and this can make coding easier. It can certainly be annoying having to go back each time you want to use a new class and add the `import` statement for it. Eclipse is pretty smart and shouldn't include any classes unless they are actually being used when it compiles your application, so there shouldn't be any negative impact on performance. Having said all that, the established convention is not to use wildcarding because it also makes it less clear for someone looking at your application later on to know exactly which classes are being used. In the end, it is probably best to stay with the established convention, which we will do in this book.

```
import net.rim.device.api.ui.UiApplication;
```

Next, we have the class declaration itself. Again, notice that the `extends` keyword is already added and the class chosen to be the superclass, `UiApplication`, is added as well. These are added because we chose the `UiApplication` to be the superclass in the **New Class** dialog.

```
public class TipCalcApplication extends UiApplication {
```

Lastly, notice that the `public static void main` method is also created. Remember that every application must have a `main` method, and this is that method. The method was added because we checked the checkbox for it. Very simple and easy! The words `public` and `static` are special keywords that allow the `main` method to be called by the system before any of the objects in your application are created.

```
    public static void main(String[] args) {
        // TODO Auto-generated method stub
    }
```

Time for action – expanding TipCalcApplication

Now that you have the class created with some of the boilerplate code it's time to expand it and make the application actually do something.

1. You can start off by giving the static `main` function something to do. Replace the `main` method with the following code.

    ```
    /**
     * @param args
     */
    public static void main(String[] args) {
        // TODO Auto-generated method stub
        // Create a new instance of the application.
        TipCalcApplication theApp = new TipCalcApplication();
    ```

Creating your First BlackBerry Project

```
        // To make the application enter the event thread and start
          processing messages,
        // we invoke the enterEventDispatcher() method.
        theApp.enterEventDispatcher();
    }
```

2. Secondly, you need to add the `TipCalcApplication` constructor to the class so add the following code.

```
private TipCalcApplication()
{
  // Push the main screen instance onto the UI stack for rendering.
    pushScreen(new TipCalcMainScreen());
}
```

What just happened?

The code that you just added takes the simple generated code that you got from the **New Class** wizard and expands it to set up and start the application.

The first thing you did was to put some code in the initially empty `main` method. This code in the `main` function is used to actually create an instance of the application's object, which happens to contain the `main` method. This may seem strange unless you are used to it and understand what the `static` keyword means. If not, then just understand that `static` means that the `main` method can be called without an instance of the object that contains it. You still do need to create an instance of the application though, and so that's the first step.

```
    theApp = new TipCalcApplication();
```

The next line of code in the `main` method is the call to the `enterEventDispatcher` method on the application that you just created. This is a method already implemented in the `UiApplication` class. It does all of the setup necessary to get the application started, runs the application, and waits until the application is finished.

```
    theApp.enterEventDispatcher();
```

As we said earlier, an `Application` object is required, but it's the `main` function that is the actual entry point of the program. When the `main` function is exited the application is terminated and cleaned up by the operating system. The `Application` object, and more specifically the call to `enterEventDispatcher`, is why a class derived from `Application` is required.

The last thing to do for this class is to create the constructor and show the first screen. We haven't created the screen yet, but we can go ahead and create the code to use it.

The constructor is also very simple and does only one thing. You could do more in the setup and initialization of things in the application constructor of course (if your application needs it), but this simple application does not. Here we create a new instance of the `TipCalcMainScreen` class and then push it onto the UI stack. The `TipCalcMainScreen` is the class that you will create next and is the screen that you will display to the user. We will come back to `pushScreen` and the UI Stack later.

```
pushScreen(new TipCalcMainScreen());
```

Pop quiz

1. What is the base class for our application in this project?
    a. `Application`
    b. `UiApplication`
    c. `TipCalcApplication`

2. What is the special keyword on the `main` method that allows it to be called before the application is created?
    a. `public`
    b. `static`
    c. `void`
    d. `main`

MainScreen

A `MainScreen` is a specific class in the BlackBerry SDK and not just the name of our first screen. The `MainScreen` class provides a lot of services for you by providing a standard framework to work in. This framework helps you in the following tasks:

- Making menus
- Detecting a prompt for save
- Laying out fields by providing a field manager
- Providing a standard title bar
- Adding standard menu items to menus

Because of this support, making your `TipCalcMainScreen` class derive from `MainScreen` is an easy choice. Again, don't let the name `MainScreen` box you in. Generally, *every* screen class that you create should be derived from `MainScreen` because of these features that are automatically provided.

Creating your First BlackBerry Project

Time for action – adding a MainScreen

Now it's time to add that screen just mentioned to your project. Adding the screen follows the same steps that you just did to add the `UiApplication` class.

1. Right-click on the package and select **New | Class**.
2. In the **New Java Class** dialog, enter **TipCalcMainScreen** as the class name.
3. Select the `MainScreen` class to be the superclass by using the **Browse** button (just like we did before).
4. Unlike last time, make sure that the **public static void main (String args[])** checkbox remains unchecked.
5. Click on **Finish**.

What just happened?

Much like before, the package declaration, the `import` statement, and the class definition are created automatically for you. It should look a great deal like the code generated for the `TipCalcApplication` class except the `main` method is not there. Just like before, this is just a starting point and now we need to start modifying it.

Determining your screen requirements

So, what kind of screen should this application have? Well, in order to calculate a tip, you need:

- Some way to collect the total bill amount
- Some way to trigger the calculation
- Some way to display the result

There are a lot of different ways in which you can accomplish these three requirements. Laying out a screen, even a simple one such as this, is partially an art and partially a science. You could, for instance, collect the bill amount in two separate fields—one for dollars and one for cents. You might choose to use a button to trigger a calculation, or use a menu item to do it instead.

The topic of good UI design is well beyond the scope of this book. I will generalize and summarize development guidelines and best practices throughout this book, but for those seeking a deeper look at the topic, BlackBerry provides a set of UI development guidelines at this link (`http://docs.blackberry.com/en/developers/subcategories/?userType=21&category=Java+Development+Guidelines`), which you can examine for all the details.

For this application, we need to make some choices and keep going even though we haven't talked about the kinds of fields available yet. To simplify things, let's just say that we will:

- Use one edit type of field to collect the amount
- Use a menu to trigger the calculation
- Display the results in a dialog box

Alright, let's get to it!

Creating your First BlackBerry Project

Time for action – expanding the TipCalcMainScreen

OK, so we have a plan for what we want the screen to look like. Let's start by adding the field to accept the bill amount into the application.

Add the following code to the `TipCalcMainScreen` class as a data member.

```
protected EditField amount = new EditField();
```

What just happened?

Talk about baby steps! This one line didn't accomplish much, but a couple of things happened that need more explanation. First, you need to know a bit more about the `EditField` class. It may seem obvious, but an `EditField` is another class in the SDK that is designed to work with the `MainScreen` class in order to provide standard functionality. As the name implies, an `EditField` is meant to allow the user to enter text data.

Secondly, as you can see in the following screenshot, `EditField` is underlined within Eclipse with a red squiggly line, which indicates that there is an error.

```
import net.rim.device.api.ui.container.MainScreen;


public class TipCalcMainScreen extends MainScreen {
    protected EditField amount = new EditField();

}
```

Hovering over the line shows a dialog with some suggestions about how to solve the problem as shown in the next screenshot:

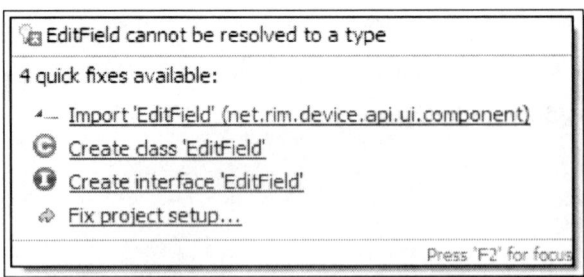

Chapter 4

In this case the editor is letting you know that the class `EditField` is not defined yet. The dialog offers a few suggestions about how to fix the error, such as to create a new class or interface called `EditField` or to go back to the project setup, in case something there is wrong. In this case, all you really need is to make sure that the class has been imported. If you select the first item in the list, Eclipse will add an `import` statement to your class for the `EditField` class. You can manually add these `import` statements if you wish.

```
import net.rim.device.api.ui.container.MainScreen;
import net.rim.device.api.ui.component.EditField;

public class TipCalcMainScreen extends MainScreen {
    protected EditField amount = new EditField();

}
```

Time for action – adding more to the MainScreen

You can continue by adding the constructor for the screen and setting up the rest of the fields. This constructor does a number of things to set up the screen. In general, it is creating and adding all of the screen elements that will be displayed.

1. Add the following code to the `TipCalcMainScreen` class.

```
public TipCalcMainScreen()
{
   // Each screen can have a field in the Title section.
   LabelField title = new LabelField("TipCalc" ,
               LabelField.ELLIPSIS | LabelField.USE_ALL_WIDTH);
   // Set the title to the label.
   setTitle(title);
   // setup the EditField to accept the Bill Amount
   amount.setLabel("Bill Amount: $");
   // add the field to the screen
   add(amount);
}
```

Creating your First BlackBerry Project

2. Add the `calculateTip` method to the `TipCalcMainScreen` class.

```
protected double calculateTip()
{
    double billamount;
    // Convert the text entered into the textfield into
    // a floating point number.
    try
    {
    billamount = Double.valueOf(
        amount.getText().trim()).floatValue();
    }
    catch (NumberFormatException nfe)
    {
        billamount = 0;
    }
    double tipamount = billamount * 0.10;
    // round the computed amount to two decimal places.
    tipamount += 0.005;
    tipamount *= 100.0;
    int tip = (int)tipamount;
    tipamount = (double)tip / 100.0;
    return tipamount;
}
```

What just happened?

The previous section just set up the data member variables for the screen elements but in this section you actually used them to set up the screen in the constructor. The first step is to create a field for the title portion of the `MainScreen`. The `MainScreen` class reserves a field to be displayed at the top of the screen as a title and automatically adds a line under that field. This is part of the standard look and feel of an application that you get by using the `UiApplication` framework and the `MainScreen` class.

In this case, set the title of the screen with a `LabelField`. Much like the `EditField`, a `LabelField` also displays text but it is intended to be a label only and therefore is not editable. The `LabelField` is given two `style` attributes as well—ELLIPSIS and USE_ALL_WIDTH. The ELLIPSIS property indicates that if the text of the `LabelField` is too large for the screen (remember there are many different screen sizes on the various BlackBerry handhelds), then the text will be trimmed and an ellipsis (that is, three dots in a row) is shown to indicate that it was trimmed. The USE_ALL_WIDTH property indicates that the `LabelField` should use as much of the screen as it is allowed.

```
LabelField title = new LabelField("TipCalc" ,
            LabelField.ELLIPSIS | LabelField.USE_ALL_WIDTH);
```

After creating the `LabelField` for the title, you need to use it by calling the `setTitle` method with the new `LabelField` object. The `setTitle` method is one of those methods provided by the `MainScreen` as part of the framework. Don't forget to add the import statement for `LabelField`!

```
setTitle(title);
```

The `amount` field was previously created as a member of the class, but there is still some setup work to do on it—specifically setting the label and adding it to the screen. Unlike some development environments, many fields include a label portion automatically. You could, of course, not set the label, in which case you would get just an empty `EditField`, but the label is desired so often that it was just included with the `EditField` and many other fields. However, not all fields have a label portion to them. For some, such as a `ButtonField`, it just doesn't make sense. For those fields where it does make sense, the `Label` is already included.

```
amount.setLabel("Bill Amount: $");
```

It should be noted that the label portion of a field is not the same as a `LabelField`, but is simply a portion of the `EditField` that is dedicated to a label function and which cannot be edited.

Once the label has been set for the `amount` field, the last step is to add it to the screen. This is done by using the `add` method. The `add` method is one of those framework methods which is part of the `MainScreen` class. Using it will add the `Field` object to the screen so that it can be displayed. Notice that you didn't have to use the `add` method for the title. Using the `setTitle` method does this for you under the covers.

```
add(amount);
```

Lastly, you must add the `CalculateTip` method—a method which is just pure Java programming and has nothing BlackBerry-specific in it, so we won't go over it line-by-line. The only line worth noting is the call to `amount.getText()`. Remember, `amount` is the name of the `EditField` where the user will enter the bill amount. Therefore, the `getText` method is used to retrieve the text that the user had entered there.

Pop quiz

1. What kind of field is often used in the title portion of the `MainScreen`?
   a. EditField
   b. LabelField
   c. TextBox
2. What method is used to add a field to the screen?
   a. `add()`
   b. `addField()`
   c. `setLabel()`

Adding a menu to the application

Menus are important user interface components on a BlackBerry. It is the preferred way to enable a user to trigger an action in an application and generally speaking, every application should have at least one.

The framework provides a great deal of support for menus and even adds some standard menu items automatically for you in proper situations. This support helps to provide a standard look and feel that makes working with your application just as easy and familiar as it is to work with any of the other standard applications.

So far, your program has a screen and a method to calculate a tip, but nothing is using that method yet. This last step sets up a menu item for your program to calculate the tip and display the results.

Time for action – adding a menu to the MainScreen

1. Add the following code to create the menu.

```
// Menu items
MenuItem _calculateAction = new MenuItem("Calculate" , 100000, 10)
{
  public void run()
  {
    Dialog.alert("The tip is $"+Double.toString(calculateTip()));
  }
};
```

Chapter 4

2. Add the menu to the screen by adding the following code snippet to the class.

```
protected void makeMenu(Menu menu, int instance)
{
    menu.add(_calculateAction);
    super.makeMenu(menu, instance);
}
```

What just happened?

The first step is the declaration for the menu itself. This style may look unusual if you aren't used to it. The style is a shorthand style of declaring the menu item and utilizes a technique called **anonymous classes**. This shorthand style contains the member declaration, creation, and inner member code for the `run` method, all wrapped together in one concise fragment. This technique certainly makes the coding easier to make and read, but you should understand that this is just a shortcut and that behind the scenes, the compiler is generating a lot of boilerplate code for you.

The important thing to get here is that the member `_calculateAction` is actually a data member of the class because this line of code is not part of a method. It MUST be done this way in order to take advantage of the shortcut. If you ignore the `run` method under it, this looks just like any other member declaration and creation statement.

```
MenuItem _calculateAction = new MenuItem(...)
```

In the creation of the `MenuItem` the text of the menu is set to `Calculate` and two more numbers are given to the constructor. These numbers are weighting values that tell `MainScreen` how to organize the menu that it is creating. The first number, `100000`, is somewhat arbitrary and can just be thought of as "a big number" for this application. This is actually a sort order and a larger number will get sorted to the top of the menu. Menu items at the top of the menu should be the most commonly used functions.

```
new MenuItem("Calculate" , 100000, 10)
```

The second number is a priority. **Priority** is used to determine which menu item will be selected by default, and in this case, a low priority number is more likely to be selected.

Lastly, the `run` method is also implemented. This `run` method is very simple, it displays the computed tip amount in a dialog. The point of all this is that when the `Calculate` menu item is selected, a dialog will be displayed with the tip amount. But, simply creating the menu isn't enough, we still have to add the menu item to the screen.

```
public void run()
{
    Dialog.alert("The tip is $"+Double.toString(calculateTip()));
}
```

By overriding `makeMenu` we can add the menu items that we want to the menu, which the `MainScreen` is already creating. The menu being created is passed in as a parameter and we can add more menu items to it by using the `add` method. When the menu button is pressed the framework calls `makeMenu` for your application so that you can supply the menu items to be displayed. This method is called each time the menu button is pressed, so you could add different menu items to the screen depending on other situations or problems, depending on your application. In our case, we need only one menu item to calculate the tip amount.

```
menu.add(_calculateAction);
```

The second parameter to `makeMenu` is an instance value that lets you know what kind of menu is being created. By checking this value you can put different menu items on the different menus, depending on what makes sense for your application. Generally, the full menu should have every menu item available, but the context menu (aka short menu) should have only the bare essentials and most commonly used items in it. Because we are ignoring the context value in this case, the menu will be added to each kind of menu.

If you are adding more than one menu item it doesn't matter in what order you add them. Remember, all of the ordering is done based on the "sort order" and "priority" parameters passed in when constructing the menu item objects.

The last line in the `makeMenu` method, `super.makeMenu`, is like saying "Ok, I'm done interrupting you; please continue with what you were going to do." When you override a method you get in the way of what would normally happen. Sometimes, this is desirable, such as if you don't want the normal response to happen, but sometimes it is not. `super` is a Java keyword meaning the superclass of your derived class. Calling the same method on super lets the superclass execute the code that it normally would execute if you hadn't overridden the method and interrupted it.

```
super.makeMenu(menu, instance);
```

 Forgetting to call `super.makeMenu` will cause all of the menus that are added by the system automatically on your behalf to be missing!

So there you have it! At this point, the application should work, assuming you don't have any copy/paste errors. It may seem hard to believe that an application can be made with such little code. This is mostly because the framework just does so much for you and you have to concentrate only on the basics of application design.

Pop quiz

1. In order to display a menu item high in the menu, what kind of number should be used as the weighting value?

    a. Any positive number

    b. A small positive number

    c. A large positive number

    d. Any negative number

2. In order to get a menu item selected as the default item, what kind of number should be used as the priority?

    a. Any positive number

    b. A small positive number

    c. A large positive number

    d. Any negative number

Setting the SDK version

Early on in this chapter, we spent a little time to decide which version of the SDK we wanted to use. However, we haven't done anything to make that selection a reality yet. Even though the application could be compiled and executed successfully right now, we need to take a moment to make sure that we are using the right SDK version. If you've done nothing since installing Eclipse, then the SDK version is probably 4.5. We need to change the build settings to use 4.2 instead.

Time for action – selecting the right component package

Eclipse can have multiple component packages installed and each workspace is configured to use one component package. You can change the package from the **Configure BlackBerry Workspace** menu item on the BlackBerry menu.

1. Navigate to **BlackBerry | Configure BlackBerry Workspace.**

    From this dialog, you can change many of the settings specific to this BlackBerry workspace. (We will come back to this part later.)

Creating your First BlackBerry Project

2. Expand the **BlackBerry JDE** branch of the tree and select the **Installed Components** node. This should present a drop list with the list of installed components in it. It really doesn't matter which version you use for this sample, but this is part of choosing the version ahead of time based on which models you want to support.

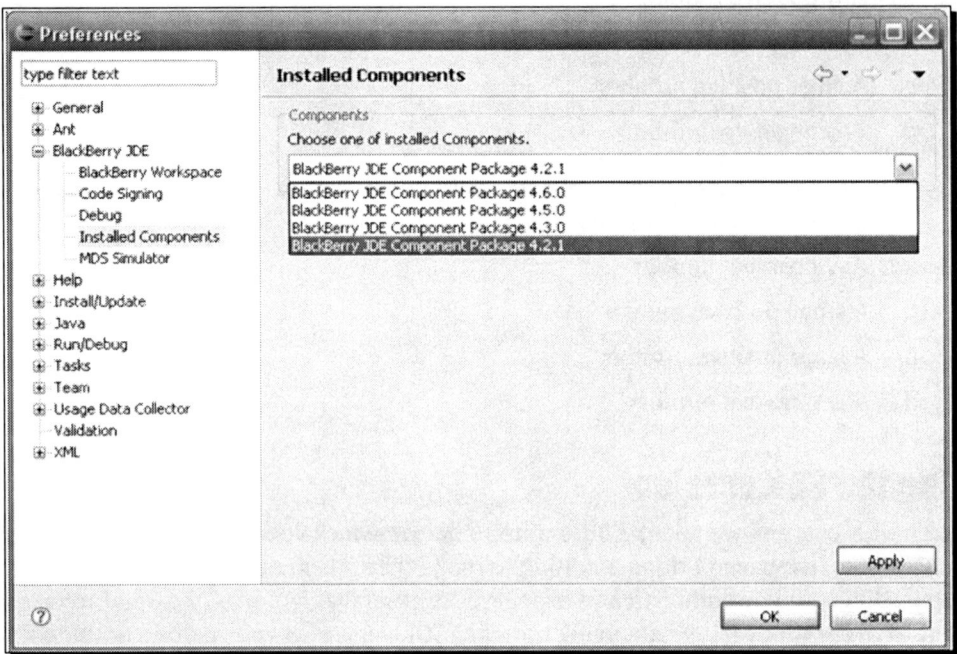

3. If you don't have the JDE Component Pack v 4.2 installed yet, follow the directions in *Chapter 2, Installing the Development Environment* and install it.

4. Once it is installed, make sure that the BlackBerry JDE Component Package 4.2.1 is selected in the list.

5. When done, click on the **OK** button.

What just happened?

Because a workspace is tied to a specific component package, when you need to change the JDE component you will see a progress meter (like the one shown in the next screenshot) while the changes are being applied. Eclipse is actually recreating the workspace from scratch in order to properly be configured to work with the new component package.

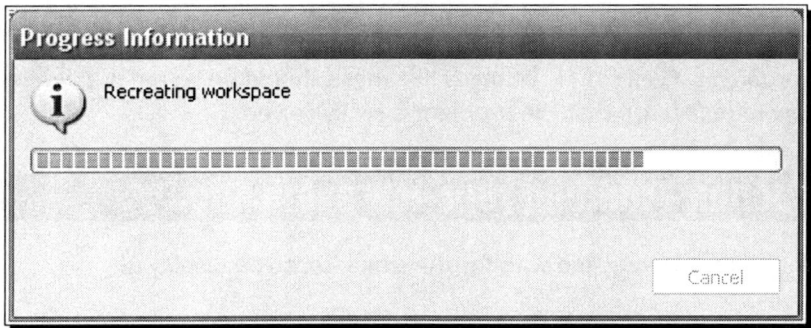

Afterward, another dialog will be displayed to clean and rebuild the workspace. Any compiled output needs to be deleted because you changed the BlackBerry libraries that the project uses. Accepting the defaults will clean and rebuild all of the projects in the workspace.

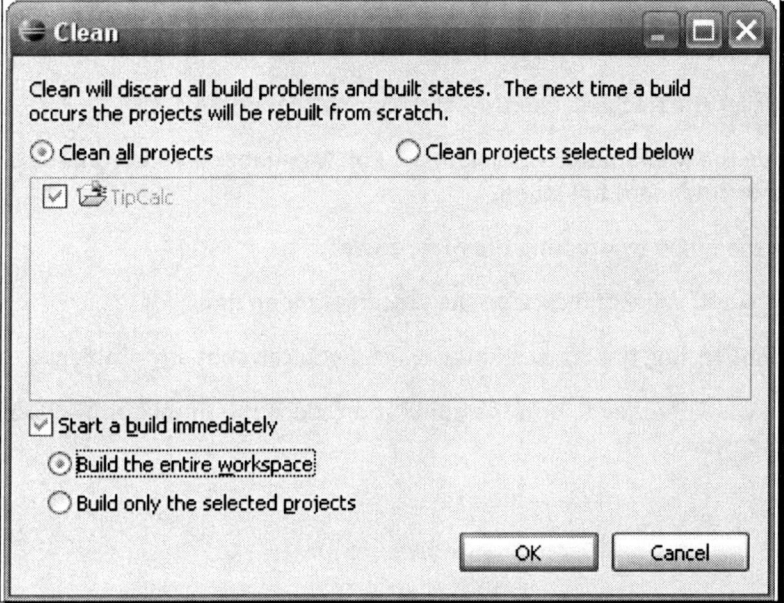

Creating your First BlackBerry Project

Testing it out

Now that we are done with the code, let's build and debug it. Because you copied all of the code there won't be any compile errors, right? Good. Eclipse is pretty good about flagging compile errors before you actually try to compile the application by placing the red squiggly line under any code with problems. At a quick glance, if you have none of these red squiggly lines in your application, then chances are good that it will compile.

Of course, just because your program will compile doesn't mean it's right and that there aren't other problems. Even simple changes like these should be tested out, which is what we will do now to make sure that the problem is really solved.

Time for action – running your new application

1. Click on **Run | Debug** and wait for the simulator to be displayed.

    Note that you may get warnings from your firewall or antivirus system about the simulator trying to access the Internet. There are a number of reasons why the simulator does this so don't worry about the warnings. If you do get any, acknowledge them so that you can continue.

2. Once the simulator starts, activate the `TipCalc` application and you can see the simple screen that you created.

3. Next, click the trackball and the "short menu" comes up.

4. Click on the **Menu** button or select the **Full Menu** menu item from the short menu to show a standard full menu.

5. Close the menu by pressing the *Escape* key.

6. Enter a valid value and click on the **Calculate** menu item.

7. Continue testing the application and see if you can spot any problems.

8. When you are ready to quit the application, close the simulator by clicking on the **Close** button.

What just happened?

Going through those steps should give you a good idea of how the application is used. Think back to the code you used to set up the screen and look at the screen of the application. Notice the title bar at the top and the edit field with the **Bill Amount: $** label. The **$** looks like it is part of the edit field, but it is really not. So, while the screen is very simple, you did get everything on the screen and it's looking good.

When you will open the short menu you will notice that the **Calculate** menu item is displayed there. Because you didn't check the instance parameter of the `makeMenu` method, the **Calculate** menu will be added to all of the menus of this application.

Once you open the full menu you will notice that the **Calculate** menu item is present and that there are a few other menu items shown as well. We didn't add these menu items. Instead, these were added by the framework automatically and is one of the reasons we are using it. The presence of these menu items adds to the standard look and feel of a BlackBerry application.

Now that you've explored the menus you can test out the **Calculate** menu item. You can see that the tip was calculated and displayed in a dialog box (just as we intended). Thanks to the nifty math in the `CalculateTip` method, it rounds up the value properly as well.

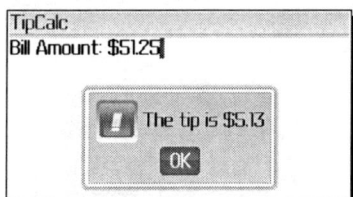

Creating your First BlackBerry Project

Once you quit the simulator you may notice that Eclipse is still showing the **Debug** perspective. If this happens it will be because you encountered an error or had a breakpoint in the code that caused the debugger to stop and switch to the **Debug** perspective. If you recall from *Chapter 3, Getting Familiar with the Development Environment*, you can switch back to the "Workbench" perspective; click on the **Java** button in the upper-right corner of the screen.

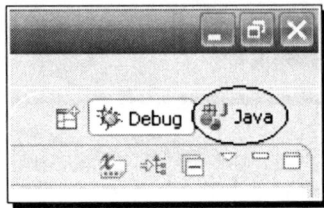

There are quite a lot of things wrong with this application still, but in a short period of time, and with relatively little source code, you've got a basic application complete and running in the simulator. This shows the power and ease with which a basic application can be put together. As with all programs though, the little details make a big difference, and that's what we will focus on next.

Giving TipCalc some polish

Now that we have covered the basics, let's go back and give it some polish. Did you play with it enough to know what needs to be improved? Here are a few of the obvious ones that I will address.

- There is no application icon. When you select the application on the simulator, there is a plain black window icon—a default icon supplied by the operating system if an icon is not presented.

- The name of the application is the same as the project name. This isn't horrible, but it could be better.

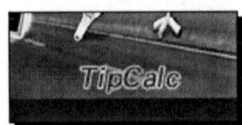

- The edit field on the application for the bill amount will accept any value. The bill amount needs to be limited to valid numbers.

- When exiting the application, a standard save prompt is shown. This is not useful, and is annoying, so it should be removed.

So let's start going through and addressing these issues!

Adding an icon to TipCalc

Adding an icon is very easy, but choosing the right size and shape of the icon can be very confusing. Each class of device has a different screen resolution and uses different sizes for the icon. Furthermore, the rules for handling icons that are not of the right size have also changed over time. We won't worry about that right now. Instead, we will just focus on adding an icon.

The icon that I made for this application is 52 x 52 pixels. Most of the icons are square-shaped and 52 pixels seems to be a pretty common size.

Icons can be in either GIF or PNG formats. When creating an icon be sure to use a tool that will let you specify the transparent color for the image; and no, MS Paint won't work. In this case, gray is the transparent color and the black border is not part of the image, but is displayed by the image viewer.

Creating your First BlackBerry Project

First, you need to add the image to the project in Eclipse. Eclipse does not have an image editor component, nor does it have the ability to add an existing file to a project. Instead, just use the Windows Explorer to copy and paste the file into the proper directory or, when creating the image using an editor, save the file directly to the project directory. What directory is that? Remember when you first launched Eclipse, it asked which directory would be used for the workspace. If you don't remember where that is you can view the project properties and the path is shown there.

Time for action – adding an icon

1. View the project's **Properties** window to get to the workspace directory.

Once the **Properties** dialog is shown, you will find the path to the project at the top of the **Resource** properties page in the **Location** field.

2. Using the path in the **Location** field, open a Windows Explorer window and browse to that location.

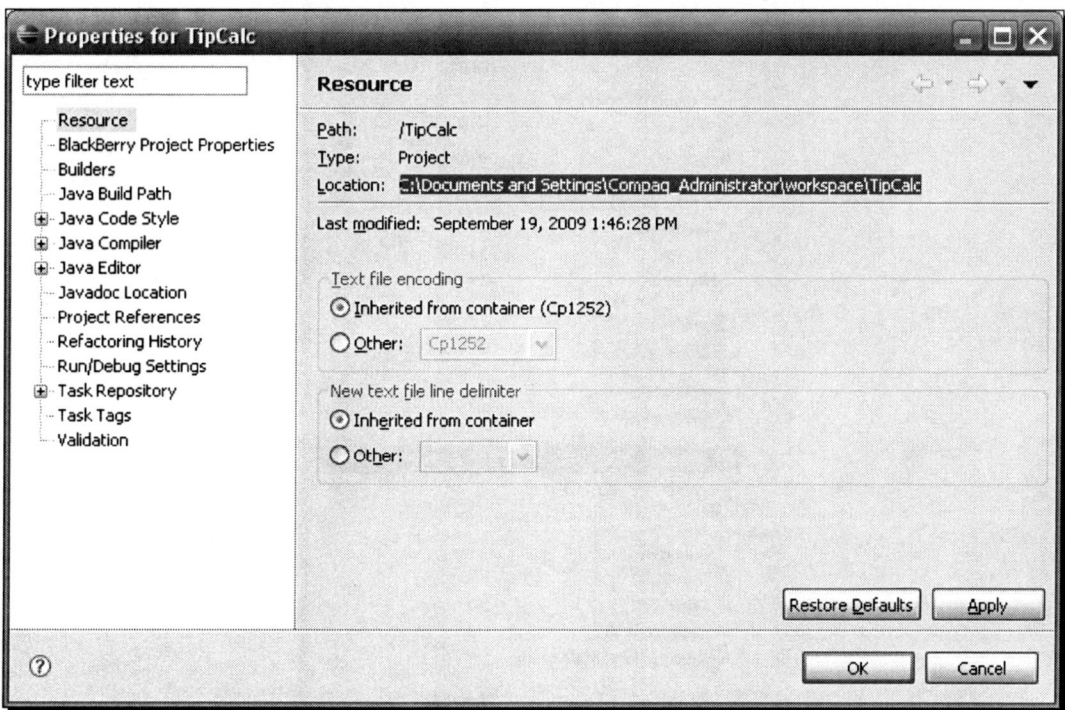

3. Using Windows Explorer, move the icon's image file into the project's directory in the workspace.

Once the file is in the proper directory you may notice that it does not show up in the project list in Eclipse. Eclipse won't automatically pick it up so you need to tell Eclipse to refresh the project by selecting **Refresh** from the right menu or by pressing the *F5* key.

Creating your First BlackBerry Project

4. Refresh the **Package Explorer** by pressing the *F5* key.

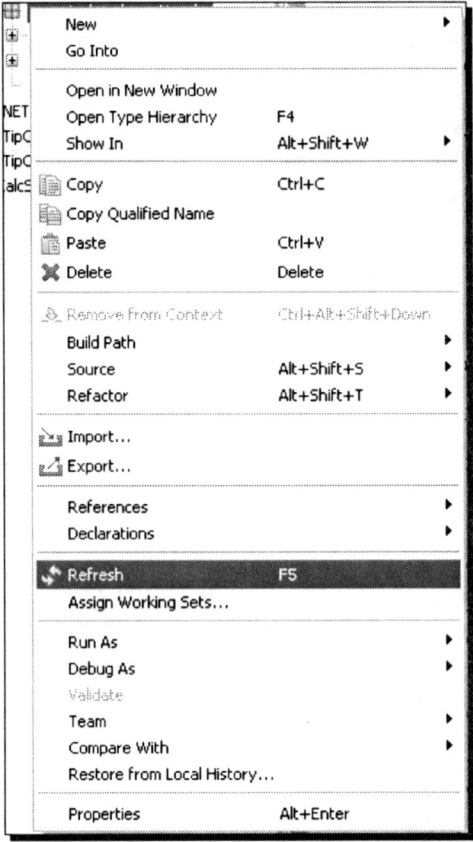

5. Once the image is listed in the project by Eclipse, open the file properties by right-clicking the image and selecting the **Properties** menu item. This will look similar to the project's **Properties**, but have only a few property pages.

In this case, we want to see the **BlackBerry File Properties** dialog, which is done by selecting the **BlackBerry File Properties** group on the left-hand side of the dialog to display the **BlackBerry File Properties** tab on the right. There are quite a few options here, most of which are used in advanced situations, but here, the **Use as application Icon** checkbox is what we are after. Checking this checkbox is all there is to do; Eclipse will handle the rest. Now, when you run the application the icon will be shown instead of the default black window icon.

Chapter 4

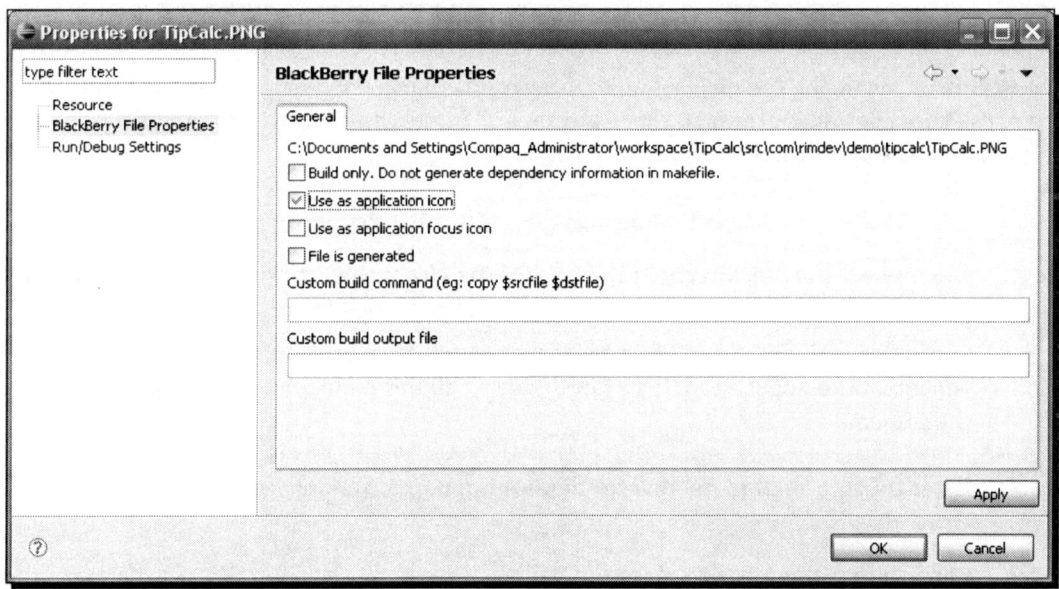

6. Check the **Use as application icon** checkbox in the **BlackBerry file Properties** page of the image properties dialog.

What just happened?

Setting the application icon is straightforward, once the file is in the proper place. There were a number of steps partly because we first looked up where the workspace directory is located and then even more steps because we had to copy the files into place using a Windows Explorer. Once the file was in the right place, setting the image file to be the application icon is simply a matter of checking the checkbox.

You can test this out by running the application again in the debugger and seeing that the icon is set properly. Notice that the background yellow disc shows up properly because this image file has the transparency color set properly.

Creating your First BlackBerry Project

Time for action – changing the application title

The next issue, changing the display name, is also solved by changing properties in the project's **Properties** dialog. In fact, there are several project settings that should be addressed at the same time!

1. Right-click on the project name and then select the **Properties** menu item.

2. Next, select the **BlackBerry Project Properties** from the list on the left-hand side of the screen to display the **BlackBerry Project Properties** tab.

   In the **General** tab you will find fields for several attributes, including the title and version of the application. It's a good idea to fill this dialog out as soon as you create the project.

3. Enter the information needed for application name, vendor, and version in the dialog.

4. Click on the **OK** button to close the dialog.

   Next time you compile and debug the application, the changes will be there!

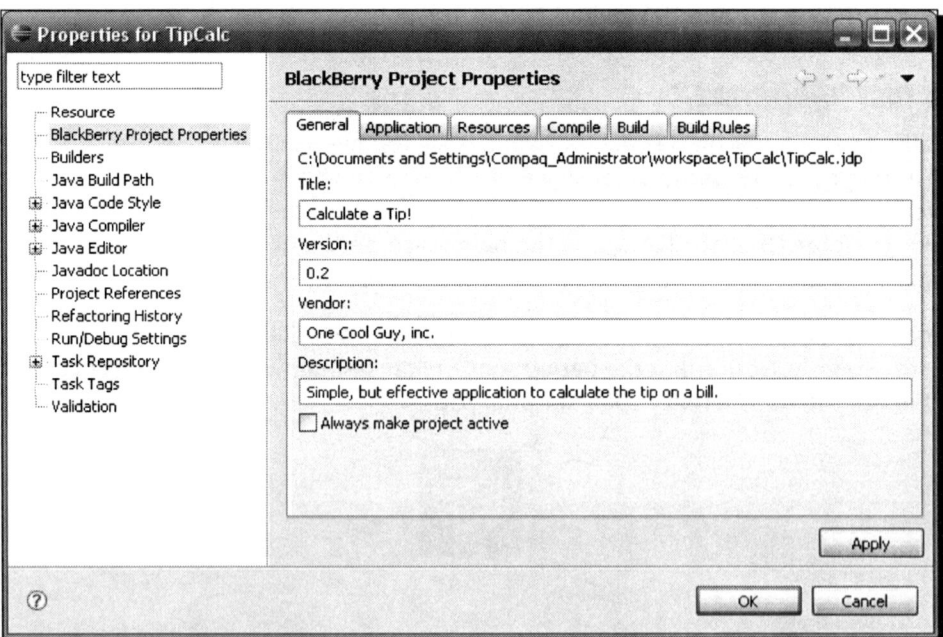

What just happened?

Changing the title is an easy step and one that doesn't really have any effects on the application; it simply changes what is displayed on the screen when the application icon is selected.

Although we came to this screen just to change the title, the other values here should be given a value as well. Obviously, the system will allow the **Version**, **Vendor**, and **Description** fields to be empty, but it is good practice to make sure these are populated. These will be used later when you build your application for distribution. These values will show up in the BlackBerry App World or in the Application Loader when you go to install it on a device.

Fixing the Bill Amount field

The third issue is one that must be solved with code. The issue here is that the **Bill Amount** text box will allow any kind of text, when we really want to allow only numbers. We aren't the first to want to do this, so as you might expect, there is a way to do this already and it is called a TextFilter. A TextFilter is the base class and can support many different kinds of filters such as phone number, e-mail address, and more. A more specific class, called the NumericTextFilter, is geared toward handling numbers, so we will use that one. The EditField class knows how to interact with a TextFilter, so to add this capability is as simple as creating the filtering object and calling setFilter on the EditField.

Time for action – fixing the bill amount field

1. Add the following code to the TipCalcMainScreen constructor.

   ```
   // In order to keep things nice and easy for the user, set a filter
   // preventing them from entering anything but numbers
   NumericTextFilter amt_filter = new NumericTextFilter(
       TextFilter.REAL_NUMERIC);
   amount.setFilter(amt_filter);
   ```

2. Of course, you need to add a couple of imports to tell the compiler about the new classes that you are using. Add these as well with the other import statements at the top of the file.

   ```
   import net.rim.device.api.ui.text.TextFilter;
   import net.rim.device.api.ui.text.NumericTextFilter;
   ```

Creating your First BlackBerry Project

What just happened?

The `NumericTextFilter` needs the additional style of `TextFilter.REAL_NUMERIC` to let the filter know what kind of numeric is needed. Without this parameter, a decimal point would not be allowed and only whole numbers could be entered into the **Bill Amount** field. After creating the new filter object, we call `setFilter`, so that the amount field will start using it.

The result is that the amount field will now accept characters that make up only a real number.

Disabling the save prompt

The next issue to tackle is to disable the save prompt on exiting the application. Something like this is usually a good feature and the fact that it is already supported automatically by the `MainScreen` is a nice benefit. However, in this case it doesn't make sense and you need to stop it from happening. To do this, you need to understand how the `MainScreen` handles the saving feature.

The API reference shows that `MainScreen` offers two methods related to saving—`onSavePrompt` and `onSave`. `MainScreen` implements `onSavePrompt` for us and it is this implementation that detects if the fields have changed and then displays the dialog prompt to save.

For this application though, you won't be saving the value of the **Bill Amount** field, so it just doesn't make sense to display the save dialog. Fortunately, you can shortcut that logic by overriding `onSavePrompt` and doing nothing. By simply returning `true` (and not calling `super.onSavePrompt`), you are effectively telling the `MainScreen` that the user did save the data and that the application can be closed.

Time for action – disabling the "save" dialog

1. Add the following method to the `TipCalcMainScreen` class.

   ```
   // return true to allow an exit without displaying the save prompt
   protected boolean onSavePrompt()
   {
       return true;
   }
   ```

What just happened?

Remember, when talking about overriding the `makeMenu` method that sometimes you want to call the same method of the super class (that is, `super.makeMenu`), and sometimes you don't. This was an example of a time when you don't want to call the super class because you wanted to interrupt what the super class was doing. In this case, simply returning `true` gave you the desired behavior.

Have a go hero – expanding TipCalc even more

Now that you've covered some of the basics of your first application, why not try to take it a step further and refine it even further on your own. One of the biggest problems with this application is the fact that you can calculate the tip at only one percentage. Sometimes you want to tip different amounts based on the quality of service so it can be helpful to be able to change the percentage that is used to calculate the tip.

To make this happen, add a second field to the screen where the user can change the percentage that can be used to calculate the tip. We haven't really covered any other kinds of fields so it would be best to use another `EditField` for now. Don't forget that the actual method for calculating the tip amount will need to be changed as well!

Summary

You just completed a couple of iterations of a real BlackBerry application, and it's a pretty good one too! The fact that you can do so little work and make such a good application speaks volumes to how powerful the BlackBerry framework is and how much it provides for you.

Specifically, we covered:

- We created the project files from scratch and utilized the Eclipse **New Java Class** dialog to make things a bit easier
- We created both an `Application` and a `Screen` class for the new application
- The default properties were OK, but even this simple change improves the application tremendously
- Every application needs an icon in the second iteration; we added one

Now, we did gloss over many things as we sped through the chapter. Many of these will be revisited in later chapters and is just a hint of the depth and power of the development environment.

A couple of those things we glossed over were the screen fields—`EditField` and `LabelField`. The next chapter is devoted to going into these field classes in depth as well as covering the many other field classes available to you for your own applications.

5
Learning the Basics About the UI

In the last chapter, we created a very simple but useful application using the screen framework provided by the BlackBerry SDK. We used only two of the `Field` *classes though and there are many others to explore. In this chapter, we will dig into that framework more and explore each of other* `Field` *classes in detail. The framework does a lot for us automatically, and we saw some of that in the last chapter as well. In this chapter, we will talk more about the services that are provided by the framework in detail.*

Here are a few things that we will cover as we proceed through this chapter:

- What is a `Field`
- What field styles are and how they can be used to change the appearance and behavior of a `Field`
- How to use common `Field` classes such as `EditField` and `ChoiceField`
- Gain an understanding of what makes each field different and what specific features are implemented in each class

Getting to know other Field classes

The screen framework provided by the SDK is a great way to create an application with a standard user interface. There are many possible field classes that can be used with the screen framework and so far, we've seen only a few of them. This section will cover several of the other common fields that can be used as well. You have probably already seen most of them in another application that comes standard on a BlackBerry. Applications such as **Email, Contacts,** and **Calendar** are made using these same tools and will also serve as good examples of what can, and should be done when creating an application.

All of the specialized field classes are based on the `Field` class and so have many common features. Because the `Field` class is a base class you can't actually create a `Field` class on the screen. If we can't create one, why do we care? The `Field` class provides the architecture for how other classes can interact with any of the specialized `Field` classes and establishes patterns that apply to every specialized `Field` class. One of these patterns is the concept of a style that can slightly change the way a field behaves.

The `Field` class defines many of these styles and they can be applied to any of the specialized field classes. The field's style is usually set in the constructor as a `long integer`, but it can also be set and retrieved through the `setStyle` and `getStyle` methods. We will use styles a couple of times in the chapter, so understanding the concept of styles and how they work is important.

One interesting example of a style is the `FIELD_RIGHT` style. There is a `FIELD_LEFT` style as well, which is the default. Creating a field with the `FIELD_RIGHT` style causes it to place the label of the field on the right-hand side of the screen instead of the left. Here is a quick example. The following piece of code shows how to create two label fields—one of the two fields created has the `FIELD_RIGHT` style.

```
add(new LabelField("Label Field",Field.FIELD_RIGHT));
add(new LabelField("Label Field"));
```

If you were to run the application you can see how the fields are arranged differently based on the styles given. The label of the first field is now right justified while the label on the second field is left justified. This is just one example of how styles can be used to slightly change the behavior of a field class.

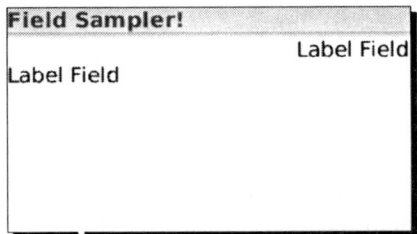

There are several styles defined in the `Field` class that can be used in any `Field` class that we cover, though it is possible that a style does not apply to a particular class. You can use just one style (like we did in the previous example), but more commonly you will be combining the styles together. The style values themselves are actually bit masks and can be combined together using the OR operator, which is the | symbol, sometimes called the "pipe symbol". Therefore, you can combine the `Field.FIELD_RIGHT` and `Field.EDITABLE` together if you needed to.

```
add(new LabelField("Label Field", Field.FIELD_RIGHT|Field.EDITABLE));
```

When it comes to user interfaces there is no better way to learn what they look like and how they work than to make a sample application that uses the fields as we cover them. For the this chapter, we will create an application called `FieldSampler` to do just that! For each field type that we encounter we will add code to the `FieldSampler` application showing how to create it and how to retrieve information from it.

So here is your chance to apply what we went over in the previous chapter. Create a new project in Eclipse called `FieldSampler`. You probably should add this project to the same existing workspace where `TipCalc` is located. Then, add a typical `UiApplication` class called `FieldSamplerApplication` (hint: it's just like `TipCalApplication` except that the class name is changed to `FieldSamplerApplication` and it references `FieldSamplerScreen` instead of `TipCalcScreen`). Lastly, create an empty `FieldSamplerScreen` derived from `MainScreen` and insert the following skeleton code:

```
import net.rim.device.api.ui.container.MainScreen;
import net.rim.device.api.ui.*;
import net.rim.device.api.ui.component.*;
import net.rim.device.api.system.Bitmap;
import net.rim.device.api.i18n.DateFormat;
import net.rim.device.api.ui.text.*;
import java.util.Date;
import net.rim.device.api.system.*;
import net.rim.device.api.lbs.MapField;
import javax.microedition.location.Coordinates;
import net.rim.device.api.ui.container.FlowFieldManager;
import net.rim.device.api.ui.container.VerticalFieldManager;

public class FieldSamplerScreen extends MainScreen
{
   public FieldSamplerScreen ()
    {
       setTitle(new LabelField("Field Sampler!"));
       createFields();
    }

   private void createFields()
   {
   }

   MenuItem _getValueAction = new MenuItem("GetValue" , 100000, 10)
   {
   // This function will demonstrate getting the value from the field
   // with focus. To do this, we must determine which field has
   // focus.
```

```
        public void run()
        {
            getValue();
        }
    };

    protected void getValue()
    {
        Field f = getFieldWithFocus();
    }

    public void makeMenu(Menu m, int instance)
    {
        m.add(_getValueAction);
        super.makeMenu(m,instance);
    }
}
```

In the preceding skeleton code we have two major parts. The first is the `createFields` method where we will be creating each field and adding them to the screen. The second is a `getValue` method where we will be retrieving the value and displaying it in a dialog box. Typically, you will keep a member variable reference to each field on the screen that you later want to retrieve data from. However, we're not going to do that in this demo for a couple of reasons.

Most of the time, one menu click will access many fields; in many cases all of them are on the screen and perform one action. What we really want to do here is to retrieve the value of the current field, whichever field currently has focus. If we held references the code would have to test every reference to see whether it is the current field with focus. Instead, I think it clears up the code to simply test which kind of field has focus using the `instanceof` operator. In short, we don't care which specific field we are getting data from, but instead only care about what kind of field it is.

The term Focus is used to describe that specific `Field` object that will receive user input when the user does something on the device. Obviously, if you start typing you want those characters to go into just one specific field; this is the field with focus. The screen keeps track of which field has focus for us so we don't have to do anything at all to implement it.

The code that we have in the `getValue` method so far simply gets a reference to the `Field` object that currently has focus using the `getFieldWithFocus` method. Later on, as we add code to this method, it will use this field reference in order to determine how to get data from it.

```
    Field f = getFieldWithFocus();
```

The downside to this approach is that we have to do some additional work to cast the value to the correct type and, in some cases, dig into the field a bit to get to information that would otherwise be available using member references. But, because we don't have to worry about holding references to the fields and the extra comparison logic that goes along with that approach, I think this code is cleaner as a result. So, let's jump in and start with some read-only fields.

SeparatorField

The `SeparatorField` is one of the most basic fields available. Its only job is to display a small line across the screen to separate one field from another. You see it in many of the standard applications, such as in the **Compose Message** screen between the subject and the body of the message. The `SeparatorField` is even used on menus to group menu items together. Because the `SeparatorField` isn't supposed to do anything except draw a line, it won't even receive focus and cannot be selected.

Time for action – creating a SeparatorField

Creating a `SeparatorField` is as simple as creating a field can possibly be. All you have to do is create the object and add it to the screen. Most of the time it's not even worth creating a variable to store a reference to the `Field` object. Just add the following line to the `createFields` method and run the application.

```
add(new SeparatorField());
```

What just happened?

When you run the application the screen will look boring and somewhat confusing because the `SeparatorField` can hardly be seen. The field is in fact the small black line under the title portion of the screen. Can you see it? It is very easily missed because it almost looks like it is supposed to be there already. Remember, there is a field at the top of the screen, which is the title, and is provided as part of the `MainScreen` framework code.

Learning the Basics About the UI

Putting the `SeparatorField` first may not have been the best way to show the field, but this is by far the simplest field and so is a good starting point. Notice that you can't scroll down on the screen at all. This is because a `SeparatorField` is not allowed to receive focus, and as none of the fields on the screen can receive focus, the focus indicator isn't even shown.

LabelField

A `LabelField` is another very simple class, just slightly more complicated than a `SeparatorField`. A `LabelField` displays some text in a read-only manner, which is only fitting for a label. The `LabelField` does not receive focus, so as the user scrolls around the screen the cursor will simply jump over the `LabelField`.

In the `FieldSampler` skeleton application, we put a `LabelField` in the title portion of the `MainScreen`. This is one of the most common uses of a `LabelField`. However, they can be used for any other descriptive text needed on the screen. Maybe the label portion of an editable field has so much text that it really needs to be split into two lines of text—the second line should be done with a `LabelField`. Or, you could have a large multiline edit field but using the label in that field just doesn't look good. In this case, you can place a `LabelField` before the multiline edit field to properly label the field's purpose.

Time for action – creating a LabelField

Creating a `LabelField` is just as simple as creating a `SeparatorField` except that the label text is also needed. So, add the following code to the `createFields` method and run the application to see the label.

```
add(new LabelField("Label Field"));

// A separator field between each type of control
add(new SeparatorField());
```

What just happened?

At this point, we can see the `LabelField` that we just added on the screen under the `SeparatorField` that we saw last time and followed by another `SeparatorField`. Each time we add a new field to the screen we will continue to follow this pattern so that each field is separated out, making it easier to see each field as we add them. Also, notice that we still can't scroll the cursor around because none of the fields on the screen can receive focus.

BitmapField

A `BitmapField` is another display-only field that shows, you guessed it, a bitmap image. You can use your own image or one of the stock images in the system. Also, just because the name is `BitmapField` doesn't mean that you have to use BMP files. In fact, the JDE doesn't support BMP files at all. The JDE supports only JPG, GIF, or PNG files. PNG files are actually preferred though, simply because they are typically much smaller in size than the other formats. We'll show how to use both using the `Bitmap` class.

The first step to using a `BitmapField` is to create the `Bitmap` object. The operating system comes with several stock images that are used in operating system functions already. They are identified not by filenames, but by special constant values in the `Bitmap` class such as INFORMATION, WARNING, and ERROR. `Bitmap` objects can be created to use these predefined images using the static method `getPredefinedBitmap`. Most of the time you use these constants when creating dialogs, but they work well in this case too.

Most of the time custom images are used and these need to be added to the project and compiled in. We did this already in *Chapter 4, Creating your First BlackBerry Project*. Once added, a `Bitmap` object can be created by using the static method `getBitmapResource` and by providing the exact filename.

Learning the Basics About the UI

Time for action – creating a BitmapField

1. Let's create `BitmapField` objects using both techniques. Add the following code to the `createFields` method and run the application. The next code snippet shows how to add a `BitmapField` by using each of the methods mentioned previously.

   ```
   // Retrieve one of the predefined system bitmaps
   Bitmap bminfo = Bitmap.getPredefinedBitmap(Bitmap.INFORMATION);
   add(new BitmapField(bminfo));
   // Retrieve a bitmap that has been added to the project.
   Bitmap bmPackt = Bitmap.getBitmapResource("PacktLogoSmall.png");
   add(new BitmapField(bmPackt));
   // A separator field between each type of control
   add(new SeparatorField());
   ```

2. Next, add the `PacktLogoSmall.png` file to your project using the instructions from *Chapter 4, Creating your First BlackBerry Project*. You can download this image from the Packt Publishing website at www.packtpub.com.

What just happened?

Wow, those bitmaps look nice. You can see both the information image that comes from the device software as well as the Packt Publishing logo demonstrating how both types are added. Where is that cursor? It's still not here yet because `BitmapFields` are not selectable.

Pop quiz

1. What operator is used to combine attributes?

   a. Bitwise OR (`|`)

   b. Logical OR (`||`)

   c. Bitwise AND (`&`)

   d. Logical AND (`&&`)

2. What is the base class for all fields?
    a. `Field`
    b. `Control`
    c. `Screen`
    d. `BaseField`
3. Selecting a `BitmapField` will do what?
    a. Allow the field to be clicked
    b. Nothing
    c. Show a border around the image
    d. `Bitmap` fields cannot be selected

ChoiceField

The `ChoiceField` is an abstract base class that is analogous to a drop list or pick list on other platforms. You can't use a `ChoiceField` directly, instead you must use one of the two specialty-derived classes—the `NumericChoiceField` or the `ObjectChoiceField`. These classes have common functionality though, which we can outline here.

Using a `ChoiceField` type of field allows the user to choose a specific value from a short list of predetermined values. Initially, the `ChoiceField` is collapsed and shows only the selected value.

When you click the trackball while the field is selected a small dialog opens up to display the full list of possible choices. The user can scroll up and down in the list and click the trackball to select a value.

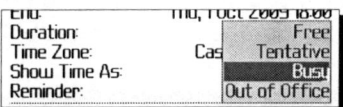

A `ChoiceField` type of class is typically used when there is a small and fixed list of possible choices that does not lend itself to the user entering free-form text. As a designer, you have to make sure that the complete list is represented because the user cannot enter any values and can choose from only one of the listed values. This means that there is no field available that operators like a Windows ComboBox control. Additionally, a `ChoiceField` type of class allows only one value to be selected. Lastly, many of the common drop list implementations allow for separate **Display text** and **Underlying value** pairs. The `ChoiceField` does not do this automatically, but such a mechanism could be easily accomplished with the `ObjectChoiceField` class.

Learning the Basics About the UI

When a `ChoiceField` type of field has focus on the screen and the menu is displayed, the framework automatically adds a menu item named **Change Option** that will expand the list of choices. This is done to create a standard user interface experience, is one of the benefits of using this framework, and is commonly added for many of the standard `Field` classes.

Additionally, there are some keyboard shortcuts that also work automatically for these kinds of fields. Pressing the *Space* key will change the selected value to the next value in the list without displaying the entire list. Scrolling up or down while pressing the *Alt* key will also change the selected value, up or down depending on the scroll direction, without displaying the list as well.

ObjectChoiceField

The `ObjectChoiceField` is the most common, and most likely, kind of `ChoiceField` derived classes to be used. It is called `ObjectChoiceField` because you supply an array of objects to the class that is used to generate the items in the list. The array can contain objects of any type and the object's `toString()` method will be used to generate the text that will be put into the list.

This approach is very flexible and makes populating the items dynamically easier. The simplest approach is to hardcode the strings into an array directly, but this works only when the values are absolutely constant and static. Many times the list will be created by populating the data from another source such as a database or over the network.

The list of values can be provided in two different ways. The most direct way is to supply them in the constructor. However, if you need to change them later, you can do so through the `setChoices` method. The next sample demonstrates both techniques.

Time for action – creating an ObjectChoiceField

1. Add the following code snippet to the `createFields` method in the `FieldSampler` project.

   ```
   String[] choices = {"Choice1","Choice2","Choice3"};
   //create an ObjectChoice
   ObjectChoiceField objChoice = new ObjectChoiceField(
           "Object Choice Field", choices);
   add(objChoice);
   ```

```
    // Another way to create the same ChoiceField.
    ObjectChoiceField objChoice2 = new ObjectChoiceField();
    objChoice2.setLabel("Another way");
    objChoice2.setChoices(choices);
    add(objChoice2);
    // A separator field between each type of control
    add(new SeparatorField());
```

2. Then add the following code to the `getValue` method.

```
if (f instanceof ObjectChoiceField)
{
    ObjectChoiceField choice = (ObjectChoiceField) f;
    int index = choice.getSelectedIndex();
    Object o = choice.getChoice(index);
    String s = (String) o;
    Dialog.alert("The selected value is " + s);
}
```

3. Lastly, compile and run the application.

What just happened?

In this example, we demonstrated creating `ChoiceFields` in two different ways. Both of the fields used the static array called `choices` as the contents for the list, but we set up the fields in different ways. The first instance put all of the important information for setting up the field in the constructor. This is good when you know for sure what needs to go into the list, but sometimes you don't. In these cases you can create the list on the fly, and then add them to the `ObjectChoiceField` by using the `setChoices` method.

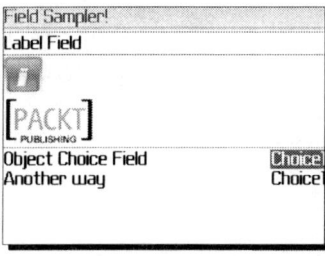

Also, note that the objects in our array are already `Strings`. This makes the sample code easy, but they could very easily be objects with some other data in them. In fact, it will be objects most of the time. Just make sure to provide a `toString` method so that the list is populated properly!

In addition, we also demonstrated code for retrieving the value from an `ObjectChoiceField` derived class. The `getChoice` method is used to get the object at the specific index given. It is worth noting that the method returns an object because it does not know the real type of the item in the list. In our case it was a `String`, but as we've said before, it could be any type. In order to use it, we need to first cast the object to the original type, in this case a `String`. Once the cast operation is done we can access the object directly and use it. This aspect of the `ObjectChoiceField` is somewhat annoying and requires some extra work, but the flexibility you gain from this approach makes up for the extra work needed.

NumericChoiceField

`NumericChoiceField` is the other specialized class in the `ChoiceField` family. Where the `ObjectChoiceField` is generic and flexible, the `NumericChoiceField` is specialized and has a narrow application. As the name implies, a `NumericChoiceField` is used to create a list of numeric values in a `ChoiceField`. It is designed to be easy to use and take advantage of the sequential aspect of numbers. Specifically, you need to specify only the beginning, ending numeric, and increment values and the `NumericChoiceField` will fill in the rest of them.

Now, you could use an `ObjectChoiceField` to accomplish the same thing. However, this class is there to make this specific case a little easier to use and code.

There are no limits to how large the range can be, but as you can imagine finding the right value in a list from 1 to 100 would be a little tough. Even though you could use this field for something like that, you must consider the user and understand that any `ChoiceField` type is not well-suited for a large number of choices. A practical limit might be to have no more than "a few dozen" choices. In general, the smaller the list of choices the better the user experience will be.

Time for action – creating a NumericChoiceField

1. Add the following code to the `createFields` method.

   ```
   // Create a numeric Choice showing values between 10 and 20
   stepping by 2s
   NumericChoiceField numChoice = new NumericChoiceField(
           "Numeric Choice Field", 10,20,2);
   add(numChoice);
   
   // A separator field between each type of control
   add(new SeparatorField());
   ```

2. Add the following code to the `getData` method.

```
if (f instanceof NumericChoiceField)
{
    NumericChoiceField choice = (NumericChoiceField) f;
    int n = choice.getSelectedValue();
    Dialog.alert("The selected value is " + Integer.toString(n));
}
```

3. As usual, debug the application and play with the new control that we added.

What just happened?

The differences between the `NumericChoiceField` and the `ObjectChoiceField` are minor, but using the right field for the right situation can make your job easier.

The first important point to notice is that the range and step values are supplied in the constructor. Actually, they must be supplied in the constructor. Unlike the `ObjectChoiceField`, there are no methods for resetting them once the field is constructed.

When it comes to retrieving the value, there are some differences here as well. All of the methods used by `ObjectChoiceField` work here as well; after all this class is derived from `ObjectChoiceField`. Because this is a specialized class and a new method for getting the value is supplied, the `getSelectedValue` method returns the number as an integer, which is currently selected in the field. Unlike the `ObjectChoiceField`, it's not an object and no casting is required, which makes the code that much easier to write. Nice huh?

GaugeField

A `GaugeField` is a dual-purpose field that can be complicated to use. It is non-editable by default, but can be editable if the proper styles are set. Therefore, what it does and how it is used depends on whether the field is editable or not.

"Gauge" is a pretty generic term that doesn't clearly identify the purpose of the field. Instead, think of this as a merger between a progress meter and a slide bar control in Windows. When the field is not editable it is most commonly used as a progress meter, but when it is editable it functions as a slide bar control.

It is drawn as a thick, blue bar filling the remainder of the screen after the label portion. How much of the bar is filled in depends on the minimum, maximum, and current values. By incrementing the current value at regular intervals you can create an animation effect filling up the bar like the progress meter, and this is most commonly how it is used.

Learning the Basics About the UI

The minimum and maximum values can be any valid number so if you wanted to count from -50 to 150 you could do that and the `GaugeField` would display the proper percentage even though the minimum value is less than zero. This kind of flexibility can be very useful when you may not know what range you are working with ahead of time. If, for instance, you need to process some records, you would probably set the minimum of the `GaugeField` to 0 and the maximum equal to the number of records that you will be processing. Then, you can simply increase the current value of the `GaugeField` for each record processed and the `GaugeField` would progress steadily regardless of whether there are 100 or 10,000 steps.

However, when a `GaugeField` is editable the user can change the current value of the control. The framework will add a **Change Option** menu just as it did for `ChoiceField`, and selecting this menu displays a dialog, allowing the user to change the value by simply scrolling the trackball right or left. When done, the new value is set by clicking the trackball in. Additionally, the dialog can be skipped by holding down the *Alt* key while scrolling the trackball left or right. Using this method the value is changed immediately.

The code we will put into the `getData` method is going to be a bit different than we have put into this method so far. For this example, we will make the menu item start a thread and update the `GaugeField` to show that animated progress effect. Working with multiple threads is a more advanced topic that will be covered later. Our focus here is on the fields themselves, so we won't be analyzing that code in detail.

Time for action – creating a GaugeField

1. Add the following code to the `createFields` method.

   ```
   // A gauge from 0 to 10 with the initial value being 8.
   GaugeField gaugeField = new GaugeField("Editable", 0, 10, 8,
               Field.EDITABLE|Field.FOCUSABLE);
   add(gaugeField);

   // A gauge from 0 to 100 with the initial value being 35 and using
   no special styles
   GaugeField progress = new GaugeField("Normal Style", 0, 100, 35,
                   Field.FOCUSABLE);
   add(progress);

   // A gauge from 0 to 20 with the initial value being 5 and using
   the NO_TEXT flag.
   GaugeField notext = new GaugeField("NoText Style",0, 20, 5,
                   Field.FOCUSABLE|GaugeField.NO_TEXT);
   add(notext);
   ```

Chapter 5

```java
// A gauge from -19 to 17 with the initial value being 4 and using
the PERCENT flag.
GaugeField percent = new GaugeField("Percent Style",-19, 17, 4,
                    Field.FOCUSABLE|GaugeField.PERCENT);
add(percent);

// A separator field between each type of control
add(new SeparatorField());
```

2. Then, add the following code to the `getData` method.

```java
if (f instanceof GaugeField)
{
 new Thread(new Runnable()
 {
  public void run()
  {
    GaugeField g = (GaugeField)UiApplication.getUiApplication()
                .getActiveScreen().getFieldWithFocus();
    g.setValue(g.getValueMin());
    for (int i = g.getValueMin(); i < g.getValueMax(); i++)
    {
      try
      {
        Thread.sleep(1000);
      }
      catch (InterruptedException e)
      {
        // TODO Auto-generated catch block
        e.printStackTrace();
      }
    UiApplication.getUiApplication().invokeLater(new Runnable()
    {
     public void run()
     {
       GaugeField g = (GaugeField) UiApplication.getUiApplication()
                   .getActiveScreen().getFieldWithFocus();
       g.setValue(g.getValue()+1);
     }
  });
```

```
            }
        }
    }).start();
}
```

3. Finally, run the application and give it a spin. Be sure to use the **Get Value** menu while a `GaugeField` is selected to see the progress meter work.

What just happened?

As we said before, `GaugeField` is not editable by default. In order to make it editable we need to set the style to `Field.EDITABLE` and `Field.FOCUSABLE`, which is what we did for the first field in the sample. Because this field is editable you can also change the value by using the **Change Option** menu or the *Alt + Scroll* technique.

The second field is intended to show what a `GaugeField` looks like with no other styles applied. Normally the field wouldn't be given the `FOCUSABLE` style when it is used as a progress meter, but in order to test it out with the **Get Value** menu item it has to be able to get focus. When you click on the **Get Value** menu a separate thread is created to slowly increment the current value of the `GaugeField` in order to demonstrate the progress meter.

It is also worth noting that for both the first and second field, neither of the `GaugeField`-specific styles is being used. You can see that when this is the case the actual value of the field is shown in the middle of the progress bar itself. Each time a new value is set for the `GaugeField` the value changes on the screen.

The other two fields in the sample demonstrate the two `GaugeField`-specific styles—the `PERCENT` style and the `NO_TEXT` style. These styles don't have any impact on how the `GaugeField` operates, but they change the way it is displayed. The third field in the sample uses the `NO_TEXT` style and you can see that there are no numbers in the bar, like there were in the first two fields.

The fourth field demonstrates two different things. First is the use of the `PERCENT` style. As the name suggests, this causes the actual value of the `GaugeField` to not be displayed and instead to display the percentage of completion in the bar. Second, the minimum and maximum values for this field are very unusual. It has a negative minimum value, a positive maximum value, and neither of them is a nice round number. In spite of these things, the percentage is calculated properly and the result is a nice and clean display.

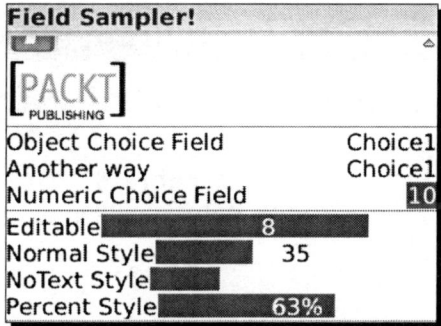

Lastly, we should note that these three different styles, numbers, percent, and nothing being displayed in the `GaugeField`, are the only options available. If you want to change what is displayed in the `GaugeField` you will not be able to do so with writing a custom control.

DateField

A `DateField` is not related to a `ChoiceField` through the object hierarchy, but it obviously uses it. Don't let the name fool you though, the `DateField` can handle `Date`, `Time`, and `Date/Time` data. This specialized class is here to make entering date and/or time values easy for the developers by encapsulating several choice fields into one `DateField`. Each component of the date or time becomes a separate `ChoiceField` that can be selected and changed. Additionally, the fields act as one unit because they handle "rolling over" date or time boundaries. If you have a field with a date value in it and you scroll the day past the end of the month, the month field will advance as well.

One thing that may be confusing is that there are actually two `DateField` classes listed in the class list in the documentation, and that is because there are actually two separate classes. One is a standard Java class in the `javax.microedition.lcdui.DateField` package. The other (the one we are interested in) is part of the RIM API and is found in the `net.rim.device.api.ui.component.DateField` package.

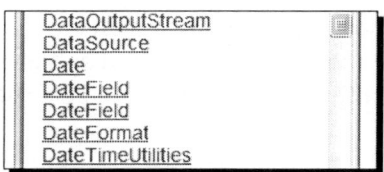

The `DateField` also requires the `DateFormat` class to know how to format the date or time on the screen so you have to make sure to include the `net.rim.device.api.i18n.DateFormat` package in addition to the `net.rim.device.api.ui.component.DateField` package. Also, you will probably need to use the `java.util.Date` package as well to get the current date or time or convert it to something more useful.

Learning the Basics About the UI

Time for action – creating a DateField

1. Add the following code to the end of the `createFields` method.

   ```
   Date now = new Date();
   DateField datetimeField = new DateField("DateTime Field",
       now.getTime(), DateFormat.getInstance(
       DateFormat.DATETIME_DEFAULT));
   add(datetimeField);

   DateField dateField = new DateField();
   dateField.setLabel("Date Field");
   dateField.setDate(now);
   dateField.setFormat(DateFormat.getInstance(
                   DateFormat.DATE_DEFAULT));
   add(dateField);

   DateField timeField = new DateField("Time Field", now.getTime(),
                   DateFormat.getInstance(DateFormat.TIME_
   DEFAULT));
   add(timeField);

   // A separator field between each type of control
   add(new SeparatorField());
   ```

2. Next, add the following code to the `getValue` method.

   ```
   if (f instanceof DateField)
   {
     DateField df = (DateField) f;
     long datevalue = df.getDate();
       Dialog.alert("The date is " + DateFormat.
   getInstance(DateFormat.DATETIME_DEFAULT).formatLocal(datevalue));
   }
   ```

3. Lastly, run the application and experiment with the `DateField`. Be sure to change the value using the *Alt + Scroll* method and to move the day portion past the end of the month to watch the month field change as well.

What just happened?

Like most computer systems, the date or time is represented by counting the number of ticks (a.k.a. milliseconds) from "the epoch", or midnight on January 01, 1970. This number is very large and is represented by the `long` data type. The example here creates a new `Date` object, which is initialized to the current time, and then calls `getTime()` to get the long value of that time.

The first field demonstrates the `DateField` with a date or time format specified. To make the sample code easy we get the default format and use it, but you could potentially create your own `DateFormat` class, if you needed to display the date or time in a custom way. It also demonstrates setting the date value by using the constructor. When this is done, you must use the `long` value of the date and not the `Date` object directly.

The second example shows how to set up the `DateField` without using the constructor parameters. Using this approach also allows the `Date` class to be used directly in the `setDate` method instead of using the `long` value.

The last field simply demonstrates using the `DateField` to display only the time portion of a date or time.

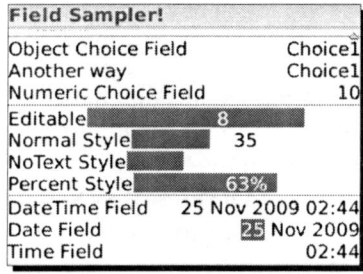

Notice that each portion of the `DateField` is a `ChoiceField`, and that these ChoiceFields have all of the same behaviors that we discussed earlier, including the **Change Option** menu and the ability to *Alt + Scroll* to change the value.

In the `getValue` method, the code is much simpler. All we really need to worry about is the getDate method, which returns the long timestamp value regardless of whether the formatting specified a Date, Time, or Date/Time. In order to display the value neatly though, we once again used the DateFormat class and the default formatter.

Learning the Basics About the UI

Pop quiz

1. What field control is equivalent to the Windows ComboBox control?
   a. `ObjectChoiceField`
   b. `ChoiceField`
   c. `ComboField`
   d. None of the above

2. What kind of field will allow a user to enter a time?
   a. `TimeField`
   b. `DateField`
   c. `DateTimeField`

3. What attribute is used to change the behavior of a `GaugeField`?
   a. `Field.EDITABLE`
   b. `GaugeField.PROGRESS`

CheckboxField

The `CheckboxField` is one of those basic fields that *almost* need no explanation. The `CheckboxField` follows many of the standard conventions in other systems, such as HTML and Windows, by placing the checkbox on the left-hand side of the screen with the label on the right. This is consistent with many other systems even if it is opposite of most other field classes in BlackBerry. A checkbox is best used to represent a Boolean value or simple on/off or yes/no values.

The checkbox itself is square and shows a nice checkmark image when the checkbox is checked. You can toggle the checkbox by pressing the *Space* key.

Additionally, when a `CheckboxField` has focus on the screen and the menu button is pressed, the framework adds a **Change Option** menu item to the menu in much the same way it does with the `ChoiceField`. Clicking on this menu item will toggle the checkbox as well.

Be sure to phrase the label in such a way as to make the choice clear. A checkbox can be used to enable a feature which is not enabled by default, but it can also be used to disable a feature which is enabled by default. Simply providing a label of "JavaScript" doesn't give the user any indication about what the result will be from checking or unchecking the `CheckboxField`. Instead, using a label like **Support JavaScript** is clearer.

`CheckboxField` does have some limitations as well. Some systems might allow a checkbox to have three states—checked, unchecked, and unknown—but the `CheckboxField` does not allow for this. Also, it is not possible to change the orientation of the checkbox from the left side of the field to the right side. Using the `FIELD_RIGHT` style right justifies the entire field, but the checkbox is still displayed on the left side of the label.

Time for action – creating a CheckboxField

1. Add the following code to the `createFields` method in the `FieldSampler` project.

   ```
   CheckboxField chkField = new CheckboxField("Checkbox Field",
                                                   false);
   add(chkField);
   CheckboxField chkField2 = new CheckboxField("FIELD_RIGHT", false,
                                                   Field.FIELD_RIGHT);
   add(chkField2);

   // A separator field between each type of control
   add(new SeparatorField());
   ```

2. Next, add the following code to the `getValue` method in the `FieldSampler` project.

   ```
   if (f instanceof CheckboxField)
   {
       CheckboxField check = (CheckboxField) f;
       String value;
       if (check.getChecked())
       {
         value = "Checked";
       }
       else
       {
         value = "Unchecked";
       }
       Dialog.alert("The checkbox is " + value);
   }
   ```

3. Finally, compile and debug the application.

Learning the Basics About the UI

What just happened?

The `CheckboxField` is one of the simplest editable fields available. In this example, we showed how to create a `CheckboxField` normally and then a second time by using the `FIELD_RIGHT` style. It is important to note that unless you are using the default constructor (the one that takes no parameters), you need to supply an initial state in the constructor, and generally speaking this is the best practice.

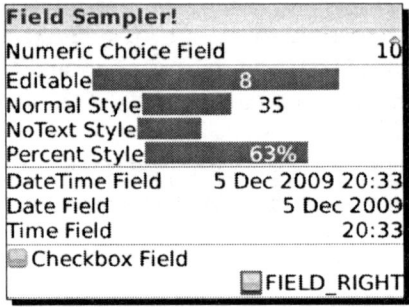

You can see how the `FIELD_RIGHT` style works in the second `CheckboxField` that you created. Using this style did not put the checkbox on the right of the label as you might expect. The `CheckboxField` does not define any styles either, so this shows that there is no way to create a checkbox with the box on the right-hand side of the label by using the `CheckboxField` class.

Lastly, the code in `getValue` to get the state of the checkbox is shown as well. The `getChecked` and the corresponding `setChecked` methods are the only methods of interest that are added by the `CheckboxField` class. Oftentimes, there are several ways to accomplish a task by using various methods. However, in the case of the `CheckboxField` there is only this one way.

RadioButtonField

A radio button is a close cousin to a checkbox. Unlike the checkbox though, it is meant for many radio buttons to be grouped together so that only one radio button in a group may be selected at a time. It is commonly used when there are a small, fixed number of choices that require different text for each one such that a `ChoiceField` might not be the best way to present the information to the user.

The `RadioButtonField` uses a small circle, or dimple, instead of a square like the `CheckboxField`. They do follow the industry standards, meaning they are arranged the same way as a checkbox by putting the radios on the left-hand side of the screen and the labels on the right.

RadioButtonField cannot be used without a RadioButtonGroup to go along with it. Using just one radio button doesn't make sense—that would essentially be a broken checkbox—and attempting to do so causes your application to crash; so don't do it. The RadioButtonGroup does the real work when it comes to making the RadionButtonField work right. Each RadioButtonField must be added to one, and only one, RadioButtonGroup. When a RadioButtonField is selected, it is the RadioButtonGroup that makes the other radio button fields become deselected, enforcing the mutually exclusive nature that we want to see in radio buttons. Radio button groups are not fields and do not need to be added to the screen, but each RadioButtonField does need to be added to the screen.

In the same way as other fields, such as the CheckboxField, if a RadioButtonField has focus and the menu is displayed, the framework adds a **Change Option** menu item. Clicking on the **Change Option** menu item will select the focused RadioButtonField and deselect all other radio button fields in the RadioButtonFieldGroup. You can also select a RadioButtonField by clicking the trackball or by pressing the *Space* or *Enter* keys.

Time for action – creating a RadioButtonField

1. First, add the following code to the createFields method in the FieldSampler application.

   ```
   // Create a radio button group
   RadioButtonGroup rdoGroup = new RadioButtonGroup();
   RadioButtonField rdo1 = new RadioButtonField("Radio Field 1");
   RadioButtonField rdo2 = new RadioButtonField("Radio Field 2");
   RadioButtonField rdo3 = new RadioButtonField("Radio Field 3");
   // add the radio buttons to the radio button group.
   //Adding them to the group is what ensures only one field is
   selected
   rdoGroup.add(rdo1);
   rdoGroup.add(rdo2);
   rdoGroup.add(rdo3);

   // Each field must still be added to the screen.
   // They do not need to be added in the same order as the they were
   with the group
   add(rdo3);
   add(rdo2);
   add(rdo1);

   rdoGroup.setSelectedIndex(0);

   // A separator field between each type of control
   add(new SeparatorField());
   ```

Learning the Basics About the UI

2. Next, add the following code to the `getValue` method.

```
if (f instanceof RadioButtonField)
{
    RadioButtonField rdo = (RadioButtonField) f;
    RadioButtonGroup rdogroup = rdo.getGroup();
    int index = rdogroup.getSelectedIndex();
    Dialog.alert("The radio button index is " + index);
}
```

3. Finally, compile the application and run it!

What just happened?

This example shows adding three radio button fields to a `RadioButtonGroup` and adding them all to the screen. After adding them to the screen, we call `setSelectedIndex` to select one of the radio button fields initially. Notice that `setSelectedIndex` is a method of the `RadioButtonGroup` and not one of `RadioButtonField`. This is because the `RadioButtonGroup` is responsible for ensuring that only one `RadioButtonField` in the `RadioButtonGroup` is selected. It stands to reason then that the call to `setSeleccctedIndex` cannot be made until all of the radio button fields have been added to the `RadioButtonGroup` as well.

When adding radio button fields to the `RadioButtonGroup`, order is important only for setting the selected field and later retrieving the selected field. In the previous example, the fields are added to the group one way, but the fields are added to the screen in reverse order. After adding the fields to both the screen and the group, the `setSelectedIndex` method is called to select the field at position 0. Which one is at position 0? That would be the field `rdo1`. In this case, position 0 is the position in the `RadioButtonGroup`, not the screen. The net result is that the radio button at the bottom of the screen is selected. This can lead to a lot of confusion, so it's just best to add the radio buttons to the group and to the screen in the same order.

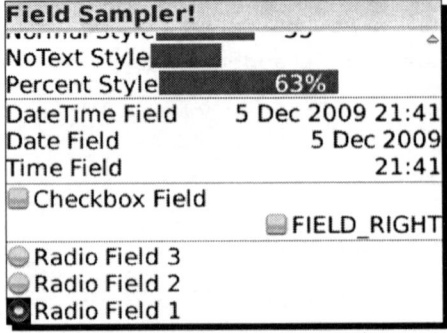

The code in the `getValue` method is a little more complicated than it would otherwise normally be, and this bears some explanation. The reason for this is that you chose not to store any member variables for the fields that you are adding. In order to find which `RadioButtonField` is selected you must use the `getSelectedIndex` method on the `RadioButtonGroup`. However, the `RadioButtonGroup` is not a field and does not get added to the screen. In the `getValue` method we have only the `RadioButtonField` objects. Therefore, we have to *dig* into the `RadioButtonField` class and get the `RadioButtonGroup` object by using the `getGroup` method. Normally, the `RadioButtonGroup` would be stored in a member variable and this step would be unnecessary. Once you have the group object you can call the `getSelectedIndex` method. Also, remember that this index is the order in which the `RadioButtonField` has been added to the `RadioButtonGroup`.

If you have also saved the radio button fields as member variables you could use the `isSelected` method to determine if a specific field is selected. This may be a lot more code because each `RadioButtonField` must be checked individually.

As radio buttons are mutually exclusive, one common technique is to use the index value as an enumeration for each radio button selection. For instance, you could have three radio buttons to represent a volume level of soft, medium, or loud. By making sure that they are added to the group in the proper order, the index of 0 could mean soft, 1 could mean medium, and 2 could mean loud. These values of 0, 1, and 2 could be saved or used instead of some other approach.

You may notice that the `RadioButtonField` has a `setSelected` method available as well. In general, you should not use this method because selecting the `RadioButtonField` directly also bypasses the `RadioButtonGroup`. You could end up with multiple selections in a group or accidently deselecting the selected `RadioButtonField`. In short, the `RadioButtonGroup` class should be used to control selection, and the `setSelected` method is what it uses to do that; not you!

Pop quiz

1. What is the maximum number of radio button fields that you can have in a `RadioButtonGroup`?

    a. 5

    b. 12

    c. 25

    d. There is no limit

2. What order is used to determine the index of `RadioButtonGroup.getSelectedIndex`?
    a. The order in which radio button fields are added to the screen
    b. The order in which radio button fields are added to the `RadioButtonGroup`
    c. The value used to call the `setIndex` method on each `RadioButtonField`

3. A single `RadioButtonField` is the same as a `CheckboxField`.
    a. True
    b. False

TextField

The `TextField` is the granddaddy in a very large family of specialized `Field` classes. It's another one of those base classes and as a result, you cannot create an instance of it. Instead, the `TextField` is there to provide some basic architecture that all of the specialized classes will use. It handles getting the keystrokes from the operating system and adding them to the field as well as providing the standard label functionality. All of the other specialized functionality is handled by the specialized classes and are added in layers of complexity. By taking this approach, it allows you to choose the right level of features based on your needs. So, without further delay, let's move on!

BasicEditField

As the name implies, the `BasicEditField` is the most basic of the `TextField` classes and is a base class to any field that can be edited. You can create instances of this class, but most often you would favor the slightly more specialized `EditField` or `PasswordEditField` classes. We will add it to the `FieldSampler`, but mostly as an exercise so that you can see the differences between the `BasicEditField` and `EditField`.

In the `TipCalc` application that we created in *Chapter 4, Creating your First BlackBerry Project*, we used a `TextFilter` to prevent non-numeric characters from going into the `Amount` field. This filtering functionality is added in the `BasicEditField` class as well as the ability to select text in a field for copy or paste operations. Because of these important features you could probably use the `BasicEditField` and be happy with it. Indeed, the differences between the `BasicEditField` and the `EditField` are very minor, but even minor differences need to be understood so that you can use the right field for the task when developing applications.

There is no real user interface change related to filtering, but selection, copy, and paste add several new aspects to a user's experience. Just like in the previous classes that we've seen when a `BasicEditField` has focus and the menu is displayed, several menu items are added to support the new features in this field.

All of these menu items do things that the user can do to make entering text easier because of the limitations of the operating system. Generally, your application doesn't care how the user enters data so the existence or use of these menus is purely for the benefit of your users and will have no impact on your application development.

The **Show Symbols** and the **Switch Input Language** menu items are always shown regardless of what the state of the field is. The **Show Symbols** menu item will display the symbols dialog in just the same manner as if the user pressed the symbol key on the keyboard. The **Switch Input Language** menu item will display a dialog listing the installed languages and allowing the user to change the language.

The next three menu items can change depending on the state of the field and are specifically related to the selection capability that is part of the `BasicEditField`. If the field has data in it when the **Menu** button is pressed, the **Select** and **Clear Field** menu items will be shown. As the name suggests, the **Clear Field** menu item will remove all of the text currently in the field.

The **Paste** menu item is shown only if some text is already in the clipboard. The **clipboard** is the area where data that has already been copied is stored until it is used. Therefore, the **Paste** menu is shown only if you have previously done a **Copy** operation.

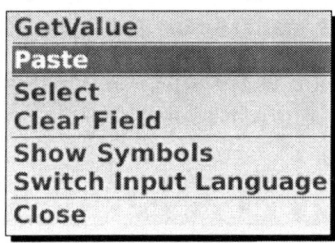

The other menu item, **Select**, is also shown only if there is some data in the field, but that's where the similarity ends. Clicking on **Select** will put the field into a *selecting* state and a couple of things change when this happens. You can also start selecting, or put the field into the *selecting* state, by scrolling the trackball while holding the *Shift* key.

The first change is that the cursor changes from a full-height flashing rectangle to a half-height flashing rectangle. This indicates that the field is in the *selecting* state and sets an anchor to the current location. At this point, scrolling the trackwheel will cause the text between the current cursor location and the anchor location to be highlighted, which is to indicate that the text has been selected.

Learning the Basics About the UI

Selecting text doesn't do anything by itself though. For this, you need the other menu items that we spoke of earlier. When the field is in a *selecting* state, the **Select** and **Clear Field** menu items disappear because they are no longer useful. Instead, a **Copy** and **Cut** pair of menu items is shown in place of the **Select** menu item and a **Cancel Selection** menu item is shown in place of the **Clear Field** menu item.

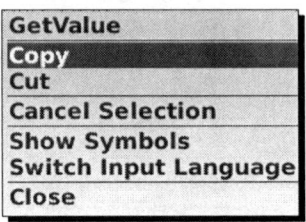

These menu items are very straightforward in their function. The **Cancel Selection** menu item cancels the whole *selecting* state of the field. The anchor point for the selection is removed, the cursor is returned to normal, and any text that has been selected is once again displayed normally and no action is taken on it.

The **Copy** and **Cut** menu items both place a copy of the selected text into the clipboard for later use. **Cut** also takes the additional step of removing the selected text from the field. In either case the selection process ends in the same way as the **Cancel Selection** menu item.

That's a lot of overhead stuff but it is important to understand why these menu items are added and what they do for you. Let's write some code!

Time for action – creating a BasicEditField

1. Add the following code to the `createFields` method.

```
// A separator field between each type of control
add(new SeparatorField());

String initialValue = "";
BasicEditField basic = new BasicEditField("Basic: ",initialValue);
basic.setMaxSize(25);
add(basic);

BasicEditField phone = new BasicEditField("Basic: ", initialValue,
                     25, BasicEditField.FILTER_PHONE);
add(phone);

BasicEditField phone2 = new BasicEditField("Phone2: ",
                     initialValue);
```

```
         phone2.setFilter(new PhoneTextFilter());
         phone2.setMaxSize(25)
         add(phone2);
```

2. Then add the following code to the `getValue` method.
```
   if (f instanceof TextField)
   {
      TextField t = (TextField) f;
      Dialog.alert("The text is " + t.getText());
   }
```

3. Finally, run the application.

What just happened?

We just experimented with the `BasicEditField` in the `FieldSampler` application as a way to understand what features this field has. Most notably, the `BasicEditField` offers an editable text field that supports selection, copy, and paste operations as well as text filtering.

As for the code, it demonstrates creating a `BasicEditField` in several different approaches. The first approach simply creates a text field without any filtering requirements on it. This form of constructor requires an initial value that is defined in the string named `InitialValue`. If you are retrieving the value from another system, this is handy; or you can simply use the constant empty string ("") as well, but by making the variable the code is easier to read and understand. Notice also that the code calls `setMaxSize` with a length of 25. This isn't strictly necessary, but every system is going to have limits on the amount of data that they can accept. For this reason, it is good practice to always define limits on the `TextField` family of classes.

The second example shows how we can create a field and apply a filter to it. This form of the constructor requires the maximum field size as well, so it has been set here again to 25. In this case, the filter is specified using a style as the last parameter. There is a style for each of the standard `TextFilter` available in the system.

The third form shows how the same field can be created, but this approach sets the `TextFilter` directly by creating a new `PhoneTextFilter` object and calling the `setFilter` method. This is the same thing that is done automatically for you when using the `BasicEditField.FILTER_PHONE` style. The important thing to note here is that you can create your own filter classes and use them in this manner if the standard filters supplied by the system don't work for you.

Learning the Basics About the UI

It's important to understand that filtering is not the same as formatting. Filtering will only prevent invalid characters from being entered into the field, but it does not make sure that the data is well formatted or in the correct order. Later on, we will see that there is an `EmailAddressEditField` class and this may seem unnecessary considering that there is a `BasicEditField.FILTER_EMAIL` filter as well. As we've said before, the filter simply stops invalid characters from being entered. Therefore, an ampersand could be entered many times using the filter, but this would still not be a valid e-mail address.

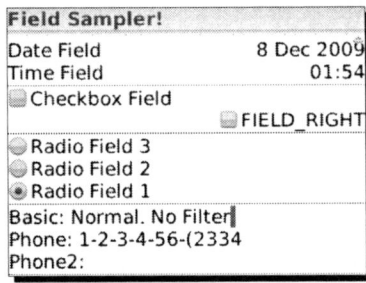

When it comes to retrieving the text from a `BasicEditField`, or any of the fields in the `TextField` family, the main method to use is the `getText` method. Unlike many of the fields we've looked at so far getting data from a field in the `TextField` family is simple and doesn't require any other operations, lookups, or conversions.

EditField

The `EditField` class adds one more feature to the `BasicEditField`—the ability to hold a key down and scroll the trackball to display similar characters from other character sets. The feature isn't nearly as important as those in the `BasicEditField`, but it is something that a user would feel is standard and so this field should be the one that is used most often and preferred over the `BasicEditField`. It isn't one commonly used for English, but is very important for other languages that need these characters.

Time for action – creating an EditField

1. First, add the following code to the `createFields` method.

    ```
    // A separator field between each type of control
    add(new SeparatorField());

    String initialValue = "";
    EditField edit = new EditField("Edit: ",initialValue);
    edit.setMaxSize(25);
    add(edit);
    ```

2. Run the application and test out the rolling character feature.

What just happened?

Wow, this code sure does look familiar, doesn't it? It should. It's nearly identical to the `BasicEditField` example code, well, except for the name. Everything needed to make the rolling character feature work is handled by the framework and those changes don't really affect us as developers. In fact, the only methods the `EditField` class adds over the `BasicEditField` are used by the class itself and aren't needed by outside developers.

You may have noticed that this time you didn't add any code to the `getValue` method. This is because getting the data from an `EditField` is exactly the same as getting data from a `BasicEditField`, so there is no need for new code in the `getValue` method.

So, in a nutshell, the `EditField` and `BasicEditField` classes are identical when it comes to code to use them and vary only slightly in the features they support.

PasswordEditField

Did you wonder why the `BasicEditField` and the `EditField` are in fact two separate fields when they are so similar in operation? The reason is this class—the `PasswordEditField`. Now, as the name implies, the `PasswordEditField` should be used any time you want to collect sensitive data, such as passwords. But what does this have to do with the other two fields?

As the name implies, the `PasswordEditField` should be used any time you want to collect sensitive data, such as passwords. Unlike the other fields, this class allows the user to enter characters into the field but displays only asterisks on the screen. The real data is still in the field, and you can access it, but it is hidden by the asterisks for protection. Furthermore, all copy operations are disabled so that the sensitive data cannot be copied out. If you had previously copied some text into the clipboard, the **Paste** operation can still be used.

Time for action – creating a PasswordEditField

1. Add the following code to the `createFields` method.

   ```
   PasswordEditField pass = new PasswordEditField("Password:
   ",initialValue);
   add(pass);
   
   // A separator field between each type of control
   add(new SeparatorField());
   ```

2. Next, run the application and test the `PasswordEditField`.

What just happened?

Do you get the feeling that this code is starting to look the same each time? You would be exactly right and that is part of the point of showing the code each time as well. The `EditField` family of fields is purposefully designed so that working with one kind of `EditField` is very similar to working with another.

Notice that we didn't add any code to the `getValue` method either. The same code still works for the `PasswordEditField` as did for the other `EditField` classes. Also notice that even though the data you entered in the `PasswordEditField` is not shown when calling `getText`, the true data is still returned to you in the code.

EmailAddressEditField

We mentioned the `EmailAddressEditField` once before, but at this point we can talk about it in more detail. Previously, the `EmailAddressEditField` was used as an example for the "how a filter can sometimes not do everything you want". For instance, using the `FILTER_EMAIL` filter will prevent illegal characters from being entered into the field, but will not enforce formatting rules, such as the rule that there can be only one ampersand in an e-mail address. Using just the filter will allow multiple ampersands and therefore, allow the user to enter an invalid e-mail address.

This field addresses that shortcoming and more! Not only does it enforce the formatting rules, but it also helps out the user. Entering an e-mail requires at least two punctuation characters—an ampersand and a period. Additionally, a space is not allowed in an e-mail address so the `EmailAddressEditField` uses this to help the user. When entering an e-mail address using this field, pressing the *Space* key will insert an ampersand or period if an ampersand has already been entered. This makes things a lot easier for the user because the user would otherwise need to access the **Symbol** menu or use an *Alt* key to put these required pieces in.

Time for action – creating an EmailAddressField

1. Add the following code to the `createFields` method.

   ```
   EmailAddressEditField addr = new EmailAddressEditField("Email: ",
                                   initialValue);
   add(addr);
   // A separator field between each type of control
   add(new SeparatorField());
   ```

2. Run the application and experiment with the `EmailAddressEditField` control.

What just happened?

I'm afraid this is starting to sound like a broken record, isn't it? Be that as it may, it is still important to demonstrate all of the fields as we talk about them in the `FieldSampler` application. As we've covered the code twice already there isn't much more to do except that these fields are so well done that they almost code themselves.

AutoTextEditField

The next feature to be added to the humble `TextField` is support for AutoText in the form of the `AutoTextEditField`. You've probably used `AutoText` and didn't even realize it while working on a BlackBerry at some point. **AutoText** is sometimes confused for spellchecking; it does do some auto-correction type of work, but it isn't a spell checker. You must have likely encountered AutoText while using the mail application and found that things such as "didnt" automatically changed into the proper "didn't". AutoText is what did this for you.

AutoText uses a simple database lookup to convert one sequence of characters into another. It does not take into consideration the context that you are writing in, other nearby words, or the sentence structure and because of this, it is not a spell checker. Nevertheless, many common typos such as "teh" are corrected by AutoText. However, a word such as "ill" is not automatically changed into "I'll" because "ill" is itself a word.

Because of the autocorrection feature this field is typically used in applications where a comparatively large chunk of text can be entered, such as a mail message, memo, description, or a comment.

Time for action – creating an AutoTextEditField

1. Add the following code to the `createFields` method.

    ```
    AutoTextEditField auto = new AutoTextEditField("Auto: ",
                            initialValue);
    add(auto);

    AutoTextEditField autoNoCap = new AutoTextEditField("AutoNoCap: ",
                            initialValue, 25, AutoTextEditField.
    AUTOCAP_OFF);
    add(autoNoCap);

    AutoTextEditField autoNoPunc = new AutoTextEditField(
    "AutoNoPunc: ", initialValue,25,AutoTextEditField.AUTOPERIOD_OFF);
    add(autoNoPunc);
    ```

```
AutoTextEditField autoOFF = new AutoTextEditField("AutoOFF: ",
initialValue, 25, AutoTextEditField.AUTOREPLACE_OFF );
add(autoOFF);

// A separator field between each type of control
add(new SeparatorField());
```

2. Run the application and test the `AutoTextEditField` by entering the string "didnt foo" into each field. Notice that there are two spaces between the words and that "didnt" has no apostrophe in it.

What just happened?

This demo code is slightly more interesting than the ones we've looked at previously. We're really just showing here that the `AutoTextEditField` has three styles that can be applied to disable one aspect of the field's functionality. By entering the specific text into each field we can see that each field handled things differently based on the styles and features that were active.

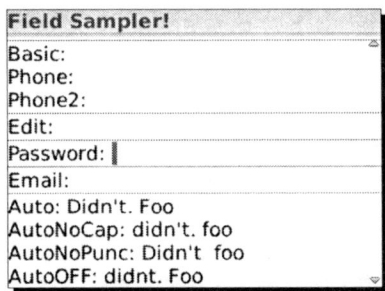

If no style is supplied then the field automatically capitalized the first letter of the word, corrected the misspelled word, and converted two spaces into a period and a space. Every other example field used a style that disabled one of these three features. `AUTOCAP_OFF` disabled the automatic capitalization of the first character. `AUTOPERIOD_OFF` **disabled the replacement of two spaces with a period and a space.** `AUTOREPLACE_OFF` **disabled the replacement of words using the AutoText database.**

 Note: These styles were added with version 4.3 of the SDK, so if you are using an older SDK version they will cause a compilation error.

ActiveAutoTextEditField

The last editable `TextField` we get to cover, and the most complex editable field, is the `ActiveAutoTextField`. Notice how the names get longer and longer each time the SDK adds more features onto and extends the previous class. This mouthful of a field is the most flexible field available. The `Active` part of the name means that there are active regions that are enabled when certain kinds of text is entered into the text field.

The regions are predefined by the operating system and include e-mail addresses, websites, and phone numbers. When data of this type is entered, the `ActiveAutoTextField` makes the text an active region. When the cursor is in one of these active regions, new menu items are added to the menu to allow the user to interact with the data in the region. For instance, if you entered a phone number, then new menu items would appear allowing you to place a call to the phone number.

It is possible to add new region types to the operating system as well, but that is a topic too advanced for this book. When done, new region types are available to all 'active' fields on the handheld.

Time for action – creating an ActiveAutoTextEditField

1. Add the following code to the createFields method

   ```
   ActiveAutoTextEditField activeauto = new ActiveAutoTextEditField("
   ActiveAuto:","Visit Packt Publishing online at www.packtpub.com");
   add(activeauto);

   // A separator field between each type of control
   add(new SeparatorField());
   ```

2. Run the application and test out the active region. Optionally, add your own phone number and e-mail address into the field.

What just happened?

The `ActiveAutoTextEditField` is still surprisingly simple to create and use. This example is very similar to the previous examples, the biggest difference here is that a different initial text is supplied to contain a website address that the field will establish as an active region. Other than that, the pattern for creating new fields remains the same and the code to get the text of the field is exactly the same as the fields we've studied previously. Much like the asterisks in the `PasswordEditField`, when the `getText` method is called only the real text of the field is returned. Any regions that are made active don't change the underlying text of the field at all.

```
Field Sampler!
Phone2:
Edit:
Password:
Email:
Auto:
AutoNoCap:
AutoNoPunc:
AutoOFF:
ActiveAuto: Visit Packt Publishing
online at www.packtpub.com
```

Pop quiz

1. What is the name of the method that is used to retrieve the text from any `TextField`?

    a. `Text()`

    b. `getText()`

    c. `setText()`

2. The term `Active` in `ActiveAutoTextEditField` means what?

    a. Text can be animated

    b. Certain text can be clicked

    c. The field actively checks spelling of the text

3. In an `EmailAddressEditField`, pressing the *Space* key will enter what character?

    a. A space

    b. An ampersand

    c. Either a period or ampersand as appropriate

    d. An underscore

RichTextField

All of the previous fields that we've discussed, starting with the `BasicEditField` all the way through the `ActiveAutoTextEditField` have been editable fields, representing one side of the `TextField` family tree. The next two classes represent the other side of the family tree—the non-editable `TextFields`. Now, any of the fields derived from `BasicEditField` can set the `READONLY` style to make any of the editable fields no longer editable.

The `RichTextField` is able to do something that no other field can do, however. Its special feature is to display text in multiple fonts within the same field. As we said already, this field is also read-only by design. It just doesn't make sense to have a field that can be edited and yet also have the text font change in the field as well.

This power and capability comes at a cost in terms of coding and setup. The code to create this field can get complicated very quickly. Let's try it out with the following code.

Time for action – creating a RichTextField

1. Add the following code to the `createFields` method of the `FieldSampler` application.

   ```
   Font someFont;
   try
   {
   someFont = FontFamily.forName("BBClarity").getFont(FontFamily.SCALABLE_FONT,10);
   }
   catch (ClassNotFoundException e)
   {
     someFont = Font.getDefault();
   }
   Font fonts[] = new Font[5];
   fonts[0] = Font.getDefault();
   fonts[1] = Font.getDefault().derive(Font.BOLD);
   fonts[2] = Font.getDefault().derive(Font.UNDERLINED);
   fonts[3] = Font.getDefault().derive( Font.ITALIC);
   fonts[4] = someFont;
   byte attributes[] = new byte[8];
   int offsets[] = new int[9];
   // must always start the offset at 0
   offsets[0] = 0;
   ```

Learning the Basics About the UI

```
attributes[0] = 0; // Default font
// The next change will happen at offset 2
// for the word 'RichTextField'
offsets[1] = 2;
attributes[1] = 1; //Bold
// then switch back to the default
offsets[2] = 15;
attributes[2] = 0; //default
//italicize the word 'display'
offsets[3] = 20;
attributes[3] = 3; //default
// then switch back to the default
offsets[4] = 27;
attributes[4] = 0; //default
// underline the word 'many'
offsets[5] = 35;
attributes[5] = 2; //default
// immediately bold italics the
// word 'different'
offsets[6] = 40;
attributes[6] = 4; //default
// then switch back to the default
offsets[7] = 50;
attributes[7] = 0; //default
// the last entry in offset is the last character in the text.
offsets[8] = 57;
// no attribute is given.
// offset array must be 1 greater than the attribute array.
RichTextField rich = new RichTextField();
// a ruler like this helps when counting characters.
//           0123456789012345678901234567890123456789012345678901
23456
rich.setText("A RichTextField can display text in many different
fonts.",
          offsets,attributes,fonts);
add(rich);
// A separator field between each type of control
add(new SeparatorField());
```

2. Then compile the application and look at how the text is displayed on the screen.

What just happened?

Now, we haven't seen a code sample like that for some time. Don't let the size intimidate you though, it's not that complicated. Well, this giant block of code sets up a `RichTextField` with several different fonts displayed in that field.

The first few lines of the code are used to create a `Font` object based on one of the standard fonts named "BBClarity". A **font family** represents all of the specific fonts that are part of the same family of fonts, that is to say are drawn using the same style. For instance, a 10 point, bold font and a 14 point, italic font are actually two separate `Font` objects. However, if they both represent, a Courier font then they belong to the same font family. Calling `FontFamily.forName()` will get the `FontFamily` object for the font of that name.

From there, calling the `getFont` method with the font size will return a specific `Font` object based on that size, if it is supported. So the `try-catch` block attempts to get a 10 point font of the BBClarity family. If it fails then we use `Font.getDefault()` to get the default font of the system—something that is always going to exist.

The next few lines of code set up an array of `Font` objects that will be used in this `RichTextField`. Several of the fonts being used in this array are derived from the default font for the system, to demonstrate how to get one of the various subtypes of fonts. The `Font.BOLD`, `Font.UNDERLINED`, and `Font.ITALIC` styles can be combined using an `OR` operator in the same way by which field's styles can also be combined.

The order of the fonts in this array is irrelevant to the `RichTextField`, but is referenced later on in the `attributes` array. The array does not have to be used exclusively for one `RichTextField` and can include other fonts as well. If you have an application with many fields of the type `RichTextField` you could use the same array of `Font` objects for all of them, even if you don't need every possible font in every `RichTextField`.

Immediately following the `fonts` array is the `attributes` and `offsets` arrays. These two arrays work together to let the field know where to apply which font. Note that the `offsets` array is one element larger than the `attributes` array. This is because the last element of the `offsets` array must be the last character in the `TextField`.

Next, and the largest portion of this sample, we populate the `attributes` and `offsets` arrays. Each element in the `offsets` array is the character offset of the text string indicating where to start applying the font. The first offset must be 0, which is the first character in the field text.

Each time an offset is set a `Font` object must also be specified, and this is done in the `attributes` array. The value of that element is the index of the font you want to use from the fonts array. It is not the font object itself, but the index into that array we previously created.

```
// must always start the offset at 0
offsets[0] = 0;
attributes[0] = 0; // Default font
```

Learning the Basics About the UI

Looking more closely at this code we can see that it is saying to apply the default font (which is index 0 of the `fonts` array) to the text in the field starting at index 0 of the text.

The first one may not be such a great example, so let's also look at the second set.

```
// The next change will happen at offset 2
// for the word 'RichTextField'
offsets[1] = 2;
attributes[1] = 1; //Bold
```

With this example we can see that at the text index of 2 (which is the start of the word RichTextField in the text) we want to use the font at index 1 of the `fonts` array, which is the bold version in this case.

The sample continues populating the `offsets` and `attributes` arrays to change the font of the text in the field at various points. After the last attribute is set, we still need to finish up by putting one more offset in place. This offset of the last character in the string.

```
// the last entry in offset is the last character in the text.
offsets[8] = 57;
```

The remainder of the sample code creates the `RichTextField` and uses the fonts, attributes, and offset arrays we've just populated.

```
Field Sampler!
Password:
Email:
Auto:
AutoNoCap:
AutoNoPunc:
AutoOFF:
ActiveAuto: Visit Packt Publishing
online at www.packtpub.com
A RichTextField can display text in
many different fonts.
```

ActiveRichTextField

The `ActiveRichTextField` adds two different features to the `RichTextField` we just discussed. You probably noticed that the name is similar to the `ActiveAutoTextEditField` seen earlier in this chapter. That is no coincidence of course. The `ActiveRichTextField` combines the "active" nature of the `ActiveAutoTextEditField` with the rich text of the `RichTextField` into one new package.

In addition to the "Active" feature, the `ActiveRichTextField` also adds the ability to display multiple colors as well as multiple fonts within the field making this an excellent field for displaying lots of text to the user. So let's get right to the example for this, our last `TextField`.

Time for action – creating an ActiveRichTextField

1. Add the following code to the `createFields` method.

   ```
   int bg[] = new int[]{Color.WHITE, Color.WHITE, Color.WHITE,
                        Color.WHITE,Color.BLUE};
   int fg[] = new int[]{Color.BLACK, Color.GREEN,
                        Color.RED,Color.PURPLE, Color.WHITE};
   ActiveRichTextField activeRich = new ActiveRichTextField("");
   initialValue = "A RichTextField can display text in many different
   fonts.  An ActiveRichTextField also displays Active regions like
   www.packtpub.com.";
   offsets[8] = initialValue.length();
   activeRich.setText(initialValue,offsets,attributes,fonts,fg,bg);
   add(activeRich);
   ```

2. Then run the application and see how the `ActiveRichTextField` is different from the `RichTextField`.

What just happened?

This example reuses some of the code from the `RichTextField`, especially the code populating the `attributes` and `offsets` arrays. The initial lines establish two arrays for the foreground and background colors that will be used on the field.

If you recall, we populated the `offsets` and `attributes` arrays in pairs. Each assignment essentially says "At this spot, start using this font". The `ActiveRichTextField` takes that a step further to say that the specified background and foreground colors will be used with each font also.

The first two lines of the sample established the colors to be used for each font that is in the `fonts` list. These color arrays, in conjunction with the fonts array, now effectively say that font 0 means to use the default font with a white background and a black foreground. Font 1 indicates that a bold font with a white background a green foreground should be used.

Learning the Basics About the UI

In order to highlight the active nature of this field the text put into the field has been changed slightly to include a URL that will get activated by the control. As a result, the `offsets[8]` needed to be changed as well because the last offset is always the position of the last character in the text.

Wow, that was a lot of `TextFields`, wasn't it? I guess it just goes to show just how much thought and effort has gone into displaying, and editing text, and doing what helps the user the most.

Pop quiz

1. What field is the only field that can display colored text?

    a. `RichTextField`

    b. `ActiveRichTextField`

2. What common class does the `ActiveRichTextField` and the `ActiveAutoTextEditField` both derive from?

    a. `ActiveTextField`

    b. `TextField`

Have a go hero – showing all fonts

One fun and educational thing to do with the `RichTextField` is to show a complete list of all fonts installed on your handheld. One easy way to do this is to simply display the same text using a different font each in a `RichTextField`. We've already shown how to set up the `RichTextField` object, but let's face it, it's not easy. This exercise will let you get familiar with all of the fonts available on the system as well as practice the somewhat complicated setup of the `RichTextField`.

You can get a complete list of all fonts by calling the static method `FontFamily.getFontFamilies()`. The previous example already shows how to get a font from a font family, so all that is left to do is to set up the `attributes` and `offsets` arrays. Using the same text for each font should make calculating the offsets easy too.

Summary

Wow, that was a lot of fields that we covered in this chapter, but that's not even all of them! Obviously, a lot of thought and planning went into creating all of these `Field` classes.

Specifically, we went over:

- Discussions and examples of each type of field available in the SDK
- Examples for both creating and retrieving data from each field

The next chapter will go even deeper into the user interface elements of the BlackBerry SDK. In it, we will cover some of the advanced fields such as lists and trees. Additionally, the next chapter will cover how to manage screens and dialogs so that you can put it all together into a complete user interface.

6
Going Deeper into the UI

In the last chapter, we covered all of the basic user interface elements of the SDK. Each of these fields have a specific purpose and implement a little more functionality. We covered them in detail so that you can choose the right field for the right job when building an application. But that's not all of them! This chapter will continue where the other left off and cover the remaining advanced `Field` *classes. I call these advanced classes because they will require more programming in order to make them work than just to create an instance and add it to the* `Screen`.

This chapter picks up where the previous one left off. In this chapter, you will:

- Learn to use the advanced fields such as `TreeField` and `ListField`
- Study what a layout manager is and how is it used
- Manage more than one screen in an application
- Create and use dialogs to notify the user of a choice or collect information
- Learn the changes that are needed to interface with touchscreens such as the BlackBerry Storm

Going Deeper into the UI

ButtonField

Okay, so the `ButtonField` isn't very interesting by itself but working with a `ButtonField` is going to be a little more complicated and involved than it was with the text fields, and in that respect, they are more interesting. Now a `ButtonField`, is in many ways, the least used field in the system. If you look at the existing applications that come with the handheld, such as **Mail** and **Address Book**, they don't use a `ButtonField` at all.

In general, you shouldn't use button fields on a screen with other fields. Anything you might want to do with a button can, and should, be done through a menu item. This is the style that has been set forth by BlackBerry in the existing applications.

So why even have a `ButtonField` if you are recommended to not use it? One word, Dialogs.

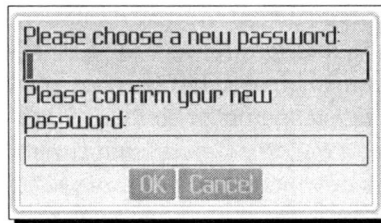

Pop-up dialogs typically do use buttons to dismiss the dialog. In fact, for dialogs one should not use menu items at all. If something is so complicated that it cannot be done with a few buttons, it is too complicated for a dialog and should be done in another screen. We'll look into displaying dialogs and multiple screens later.

Time for action – creating a ButtonField

1. Start by adding the following code to the `getValue` method.

   ```
   if (f instanceof ButtonField)
   {
      Dialog.alert("HelloWorld!");
   }
   ```

2. Next, add the following code to the `createFields` method.

   ```
   ButtonField button = new ButtonField("Button");
   button.setChangeListener(new FieldChangeListener()
   {
      public void fieldChanged(Field field, int context)
      {
   ```

```
            getValue();
        }
    });
    add(button);

    ButtonField button2 = new ButtonField("Button2",
                    ButtonField.CONSUME_CLICK);
    button2.setChangeListener(this);
    add(button2);

    // A separator field between each type of control
    add(new SeparatorField());
```

3. Replace the class declaration with the following one.

```
public class FieldSamplerScreen extends MainScreen implements
FieldChangeListener
```

4. Add the following method to the `FieldSamplerMainScreen` class.

```
public void fieldChanged(Field field, int context )
{
   getValue();
}
```

5. Lastly, run the application and click both buttons on the screen.

What just happened?

We've had some large pieces of sample code before, but this sample starts to show us some complicated code. Up until now, all of the fields haven't been very active, meaning that they didn't do anything as soon as you entered data into them. However, a button is active and we expect that when we click a button something will happen immediately. That kind of interaction takes a bit more code.

So let's go over the changes one-by-one. The first segment of code is for the `getValue` method and it simply displays a dialog saying **Hello World!**. A button has no input value to get so simply showing this alert will at least show us that the button click is working.

The next set of changes to the `createFields` method creates two buttons on the screen. They are created in much the same way, but we set the `FieldChangeListener` in two very different ways. First, we need to explain what a `FieldChangeListener` is.

Going Deeper into the UI

A `FieldChangeListener` is an interface that allows another class to listen for changes to a field. Every field can have a `FieldChangeListener` set, but so far we haven't needed it. We do need it for the `ButtonField` though, because the click on a `ButtonField` can be picked up only if you are listening for changes.

The `FieldChangeListener` for the first example is created on the fly by using an anonymous class. This anonymous class exists for the sole purpose of listening to changes for that specific `button` object. In this implementation, we call the `getValue` method on the `MainScreen` when any kind of change happens. Using an anonymous class like this makes for clean and concise code, but puts that code inside a class that cannot be referenced again. More precisely, it creates a new class that implements `FieldChangeListener` as a new inner class at compile time. Because we don't know the full name of this new class we cannot interact with it more. Also, debugging the class can be problematic because there is no source file in the project for it.

```
button.setChangeListener(new FieldChangeListener()
{
  public void fieldChanged(Field field, int context)
  {
    getValue();
  }
});
```

The second button is created by using a different approach and sets the `ChangeFieldListener` to the Java keyword `this`. When it is done this way it means that the `FieldSamplerScreen` class is also the `FieldChangeListener`, and setting it up this way requires some other new code to make this happen.

```
button2.setChangeListener(this);
```

The first change is to replace the class declaration itself to include the `implements` clause. A `FieldChangeListener` is really an interface that any class can implement. The `FieldSamplerScreen` didn't already do this. Replacing the line now declares that the `FieldSamplerScreen` implements the `FieldChangeListener` interface.

```
public class FieldSamplerScreen extends MainScreen implements
FieldChangeListener
```

Implementing the interface means that a new method must be implemented and this is our last change. Implementing the `fieldChanged` method satisfies the compiler and completely implements the `FieldChangeListener` interface. Now, when `button2` is clicked the `fieldChanged` method in `FieldSamplerScreen` will be called. This method simply calls `getValue` just like the anonymous `FieldChangeListener` of `button1`, so at this point both buttons function the same. We implemented `button2` just to demonstrate another approach to handling buttons.

Well, there is one minor difference to note still, and that is the presence of the CONSUME_CLICK style on `button2`. If you click `button1` you will get the "HelloWorld!" dialog, but once that dialog is dismissed the menu will immediately show up. However, when you click `button2` only the dialog is shown, the menu is not shown. The CONSUME_CLICK style means that processing of that click event should stop (that is, the event is consumed) once the `ButtonField` has processed the event. Most of the time if you are working with button fields you want to use the CONSUME_CLICK style.

ListField

If the `ButtonField` is one of the least used fields it seems fitting to move on to the `ListField`, which is one of the most used Fields, second only to the `TextField` family. List fields are very common and are used in nearly all of the standard applications, such as **Address**, **Tasks**, and of course, **Mail**. It is a versatile class that can be used in a lot of ways, but is also just as complex as the `ButtonField` in terms of implementation.

The `ListField` class is complicated to implement because this class requires us to implement the `ListFieldCallback` interface in order to display the items in the list. This callback is also why the field can be so powerful because we can exert a great deal of control over how the list is drawn and displayed. Let's see it all in action!

Time for action – creating a ListField

1. The first thing that you need to do is change the class declaration again to implement the callback interface. Replace the class declaration with the following list.

   ```
   public class FieldSamplerScreen extends MainScreen implements
   FieldChangeListener, ListFieldCallback
   ```

2. Next, you need to add a data member to the class to hold the items of your list.

   ```
   protected String listMembers[] = {"Item1","Item2","Item3"};
   ```

3. Next, you need to implement the methods of the callback. Add the following methods to the `FieldSamplerMainScreen` class.

   ```
   public void drawListRow(ListField list, Graphics g, int index,
                           int y,int width)
   {
     g.drawText( listMembers[index], 0, y, 0, 50 );
     switch (index)
     {
       case 0:
         g.setColor(Color.BLUE);
         g.setFont(Font.getDefault().derive(Font.BOLD));
   ```

Going Deeper into the UI

```
            g.drawText("Wow!",150,y,0,width-150);
            break;
          case 1:
            g.setColor(Color.BLACK);
            g.setBackgroundColor(Color.YELLOW);
            g.setFont(Font.getDefault().derive(Font.ITALIC));
            g.drawText("Shazam!",100,y,0,width-100);
            break;
          case 2:
            g.setColor(Color.RED);
            g.setBackgroundColor(Color.GREEN);
            g.drawText("Incredulous!",80,y,0,width-80);
            break;
       }
    }
    public Object get(ListField listField, int index)
    {
       return listMembers[index];
    }
    public int getPreferredWidth(ListField listField)
    {
       // This is a hack for now. The typical solution is below
       //return Display.getWidth();
       return 200;
    }
    public int indexOfList(ListField listField, String prefix,
                           int start)
    {
       // returning -1 indicates that a search is not allowed.
       return -1;
    }
```

4. Now, let's actually create the list. Add the following code to the `createFields` method.

```
// A separator field between each type of control
add(new SeparatorField());

ListField list = new ListField();
list.setCallback(this);
list.setSize(3);
add(list);
```

[146]

Chapter 6

5. Then, you need to make it do something. Add the following code to the `getValue` method.

    ```
    if (f instanceof ListField)
    {
        ListField l = (ListField)f;
        Dialog.alert("The selected element is: "+
                    Integer.toString(l.getSelectedIndex()));
    }
    ```

6. Finally, compile and debug the application.

What just happened?

The code that you added for the `ListField` has a lot of similarities to the one for `ButtonField`. Let's look at the changes one at a time.

The first change is to add the `ListFieldCallback` interface to the `FieldSamplerScreen` class. You have already added a `FieldChangeListenser` interface before so the `ListFieldCallback` will be another interface added to the class declaration. The `ListField` will use this interface to gather information about the items in the list and to notify the application when it is time to draw the field.

> Remember, any object can implement this interface, not just the `MainScreen`. Because this is a sample though, and creating a lot of objects can confuse the concept, we're just going to use the `MainScreen`.

One common practice is to create your own collection class for your data objects and to implement the `ListFieldCallback` in that class. The benefit here is that the collection for your objects and the code to handle the `ListField` for them are together in the same class.

The second code fragment simply adds a data member, which is an array of strings, to the class. So far we've avoided having data members. For this example though, avoiding it complicates things more than just using the data member though. Most applications will store data in a collection of some type, and this data member represents it. Now this data is very simple and convenient, but you get the point.

The next code fragment adds the methods to the `FieldSamplerScreen` class that implement the `ListFieldCallback` interface. This is where all of the work is really done as far as making the list work. The first method, `drawListRow`, is probably the most important, and the reason that the list field is so powerful. This method is called anytime a row in the list needs to be redrawn. As the second argument to that method is a `Graphics` object, which is a low-level drawing object, you can practically draw anything you want for each row.

The code in the `drawListRow` method demonstrates how you can draw each row of the list any way you want. Most of the time, you want things to be done the same for each row, but it doesn't have to be done this way. This example changes text, color, and font for each row. This implementation isn't very pretty and is very manual, but makes the point. Many applications will add small bitmaps or will draw multiple portions of the list to simulate columns in a table. The options are practically limitless.

```
case 0:
  g.setColor(Color.BLUE);
  g.setBackgroundColor(Color.WHITE);
  g.setFont(Font.getDefault().derive(Font.BOLD));
  g.drawText("Wow!",150, y, 0, width-150);
  break;
```

After `drawListRow` is the method called `get`. This method should simply return the object at the index that is passed in. If this method is implemented properly, it can be used to get the data in a `ListField` by accessing the `ListField` directly.

Next up is the `getPreferredWidth` method and some interesting comments. Most applications will return the width of the screen on the handheld, and because that varies based on model, they use the `Display.getWidth` method. This is preferred, but is a protected method and requires code-signing the application, which we haven't covered yet. Because we haven't covered code signing yet, the value is just hardcoded to 200. I wouldn't recommend doing this in your application, so just understand that this is done here only for the sake of brevity.

The last method you must implement is the `indexOfList` method—the method that is used with the search feature of `ListField`. It would have required implementing a search feature that would have just confused the sample code too much. So instead, we are returning `-1` to indicate that the search feature is not supported.

Now that the `ListFieldCallback` interface has been implemented, the next segment of code is used to add a `ListField` to the screen. Notice that there isn't a lot of work to be done at this point. Besides creating the object and adding it to the screen, we also call `setSize` and `setCallback`. The call to `setCallback` is used to let the `ListField` know which object it should call to get to the interface methods that we just implemented previously, and which will be used for each item in the list.

```
ListField list = new ListField();
list.setCallback(this);
list.setSize(3);
add(list);
```

Simply telling the `ListField` how many pieces of data you want to display may not seem like enough information, but that is all it needs at this point. Everything else is handled by the methods in the `ListFieldCallback` interface. Notice that the size is a count and not an index.

The last code segment implements the `getValue` method. The only piece of data that matters in this field is the element that is currently selected, so the `getValue` method simply displays the current selected index in the field.

TreeField

A `TreeField` is a relatively new field released with version 4.5 of the SDK, and a close cousin to the `ListField`. The `TreeField` does not inherit from the `ListField` so they aren't directly related, but I would wager that the implementation of the `TreeField` borrows very heavily from the `ListField`. As the name implies, a `TreeField` is used to display information which is organized into a hierarchical format, also called a **tree**, and can show a parent-child type of relationship in the data.

A tree always starts with a root node, which is to say a node with no parent. That root node then has child nodes, each of which can have their own child nodes and so on. This growth of nodes from a single root is much like how a tree will grow with branches that in turn have their own smaller branches. At the end of the branches are leaves, which in a `TreeField` are nodes with no child nodes of their own.

Hierarchical data, like that of a file system, is best shown using a `TreeField`. In the `TreeField`, each time there is a branch with child nodes added, the child nodes are drawn with an indentation so that it is clear that the children are nested under the parent node. Additionally, each branch of the `TreeField` can be collapsed to hide the child nodes, or later expanded to show them.

Going Deeper into the UI

This collapsing and expanding is shown by a small circle next to any branch nodes. When the circle has a minus sign, the branch is expanded and the child nodes are visible. When the circle has a plus inside it, the node is collapsed and the child nodes are hidden. We see this same functionality in desktop operating systems so the notation should be familiar. Much like some of the other fields that we've looked at earlier, when a branch node is selected and the menu is shown, a **Collapse** or **Expand** menu item is added to the menu automatically, depending on which action is appropriate for that node. When a leaf node is selected, no menu items are added.

Talking about the field is one thing, but let's see it in action.

Time for action – creating a TreeField

1. Like the ListField before, replace the class declaration with this code.

   ```
   public class FieldSamplerScreen extends MainScreen implements
   FieldChangeListener, ListFieldCallback, TreeFieldCallback
   ```

2. Add the following code to the `createFields` method so that a `TreeField` is created in your project.

   ```
   // A separator field between each type of control
   add(new SeparatorField());

   TreeField tree = new TreeField(this,Field.FOCUSABLE);
   int rootnode = tree.addChildNode(0,"Root");
   int child1node = tree.addChildNode(rootnode,"Child1");
   int child2node = tree.addSiblingNode(child1node,"Child2");
   int child3node = tree.addSiblingNode(child1node,"Child3");
   tree.addChildNode(child2node,"Grandchild1");
   add(tree);
   ```

3. Next, add this code to the `getValue` method so the menu will work.

   ```
   if (f instanceof TreeField)
   {
     TreeField t = (TreeField)f;
     int node = t.getCurrentNode();
     String str = (String) t.getCookie(node);
     Dialog.alert("The Current node is: "+str);
   }
   ```

4. Next, add this method to the class in order to implement the interface.

   ```
   public void drawTreeItem(TreeField field, Graphics g, int node,
                       int y, int width, int indent)
   ```

```
    {
       String str = (String) field.getCookie(node);
       g.drawText(str,indent,y,0,width);
    }
```

5. Finally, compile the application and run it!

What just happened?

Implementing a `TreeField` is almost identical in technique to the `ListField`, but with one major difference: where the `ListField` did not store any information about the data it was displaying, the `TreeField` does because it must. A `ListField` has a very simply structure, it is just a list so there is no need to store any additional information about the structure of the data. However, the structure of a `TreeField` can be much more arbitrary and so you must go through a process of adding data to the `TreeField` node by node. This has the side effect of simplifying the callback significantly though. Because the `TreeField` already has so much data about the structure of the tree, the only thing the callback needs to do is to draw each node of the `TreeField`.

So, much like the `ListField`, the first step is to add the interface that will be implemented to the class declaration. At this point, the declaration is getting a bit long but don't worry, you can add as many interfaces as needed!

The next step is to create the field in the `createFields` method. The constructor for the `TreeField` is a little different than that of the `ListField`. As the callback field is required to make this field useful, the `TreeField` requires the callback object in the constructor. Additionally, a style is also required. It is somewhat silly as the only styles that are allowed are either `Field.FOCUSABLE` or `Field.NON_FOCUSABLE`, but one must be supplied regardless.

```
    TreeField tree = new TreeField(this,Field.FOCUSABLE);
```

After the constructor, you can see how the nodes of the tree are added one-by-one. Each time a node is added an integer node ID is returned for it. This node ID is how the `TreeField` keeps track of the nodes in its system. We start with the root node and provide a parent node ID of `0`—a special ID indicating that there is no parent for this node.

```
    int rootnode = tree.addChildNode(0,"Root");
```

Going Deeper into the UI

Then, we make calls to `addChildNode` and provide the root node ID that was just returned when we added the root node. You can call `addChildNode` to add multiple children to the same parent node, or you can call `addSiblingNode` to add a new node after the current sibling. Which one do you choose to use will depend on how much information you have at the time that you need to add a node.

```
int child1node = tree.addChildNode(rootnode,"Child1");
int child2node = tree.addSiblingNode(child1node,"Child2");
int child3node = tree.addSiblingNode(child1node,"Child3");
```

Using the `addSiblingNode` method allows more control over the order of the children of a node than you can get simply using `addChildNode`. Using `addChildNode` though is often easier to code, and if the order of the data isn't as important, this is perfectly acceptable.

Each call to `addChildNode` or `addSiblingNode` takes a cookie value as well. A **cookie** is a generic term to mean some token that will help you later identify the object of that node. The `TreeField` does not do anything at all with these cookie values except for providing a way to set and retrieve them. The cookie may be a database ID, or it might even be the object that holds the data itself. Whatever the value is, only your application needs to understand what it means. In the case of this example, the cookie is the string value that you want to display in the tree itself. This means that the value `Child1` is being passed in as the cookie, which the callback will use to draw the screen.

The next segment of code implements the `getValue` method. As a `TreeField` has the cookie value, it is good practice to use the cookie to hold your data objects. This code gets the node ID of the current selected node and then uses that node ID to get the cookie (which is really a `String` object) and displays it in a dialog.

```
TreeField t = (TreeField)f;
int node = t.getCurrentNode();
String str = (String) t.getCookie(node);
Dialog.alert("The Current node is: "+str);
```

The last code that you have to look at is the interface implementation, which is the `drawTreeItem` method. Just like the `ListFieldCallback drawListRow` method, this provides a `Graphics` object so the sky is the limit for how you want to draw it. This time we didn't get fancy because that point was already driven home in the `ListField`.

It is important to note the indent value that is passed into the `drawTreeItem` method, which the `drawListRow` method does not use. Because a `TreeField` indents each child node, in order to draw the node properly you need to take that indent into account. The `Graphics drawText` method has a starting X position, which is the indent that you need to shift over. The `width` parameter already takes into account the indent value provided, so you don't need to do any manual adjustment for it. The `drawTreeItem` method does the same thing as `getValue` by getting the cookie for the node ID that is supplied to the method. Then, it draws that string by using the `drawText` method that we saw earlier with the `drawListRow` method.

```
String str = (String) field.getCookie(node);
g.drawText(str,indent,y,0,width);
```

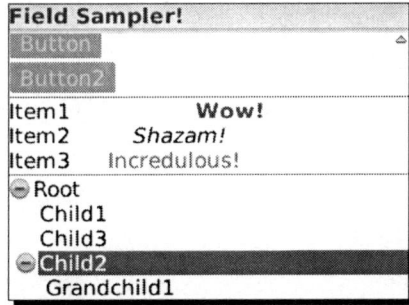

Pop quiz

1. To respond to a `ButtonField` click, what do you need to do?

    a. Implement `ButtonFieldListener` interface

    b. Set a callback object with the `setCallback` method

    c. Implement the `FieldChangeListener` interface

2. What interface is required to use a `ListField`?

    a. `ListFieldCallback`

    b. `ListFieldInterface`

    c. `IListField`

    d. `ListFieldListener`

3. What method is used to get the object at each node in the `TreeField`?

    a. `getObject`

    b. `getData`

    c. `getCookie`

MapField

The other new field addition to the version 4.5 SDK is the `MapField`. A `MapField` has a lot of potential uses in applications where the device has a built-in GPS. It is a read-only field though, so it isn't for data entry at all. As it is a read-only field, the only thing that you can do with it is to display a map to see. There are methods to move, zoom, and otherwise control the map at a pretty low level, but none of these features are directly accessible by the user through built-in controls; nor is there any integration with a GPS.

Time for action – creating a MapField

1. It's time to see a `MapField` in action! Add the following code to the `createFields` method.

   ```
   MapField map = new MapField();
   Coordinates c = new Coordinates(37.821582,-122.479362,(float) 0.0);
   map.moveTo(c);
   map.setZoom(4);
   add(map);
   ```

2. After that is done, compile and run the application and you will see a lovely map on the screen!

What just happened?

Again, because this is a read-only field the code is once again pretty simple compared to the `ListField` and `TreeField` that we just went over. Creating the field itself is very simple and setting up the field isn't much harder. In this sample, you create a `Coordinates` object with the coordinates for the Golden Gate Bridge in San Francisco, California. As you can see, these coordinates are hardcoded, meaning you aren't using a GPS to get them.

```
Coordinates c = new Coordinates(37.821582,-122.479362,(float) 0.0);
```

Next, a call to the `moveTo` method tells the `MapField` to shift the display so that those coordinates are centered within it. Lastly, `setZoom` is called so that you can see the road that is labeled **Golden Gate Brg**. The zoom level can be anywhere between `getMaxZoom` and `getMinZoom` level, which is between 15 and 0. However, the documentation does say that you should not rely on these value or hardcode them (like we did for this sample).

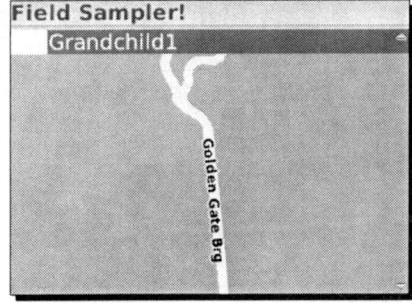

Displaying another screen

Not everything that needs to be done can be done on a single screen. The samples that we've made so far have used only one screen in order to keep things simple, but most applications will need many more. Switching between screens is a very common task and one that the SDK supports using the UI Stack. Each UiApplication has a stack of screens that you can use to manage the transition from one screen to the next. This stack actually places the entire Screen object onto the stack, so when you return from one screen to the previous one, the state of the previous screen has been preserved.

We first encountered the UI Stack in *Chapter 4, Creating your First BlackBerry Project* while setting up the TipCalcApplication constructor. This constructor does only one thing: makes a call to the pushScreen method that places the first (and only) screen onto the UI Stack. In order to display another screen to the user, all you need to do is to place another Screen object onto the UI Stack and the framework will do the rest.

```
private TipCalcApplication()
{
    // Push the main screen instance onto the UI stack for rendering.
    pushScreen(new TipCalcMainScreen());
}
```

TipCalc placed all of the screen setup code in the screen constructor because this approach of creating a new Screen object and passing it into the pushScreen method is a common approach. Let's expand on this approach and create a new screen to be added into the FieldSampler application.

One simple screen to create is an "About Screen" with your company name and contact information on it. This screen is often done by using an ActiveRichTextField because you will often want to include content such as website and phone numbers which can benefit from the "active" nature of the Field. Also, the ability to include multiple fonts and/or colors can make an otherwise boring screen much more interesting.

Time for action – creating an "About Screen"

1. First, create a new class for this screen. Add the following class declaration to the `FieldSamplerScreen` **class**.

   ```
   private class AboutScreen extends MainScreen
   {
     String _AboutText = "BlackBerry Field Sampler\n" +
         "Copyright (c) 2010 Bill Foust\n" +
         "BillFoust@rimdev.com";
     ActiveRichTextField _AboutField = new ActiveRichTextField
                                       (_AboutText);

     public AboutScreen()
       {
         setTitle(new LabelField("Field Sampler!"));
         add(_AboutField);
       }
   };
   ```

2. Next, you need to add the menu item that will show the screen. Add the following menu item to the `FieldSamplerScreen` as well.

   ```
   MenuItem _AboutAction = new MenuItem("About" , 100, 100)
   {
    public void run()
    {
      UiApplication.getUiApplication().pushScreen(new AboutScreen());
     }
   };
   ```

3. Lastly, you need to add the menu item to the menu when it is shown.

   ```
   m.add(_AboutAction);
   ```

4. After that is done, compile and run the application. Once you have `FieldSampler` running, click on the **About** menu item and see the new screen being displayed!

What just happened?

The first thing you did was to create a new screen class inside the existing `FieldSamplerScreen` class. As this new screen can be shown only from the `FieldSamplerScreen`, the `AboutScreen` can be an internal class and reside in the same Java file. Generally, you will want to create a separate Java file for each Screen class in your project. Using a separate file is essential if that screen will be shown by more than one screen in your application. "About Screens" usually aren't shown from more than one screen, and that is the case here. Because of this and the fact that they are also generally small, "About Screens" are often created as internal classes.

The setup and creation of the `AboutScreen` class shouldn't have any surprises in it. For this example, you didn't make the effort to make the screen particularly complicated with fonts and colors because that was already demonstrated in the previous chapter. You may notice that you also didn't do anything with adding menus to the `AboutScreen` either. The framework will automatically add a **Close** menu item, which is all what you really need for the `AboutScreen`. All you really did was to create an `ActiveRichTextField` and supply some text to be displayed.

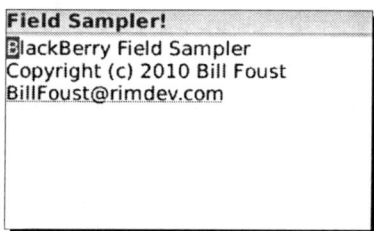

The real work comes in the menu item that is used to show the "About Screen". This menu item isn't very complicated either, but the important part to see here is how the `pushScreen` method is used.

```
UiApplication.getUiApplication().pushScreen(new AboutScreen());
```

This is the same method that we used earlier to get the application started except that this time the code is contained in the menu item's `run` method and nested inside the `FieldSamplerScreen` class. Because we don't have direct access to the `UiApplication` object, we need to get it through the `getUiApplication` static method on the `UiApplication` class itself. This method returns the current `Application` object that is being run, and so is a very useful shortcut in a situation like this.

You will note from using the application a little bit that if you select the **Close** menu item, or simply press the *Escape* key, you will return to the previous screen. How is this possible if we didn't add any code to do that? It is just another feature of the framework that saves us work. The default implementation for pressing the *Escape* key or selecting the **Close** menu item is to return to the previous screen.

Now, if you needed more complex logic in the screen you can always return to the previous screen manually by calling the `popScreen` method that is part of the `UiApplication`. `popScreen` is the counterpart to `pushScreen`. It will remove the top screen from the Ui Stack and display the screen which is next in the stack.

It is important to note that this is not the same as the call stack! By this, I mean that the program execution will not resume at the line directly following the `pushScreen` call that caused the new screen to be displayed in the first place.

If you find yourself in a situation where you need to get a value and return to the same point of code in your screen, then you really should be using a dialog, especially if you need only one or two pieces of data.

Pop quiz

1. What class maintains the UI Stack?
    a. `Application`
    b. `UiApplication`
    c. `MainScreen`
2. When adding a screen to the UI Stack, what method is used?
    a. `add()`
    b. `pushScreen()`
    c. `addScreen()`

Displaying a dialog

Another common task is to display a dialog to collect just a single piece of information or prompt the user for some confirmation. We've used `Dialog.alert` before to display a simple alert, but these aren't active and can't be used to collect any real information. The `Dialog` class is actually much more flexible! There are several forms that will display common dialogs, dialogs with custom buttons, or even dialogs with a simple `ChoiceField`.

Being so flexible can also make it somewhat confusing though, so we will add a few menu items to demonstrate each form of dialog that can be used. The first example is to use one of the stock common dialogs.

Time for action – collecting information with a common dialog

1. The first thing that you need to do is to add a menu item to the `FieldSamplerScreen` to display and demonstrate this first form of dialog.

```
MenuItem _Dialog1Action = new MenuItem("Demo Common Dialog" ,
                                        10000, 100)
{
  public void run()
  {
    int retValue = Dialog.ask(Dialog.D_OK_CANCEL,
                     "Click OK or Cancel");
    if (retValue == Dialog.OK)
    {
      Dialog.alert("You hit OK");
    }
    else
    {
      Dialog.alert("You hit Cancel");
    }
  }
};
```

2. Lastly, you need to add the menu item to the menu when it is shown. Modify the `makeMenu` method to include the following code.

```
m.add(_CommonDialogAction);
```

3. After that is done, compile and run the application. Once you have the field sampler running, click on the **Demo Common Dialog** menu item to see what this kind of dialog looks like.

What just happened?

The common dialog we chose to use here is one that simply has two buttons: **OK** and **CANCEL**. There are only a few common dialogs, but they are used for simple things such as an **OK** confirmation, **YES/NO** choices, or **OK/CANCEL** choices. There are even common dialogs for saving and deleting confirmation. All of the common dialogs can be identified by one of the static constants that are part of the `Dialog` class that begin with `D_`.

Going Deeper into the UI

Displaying a common dialog is done by using the `Dialog.ask` method. This method is a more advanced version of the `Dialog.alert` method because it returns a value corresponding to the button selected by the user. These constants are also part of the `Dialog` class, but do not begin with a `D_` and include some with simple names such as **OK**, **YES**, **NO**, and **CANCEL**.

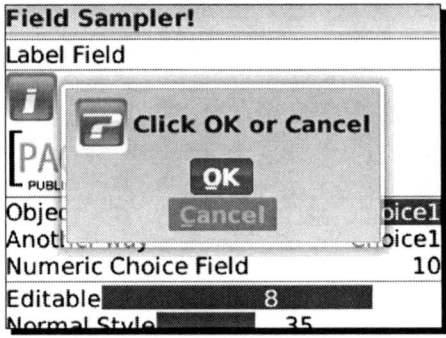

The dialogs with standard answers work most of the time, but sometimes you need something more when the standard choices just don't work. One of these situations (which is more common) is to display a few choices and ask the user to select one of them. Another variation of the `Dialog.ask` method can be used to display two or more buttons with your own custom text on them.

Time for action – collecting information with custom buttons on a dialog

1. Again you will add another menu item to the `FieldSamplerScreen` class to display this form of dialog.

    ```
    MenuItem _ButtonChoiceDialogAction = new MenuItem("Demo Button
                                            Choice Dialog", 10000, 100)
    {
      public void run()
      {
        Object[] _choices = {"Choice1","Choice2","Choice3"};
        int[] _values = {0,1,2};
        int retValue = Dialog.ask("Please select a value",
                                _choices,_values, 2);
        Dialog.alert("You selected "+_choices[retValue].toString());
      }
    };
    ```

2. Also, again, you need to add the following code to display the menu item when it is shown. Add this code to the `makeMenu` method.

```
m.add(_ButtonChoiceDialogAction);
```

What just happened?

This code isn't quite as easy as using a common dialog, but getting the power to display your own values in the buttons being shown to the user is worth the effort. The objects in the `_choices` list don't necessarily need to be a type of `String` either. Much like the `ObjectChoiceField`, the class will use the `toString` method in order to generate the text that will go into the buttons.

The second array, named `_values`, is used to assign a numeric value to each choice. These numbers can be any valid number, but in this case it makes sense to make the value be the same as the index of the item in the list. The value is returned by `Dialog.ask` and is used to identify one particular choice over another.

The list of choices should generally be small, but there is no hard limit and the text being displayed should also be fairly small. Remember, this is a dialog and not a full screen so there just isn't as much room to work with. If you need to display a large number of choices or anything with a more complicated user interface, then another `Screen` class is probably a better way to do it.

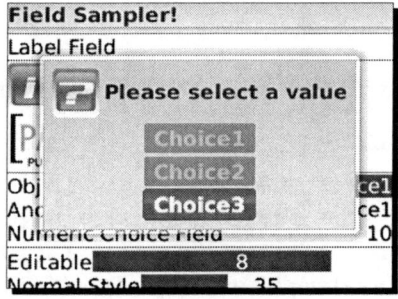

Sometimes the data just doesn't lend itself well to being in a button. Each button takes up some portion of the screen so the number of items you can display well is really limited to three or four items at the most. If you have even a few more choices, a `ListField` could be a much better way to accomplish the task.

You can show a dialog in this way, and the form is very similar to the one that is used to display buttons, but you can no longer use the static method `Dialog.ask()` to accomplish it.

Time for action – collecting information with a list on a dialog

1. One last time, add a menu item to the `FieldSamplerScreen` class so that you can display this form of `Dialog`.

    ```
    MenuItem _ListChoiceDialogAction = new MenuItem("Demo List Choice
                                                    Dialog ", 10000, 100)
    {
      public void run()
      {
        Object[] _choices = {"Choice1","Choice2","Choice3"};
        int[] _values = {0,1,2};
        Dialog d = new Dialog("Please select a value",
                    _choices, _values,2,
                    Bitmap.getPredefinedBitmap(Bitmap.INFORMATION),
                    Dialog.LIST);
        int retValue = d.doModal();
        Dialog.alert("You selected "+_choices[retValue].toString());
      }
    };
    ```

2. Then, you also need to add the menu item to the menu when it is displayed. Add the next line of code to the `makeMenu` method.

    ```
    m.add(_ListChoiceDialogAction);
    ```

3. Of course, you need to run the application and test it out!

What just happened?

This version of the `Dialog` functions is nearly identical to the previous version except instead of displaying each choice as a button, the choices are displayed in a `ListField`. Getting here was a bit more work though because you couldn't use the `Dialog.ask` method to help create and show the dialog for us. Instead, we had to do it manually.

The parameters to the `Dialog` constructor are nearly identical to those used in the `Dialog.ask` method with the same kind of object list for choices and list of integers for the values. The big difference here is the new `Dialog.LIST` style that is added to the constructor. If you leave the style off, the dialog will be displayed using buttons for each choice, just like we saw using the `Dialog.ask` method.

Another major difference is how we show the dialog. When using the `Dialog.ask` method, it handled both the creation and display of the dialog for us, but now we must do it by hand. Dialogs don't work the same way as screens do, so you need to use a different method to show them, that method is called `doModal`.

There are no other buttons on the dialog, so the user must select one of the choices in the list. The value associated with that selection is returned as the return value from `doModal()` just like it is from `Dialog.ask`.

This form which uses the list instead of buttons is more acceptable if you need to display a few more choices. Buttons are useful if there are only a few (that is, two, three, or four) choices, but a list can often be used with a few more, maybe even up to a dozen choices. A list is also preferable to buttons if the text that needs to be displayed is long, such as an e-mail address or telephone number.

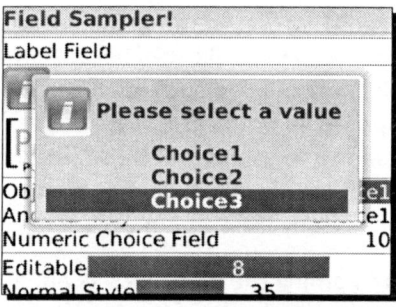

Pop quiz

1. What constant values do you use to display one of the common dialogs that are available?
   a. Constants with the `C_` prefix
   b. Constants with the `D_` prefix
   c. Constants with the `COMMON_` prefix

2. Which method is used to show a dialog with custom buttons?
   a. `Dialog.ask`
   b. `Dialog.alert`
   c. `Dialog.inform`

3. Which style is required to display a dialog with a list of choices instead of buttons?
   a. `DIALOG_LIST`
   b. `Dialog.NO_BUTTONS`
   c. `Dialog.LIST`

Listeners and callbacks

We've seen one listener and a couple of callbacks already, but it seems important to come back to this concept again because it is used for so many things in the SDK besides `ButtonField` and `ListField`.

Generally speaking, the listener pattern is used to allow one class to tell another class when something happens to it. In the cases that we've seen so far the `FieldChangeListener` is used to let another class listen for notifications that a field has changed. There can be many listeners, all listening to the same event, or there can be none at all. Things that use listeners often employ a "fire and forget" approach, meaning that a response is not required from any of the listeners that may be active. The `FieldChangeListener` is just one of the many listeners out there.

A callback is very similar to a listener, but the distinction is one of semantics. A callback is usually used when an object needs two-way communication with just one single object. The `ListField` and `TreeField` both use callbacks because the `ListField` class needs to query another class about the data being displayed. It can have only one response, so a listener pattern is inappropriate. In both cases, listeners and callbacks are always implemented using interfaces and so to use one of these listeners or callbacks, you must implement the interface methods in some class. For these examples, we've used a `MainScreen` class, but you can use any class that makes sense for your application.

The SDK does a very good job of naming the interfaces as either listeners or callbacks so it should be easy to tell what the thing is used for. For instance, implementing the `PhoneListener` interface and registering it with the `Phone` class will allow your application to receive notifications when a phone call is placed or received. This is just one of the many listeners that are available in the SDK.

Layout managers

The last topic that we have to cover is the **layout managers**. So far we've worried only about each specific class and what it does and we haven't been worried about how the fields are arranged on the screen. This task falls to the managers.

There are three managers provided by the SDK that handle most normal situations—`VerticalFieldManager`, `HorizontalFieldManager`, and the `FlowFieldManager`. Each of these managers arranges the fields within them differently. The names make their roles pretty clear. A `VerticalFieldManager` arranges the fields veritcally, or stacked on each other, as we have seen in the sample applications we have built so far. The `HorizontalFieldManager` arranges fields horizontally on a single row. In contrast to this, a `FlowFieldManager` arranges the fields horizontally and vertically by wrapping fields from one line to the next line.

A `MainScreen` class has a `VerticalFieldManager` built into it, which is one of the reasons that we are using it. When we call the screen's `add` method we are implicitly adding the field to the `VerticalFieldManager` that is contained in the class. However, as a manager is derived from the `Field` class they can be added to other managers as well, and so you can achieve complicated screens.

For instance, the `VerticalFieldManager` that is included in the `MainScreen` can have a `FlowFieldManager` added to it, and that in turn could have two instances of `VerticalFieldManager` added to it. The resulting screen might be described as a screen having two columns of fields.

As cool as all this sounds though, there is one really big catch here. There are very few `Field` classes that can be used with a `HorizontalFieldManager` or a `FlowFieldManager` and still achieve any horizontal layout. Specifically, only the `LabelField`, `BitmapField`, and the `ButtonField` can be used. Any of the other `Field` classes can be used only if you first create a custom version of that class.

Special considerations for touchscreens

Most of the BlackBerry models have a keyboard and a trackball (or trackpad) which handle cursor movement and any screen interaction that is required. The BlackBerry Storm and Storm 2 are different than all other BlackBerry devices because these models have a **touchscreen** instead of a trackball so you may be wondering what you need to do in order to support these models.

The good news is that the answer is nothing at all! There are a couple of caveats though, of course.

If you build an application using an SDK older than 4.7, a BlackBerry Storm will automatically use compatibility mode. Version 4.7 of the SDK introduced touch APIs so it only makes sense that any applications made with older versions of the SDK can still work, but using this mode. Compatibility mode essentially tries to simulate a device without a touchscreen by enforcing a couple of rules. While running in compatibility mode there will always be a keyboard displayed on the screen and the application will not change orientation from portrait to landscape when the handheld is rotated. The point is that all of the older and existing applications can be run on Storm devices, but the experience is sometimes less than ideal; in fact many Storm users dislike it a lot.

Going Deeper into the UI

It is possible for a user to disable compatibility mode, and most of the time this works just fine, but it is an extra step that is typically not done by novice users. It is also possible for a developer to request that an application not be run in compatibility mode, but in all honesty, the best approach is probably to simply create a new version of the application for handhelds running 4.7 or higher. Compatibility mode is best used for applications that do not use the standard `Field` classes for the user interface.

For any applications built using version 4.7 or higher of the SDK, things work a little differently. Using the standard `Field` classes that we've been using so far works just like you would expect it to. The on-screen keyboard is not forcibly shown and there are no restrictions about changing orientation from portrait to landscape. You don't need to do any special coding in order to get the touchscreen interaction mapped onto the screens and fields properly; the framework does this automatically for you.

TouchEvents and TouchGestures

Of course, it is possible to intercept and handle touches and gestures in your application, but if you need to do that then you are probably not going to be using the standard `Field` classes provided by the SDK.

The BlackBerry Storm uses a special system of events that are somewhat equivalent to key presses, called **TouchEvents**. These represent different kinds of touches such as CLICK, UNCLICK, MOVE, and others. These are pretty similar to key down and key up events that are available for systems with a keyboard.

Gestures are special combinations of touch events that are recognized by the OS as one action. In much the same way as a key down event followed by one or more key press events and finished with a key up event can be considered to be a key click event, a `TouchGesture` event can be represented as several touch events.

Starting with version 4.7 of the SDK, the `MainScreen` class allows you to interact with touch events and touch gestures by overriding the `TouchEvent` method on a `Screen`. This method is used to notify your application of touch events that have happened.

There are several kinds of events available so your application must query which particular `TouchEvent` has happened and process each one separately, usually by using a `switch` statement. Each event has a constant defined in the `TouchEvent` class that will be returned when calling the `getEvent` method.

```
switch (event.getEvent())
{
  case TouchEvent.CLICK:
    //do something
    break;
  case TouchEvent.MOVE:
    //do something
    break;
}
```

One of the `TouchEvent` types is GESTURE and indicates that the `TouchEvent` is really a `TouchGesture`. In order to get the `TouchGesture` object associated with the `TouchEvent` you need to make a call to the `getGesture` method. `TouchGesture` also has a `getEvent` method like `TouchEvent` that can be used to determine which specific type of gesture the user has done.

```
case TouchEvent.GESTURE:
  TouchGesture gesture = event.getGesture();
  switch (gesture.getEvent())
  {
    case TouchGesture.SWIPE:
    // do something
      break;
  }
  break;
```

Unfortunately, the framework doesn't make interacting with the `TouchEvent` and `TouchGesture` classes as easy as it does for working with fields and screens, but the tools are there to do so if you want to. This almost certainly means creating a specialized version of your application just for the Storm models, but honestly, it is best because handling touch events would be only a small part of the overall changes that would be required to make an effective and polished BlackBerry Storm application.

Have a go hero – Adding another Listener to the FieldSampler

As we mentioned earlier, there are a number of listeners available so that your application can receive information about other things that are happening on the device, which might be outside of the control of your application. One of them is called `PhoneListener`. Implementing this interface will let your application receive notification about phone events, such as when there is an incoming phone call.

One thing that you should plan for, and test, is what will happen to your application if the user receives a phone call while using the application. This is one area that developers can fail to plan for and that lead to a bug or user interface issues. Depending on what your application is doing, you may want to react to an incoming phone call. You may need to suspend a thread, save application data, or possibly even close the application.

Experiment with this aspect of development by implementing the `PhoneListener` interface and then using the simulator to receive phone calls while the application is running. Remember, you will not only need to implement the interface, but will also have to activate the listener . Do this by adding the class that implements the interface (most likely the `FieldSamplerScreen` class) calling the `Phone.addPhoneListener` method. Also, remember that you should remove the listener when closing your application as well!

Summary

Wow, that was a lot of fields that we covered in this chapter. Obviously, a lot of thought and planning went into creating all of these `Field` classes and the features available are both wide and powerful.

In this chapter, we covered:

- Advanced Field classes such as `ListField`, `TreeField`, and `ButtonField`
- Discussed the UI stack and how to display and navigate between multiple screens
- Covered dialogs and their various forms for collecting information
- Learned about listeners and callbacks
- Examined the specifics surrounding programming with a touchscreen

Now that you've covered all of these different `Field` types it's time to start looking at some of the other systems on a BlackBerry. Most applications have other requirements beyond just a nice user interface. Another important part of an application is the ability to store data once the application is closed. There are several options for this available in the BlackBerry SDK and the next chapter will dive into each of them in more detail.

7
Storing Data

Making a usable and effective screen is usually only one facet of many when it comes to making an application. An application will typically need to save and retrieve data at one point or another. In fact, making an application that does not do this and is still useful is quite a challenge!

*The BlackBerry OS has internal storage that can be accessed in a couple of different ways. These approaches allow a developer to access the storage like a non-relational database, which should be a familiar concept. In spite of these similarities, the specifics can be very different. The first approach is to use **Record Management System (RMS)**, which is part of the Java MIDP specification. The second is to use the **BlackBerry Persistent Store** which, as the name implies, is a BlackBerry-specific feature.*

Additionally, if a handheld has an SD card slot, files on the SD card can also be accessed to read or store data. In general, you should use the SD card slot if you require large amounts of data or that data is not organized into records.

Laying the ground work

In order to demonstrate the storage techniques appropriately we need a good application to work with. For this chapter, we will start with a journal application. This program is designed to be a simple diary or a journal application that allows you to create entries with some long text and a date. The only problem is that as soon as you exit the application, all of the journal entries are lost because they are not being saved into a permanent storage area.

This is obviously a contrived example, but it isn't too far off from an iterative development cycle where you might be expected to lay out the screen and basic functionality first and add storage or other features later on as the development process continues.

Creating a data class

The journal application uses a data class to store each entry in the journal simply called `JournalEntry`. The class itself is very simple, but it's also where most of the work will be done as we implement code to store the entries in each system. Generally speaking, this is the preferred approach.

The Java way: RMS

RMS is probably the simplest, and least powerful, of the three approaches because it is a Java standard that has to be implemented the same way on many different devices. It is basic and functional, but not terribly easy to use.

RMS allows an application to create one or more record stores, which in turn stores one or more records. Each record is one large array of bytes and can be of any size, subject to the limits of the OS. RMS does not provide or understand any structure of the data in each record.

The `RecordStore` class is at the heart of RMS. Because the `RecordStore` is a Java standard, it is found in the `javax.microedition.rms` package instead of the BlackBerry-related packages. The `RecordStore` class can be instantiated to represent a single `RecordStore` object, but it also contains several static methods for operating on record stores in general. Methods such as `listRecordStore` and `deleteRecordStore` are available at any time and do not require a `RecordStore` instance.

Records in the `RecordStore` are identified by a unique integer ID and serves as a system-imposed primary key. Every record added will be given a record ID and methods that act on a single record will use that record ID.

There are many things that are unique to RMS and these all should be considered before choosing RMS as the way you should store data.

- **Java MIDP standard**: RMS is a standard within the MIDP specification and as such it must be implemented on every device that supports MIDP, which is pretty much any Java-based mobile device. If you are creating an application to be built on multiple platforms, there is no other choice. The alternative, the Persistent Store, is specific to BlackBerry and therefore, not useful for applications that will be ported to other devices.
- **Records contain no structure**: As we said before, RMS records are not structured in any way. This leads to both flexibility and difficulty in coding. Each record in the `RecordStore` can contain a different type of record with a different structure. If this is done, knowing what kind of record is being read in is critical. You shouldn't rely on the order of the records in a database even if the order never has changed on you.

Additionally, any complex data must be converted or serialized into an array of bytes that can be put into the `RecordStore`. Each time a record is loaded or saved there is additional processing because that object needs to be converted from one format to the other. Lastly, if the record format happens to change after sometime then, converting old format records to new format records could be problematic.

- **Backed up as one database**: This is a BlackBerry-specific implementation of RMS and this issue may not exist on other devices. One of the maintenance tasks that you can do when you synchronize your handheld to a PC (or your IT Staff can do this for you automatically) is to back up your device onto your desktop. When you do this you can choose to back up just a single database or to back up all of them. Unlike Persistent Store databases, all RMS record stores are actually within the same BlackBerry database and are backed up as one file. Many times this lack of separation from other data isn't an issue but, depending on your application, it may be an issue for you.

- **Size limits:** Another BlackBerry-specific limitation is the limit on how much data you may put into one `RecordStore` and how much data may be in all record stores put together. Initially, the limit was set to 64 Kilobytes of data in all of the record stores combined, but over a period of time the limits have been expanded. As of version 4.6 a single `RecordStore` may have 512 Kilobytes of data and the only limit to the total data is the device memory itself.

- **Share with no one or everyone**: The RMS record stores were specifically designed to be **sandboxes**, which is to say that the data within them was secure from tampering by other processes on the device. However, it is often desirable for applications to share their data with other applications in controlled ways. This was addressed in MIDP 2.0, but not in a granular way. Therefore, there are only two ways to control access to your `RecordStore`—either you share with any application or with no other applications at all.

Just about every method related to RMS can throw an exception of some kind. Sometimes, it's fine to have an exception thrown, but most of the time it isn't. Regardless, Java requires for every possible exception that can be thrown to be handled in some way. Not handling an exception is a compile error so there is often a lot of error handling in code that deals with databases in general.

As this section is focused on storage, and not exception handling, we will be simply allowing all of the exceptions to be passed out of the methods we create and will be handled in one spot with some generic code. This isn't really the best way to do things but the code could get bogged down with exception handling very quickly otherwise.

Storing Data

For this application we're going to create a new `RecordStore` each time the application is closed instead of trying to determine if a record needs to be inserted or not. It is potentially very inefficient with a lot of records but a valid strategy under the right circumstances. If you don't want to clutter your data structures with storage details and you know the data being stored is small in size, then this approach can make a lot of sense. As with any project you need to give some thought to the data storage techniques.

So, let's start adding some code to the journal application.

Time for action – creating and opening a RecordStore

Creating a new `RecordStore` is a pretty simple operation. However, because we're going to create a new one each time the application is closed we also have to delete any previous record stores that might have been created already. This will all be done in the `onClose` method of the `JournalMainScreen`, which is called when the application is quitting.

1. Add the following method to the `JournalMainScreen` class:

```
protected void SaveEntriesRMS(Vector EntryList) throws
RecordStoreNotOpenException, RecordStoreFullException,
RecordStoreException
{
  //Delete the existing recordstore if there is one.
  try
  {
    RecordStore.deleteRecordStore("JournalEntries");
  }
  catch (RecordStoreException e1)
  {
   // Do nothing. It's entirely possible that the recordstore
      doesn't exist
   // yet and will throw an exception. Just silently ignore it.
  }
  // create a new one.
  RecordStore JournalStore = RecordStore.openRecordStore(
                    "JournalEntries", true);
  if (JournalStore == null)
  {
    //big error! quit now.
    return;
  }
  //TODO: Save the records
```

```
      JournalStore.closeRecordStore();
   }
```

2. Add the following method call and error handlers to the `onClose` method in the `JournalMainScreen` class.

```
// Save using RMS
try
{
   SaveEntriesRMS(_EntryList);
}
catch (RecordStoreNotOpenException e)
{
   e.printStackTrace();
}
catch (RecordStoreFullException e)
{
   e.printStackTrace();
}
catch (RecordStoreException e)
{
   e.printStackTrace();
}
```

What just happened?

Creating a `RecordStore` is a lot like creating the `Application` object, which we have done in our own programs here. In this case we use the static method from `RecordStore`, `openRecordStore`, in order to create an instance of a `RecordStore` that has already been opened and is ready for use. In fact, there is very little distinction between creating and opening a `RecordStore`. It is not possible to simply create a `RecordStore` without opening it. You can only open a `RecordStore`, and optionally create it if it does not already exist. You do need to close the `RecordStore` before quitting the application as well.

Record stores are identified by a name that must be unique within the scope of the application and can be up to 32 characters long. Because the name is within the scope of only this application, `RecordStore` names don't need to be complex or avoid common words. Instead, they should be clear about what they are used for, such as "Options" or, in this case, `JournalEntries`. You don't have to worry about these simple names being taken by another application or conflicting with the ones already created by the operating system.

Storing Data

This step adds a method to handle saving the data out and calls it from the `onClose` method in the main screen. The method isn't complete yet because it doesn't actually save the data out. However, it does perform the opening and closing of the `RecordStore` in preparation for the actual saving (which will come next).

Notice that the first action of the `SaveEntriesRMS` method is to delete any existing record stores with the name that you chose to use. You are doing this because this program will simply save all of the data each time so if there is any data from a previous execution it needs to be deleted first. The `deleteRecordStore` method is a static method of `RecordStore` so notice that this is done even though you don't yet have a `RecordStore` instance to work with.

```
RecordStore.deleteRecordStore("JournalEntries");
```

Also, this step is the only step with exception handling around it. This is because trying to delete a `RecordStore` that does not exist will throw a `RecordStoreNotFound` exception. In this case, you don't care if the `RecordStore` was found or not, so the exception handler simply ignores the exception and proceeds.

Next, you try to create a new `RecordStore` by using the `openRecordStore` method and making sure to set the second parameter to `true`. With the second parameter set to `true` the `openRecordStore` method will create the `RecordStore`, if it does not exist, and then open the `RecordStore` and return it. If the second parameter is set to `false`, `openRecordStore` will throw an exception if the `RecordStore` doesn't already exist.

```
RecordStore JournalStore = RecordStore.openRecordStore(
                               "JournalEntries", true);
```

After opening the `RecordStore` there is a quick sanity test to make sure that you actually have an object to work with. If for some reason there isn't, well that's big trouble and you need to quit now.

The next step will be to actually save the data, but as we mentioned already, we will get to that next. For now, there is just a comment to remind us to come back later and finish it up!

```
JournalStore.closeRecordStore();
```

After that you should be done saving the data so the only thing left to do is to close the `RecordStore`.

Back in the `onClose` method there is a call to the new `SaveEntriesRMS` method—a call that is surrounded with several exception blocks to make sure that every possible kind of exception has been handled. Several of the calls inside the `SaveEntriesRMS` method should have been wrapped in exception handling blocks as well. Instead of doing the error handling inside the `SaveEntriesRMS` method you let them be thrown out in order to make the code more readable. The special `throws` keyword in the method declaration is what keeps the compiler happy.

Now that the `RecordStore` has been created and opened you're ready to add some data to it. On the surface, this is simply adding each record to the `RecordStore` by using the `addRecord` method. When you go to use the method though, you will notice that it accepts the data only in one form—as a byte array. Now, the `JournalEntry` class isn't very complicated, but any class is more complicated than an array of bytes.

In order to add the data of a `JournalEntry` into the `RecordStore` it must be serialized into a byte array. This serialization isn't very hard, but it is one more step that definitely isn't obvious to new Java programmers. So let's look at the code.

Time for action – adding a record

1. Add the `save` method to the `JournalEntry` class.

   ```java
   public byte[] save()
   {
     ByteArrayOutputStream baos = new ByteArrayOutputStream();
     DataOutputStream outputStream = new DataOutputStream(baos);
     byte[] data = null;
     try
     {
        // Add the Entry Date as a long integer.
        outputStream.writeLong(getEntryDate().getTime());
        // Then add the entry itself
        outputStream.writeUTF(getEntry());

        // Extract the byte array
        data = baos.toByteArray();
     }
     catch (IOException ioe)
     {
       System.out.println(ioe);
       ioe.printStackTrace();
     }
      return data;
   }
   ```

2. Add this loop to replace the `TODO:` comment in the `SaveEntriesRMS` method of `JournalEntryMainScreen`.

   ```java
   for (Enumeration e = EntryList.elements(); e.hasMoreElements();)
   {
   ```

```
            JournalEntry Entry = (JournalEntry) e.nextElement();
            byte[] data = Entry.save();
            if (data != null)
              {
                JournalStore.addRecord(data, 0, data.length);
              }
        }
```

What just happened?

I'll bet that the `save` method is a little bigger than you expected. The serialization is a bit messy and a somewhat complicated process that we just can't avoid when working with RMS. The process is essentially the same as saving data to a file on your desktop.

The `DataOutputStream` and the `ByteArrayOutputStream` work together to make the conversion magic happen. The `DataOutputStream` is used to place primitive data types into an output stream that the `ByteArrayOutputStream` then converts to the required byte array. Once the stream objects are set up, you then add each piece of data to the stream one at a time. Notice that there is no `write` method for the `Date` class. Fortunately, you have access to the raw data in the `Date` class, which is the `long integer` value from `getTime`. Serialization is not natively supported by every class in Java, so you will need to write your own, even for standard classes such as `Date`.

```
    // Add the Entry Date as a long integer.
    outputStream.writeLong(getEntryDate().getTime());
    // Then add the entry itself
    outputStream.writeUTF(getEntry());
```

As you will be controlling the serialization when loading as well as saving, it doesn't matter in which order the data fields are added to the stream. In this case, the `EntryDate` was added first but the text of the `Entry` could have been added first (if we wanted to). The only requirement is that the data is retrieved in the same order when reading them back in.

You can add other data into the serialization as well, such as an application version number or something to make it easier for your application to handle revisions in the future. Imagine the scenario where you wanted to release another revision of the journal application that would encrypt the entries. You can absolutely encrypt the byte array and store the encrypted data in the RMS record. However, the application would need some way to identify whether data was from a previous version, and therefore, unencrypted or not.

It's important to think about the future revisions, but for now, we have some more code to look at back in the `onClose` method. The loop that we added simply gets each `JournalEntry` object from the `EntryList` and calls the save method on it. The `save` method returns a byte array that is then used to add a new record to the `RecordStore`.

```
for (Enumeration e = EntryList.elements(); e.hasMoreElements();)
{
   JournalEntry Entry = (JournalEntry) e.nextElement();
   byte[] data = Entry.save();
   if (data != null)
   {
      JournalStore.addRecord(data, 0, data.length);
   }
}
```

You can do even more interesting things at this point as well. You could also add a small 'header' record here if you wanted to, or encrypt the data before creating the record. Because you have such a low-level control over the data there are a lot of options available.

The `addRecord` method will return the Record ID of the new record that was just added, but you don't need to use it at this point because the application is in the process of closing down. The Record ID would be a lot more important if you had chosen a different approach for saving and loading the records from the `RecordStore`. If there are a lot of records you may not want to read them all in when the application loads up. You may instead just want to collect the Record IDs of each record and then read in a record when needed. In this case, capturing the Record ID when saving new records would be essential. Now that you have the records saved into the `RecordStore` you need to be able to read them back out. Because you've chosen to save the records when closing the application the best place to read them back in is when the application is being started.

Time for action – retrieving records

1. Add the following code for the `load` method to the `JournalEntry` class.

    ```
    public void load(byte[] data)
    {
        ByteArrayInputStream bais = new ByteArrayInputStream(data);
        DataInputStream inputStream = new DataInputStream(bais);
        try
        {
            setEntryDate(new Date(inputStream.readLong()));
            setEntry(inputStream.readUTF());
        }
        catch (IOException e)
        {
            e.printStackTrace();
        }
    }
    ```

Storing Data

2. Add the `LoadEntriesRMS` method in the next code snippet to the `JournalMainScreen` class.

```
protected void LoadEntriesRMS(Vector EntryList) throws
RecordStoreFullException, RecordStoreNotFoundException,
RecordStoreException
{
// create a new one.
RecordStore JournalStore = RecordStore.openRecordStore(
                    "JournalEntries", true);

  if (JournalStore == null)
  {
    //big error! quit now.
    return;
  }

  RecordEnumeration e = JournalStore.enumerateRecords(null,null,
                        false);
  for (e; e.hasNextElement();)
    {
      JournalEntry Entry = new JournalEntry();
      Entry.load(e.nextRecord());
      EntryList.addElement(Entry);
    }
    JournalStore.closeRecordStore();
}
```

3. Replace the TODO comment in the constructor with the following code.

```
try
{
   LoadEntriesRMS(_EntryList);
}
catch (RecordStoreFullException e)
{
   // TODO Auto-generated catch block
   e.printStackTrace();
}
catch (RecordStoreNotFoundException e)
{
   // TODO Auto-generated catch block
   e.printStackTrace();
}
```

```
catch (RecordStoreException e)
{
   // TODO Auto-generated catch block
   e.printStackTrace();
}
```

What just happened?

This is a lot of code in one bunch, but all in all it should seem similar to the code you just wrote for writing out the records. You have the same basic steps in that, there is a `load` method in the `JournalEntry` class, a `LoadEntries` method in the `MainScreen`, and code in the constructor that actually loads the data when the application starts up.

The `load` method in the `JournalEntries` class follows the same basic steps as the `save` method does, only it reverses their order. So the `DataInputStream` and the `ByteArrayInputStream` again work together to allow the various `read` methods to read data from the byte array, which are used to populate the data members in `JournalEntry`. Notice that the `Date` object for the `EntryDate` is reconstructed as well from the long time value.

In the `LoadEntries` method we again start by opening the `RecordStore` and then use the `enumerateRecords` method to read in all of the records. The `enumerateRecords` method offers a couple of parameters which can be used to search for records that match some criteria, but those are set to `NULL` because we want all of the records.

Inside the loop you do the real work of loading the records into the vector for storage in the application. First, an empty `Entry` object is created, which is then loaded with the data from the current record before being added to the list. Once all of the records have been processed the `RecordStore` is closed again.

In the third step you added some code to the constructor to kick off the `LoadEntries` method and handle any errors that might have been thrown. Well, "handle" isn't very accurate because they would be basically ignored for the sake of the sample.

By using the enumeration we effectively ignore the `RecordID` for loading purposes. There is another method in the enumeration that you can use if you want to get the IDs for each record. Instead of using the `nextRecord` method and getting the data directly you can use the `nextRecordId` method to get the ID and then use the `getRecord` method, to get the data. The net result is the same except that you can also get the `RecordID` by using the second approach.

```
int recordID = e.nextRecordId();
Entry.load(JournalStore.getRecord(recordID));
```

Storing Data

Even though there is a `nextRecord` method and a `nextRecordId` method in the enumerator you shouldn't use them both at the same time. Each call to a `nextRecord` method, whether that be `nextRecord` or `nextRecordId`, advances the enumerator one step to the next record. Therefore, you should call only one method or the other to load data.

In the code that you've done so far, the entire `RecordStore` is deleted each time the application closes so there is no real need to delete an individual record in this application. RMS allows for it of course though, by providing the `deleteRecord` method, which takes a `RecordID` as its only parameter.

Instead of deleting the `RecordStore` completely let's change that code to remove all of the records from within the `RecordStore` by deleting them individually.

Time for action – deleting records

1. Comment out the previous implementation in the `SaveEntriesRMS` method.

   ```
   //    //Delete the existing recordstore if there is one.
   //    try
   //    {
   //        RecordStore.deleteRecordStore("JournalEntries");
   //    }
   //    catch (RecordStoreException e1)
   //    {
   //    // Do nothing. It's entirely possible that the recordstore
   //    //doesn't exist
   //    // yet and will throw an exception. Just silently ignore it.
   //    }
   ```

2. Add the following enumeration in the same method after the `RecordStore` has been opened.

   ```
   for (RecordEnumeration e = JournalStore.enumerateRecords(null,
                           null, true);
        e.hasNextElement();)
   {
     int recordID = e.nextRecordId();
     JournalStore.deleteRecord(recordID);
   }
   ```

What just happened?

The program behavior didn't change at all with this latest change. Instead, you just changed how the `RecordStore` is cleaned when saving the data. Previously, you deleted the entire `RecordStore` and then recreated it with the call to `openRecordStore`.

This approach deletes any existing records from the `RecordStore` and then places new records into it so the `RecordStore` itself is never deleted. To do this you had to change the order in which things are done in the method. When you deleted the entire `RecordStore` that action was done before the `RecordStore` was opened. Since the `deleteRecord` method requires the `RecordStore` to be opened you have to make sure that this is done first.

To actually delete the records you use the same enumeration that you used in the `LoadEntriesRMS` method with one minor exception. There are several parameters to `enumerateRecords` and among them is a flag indicating whether to keep the enumeration synchronized. Because you will be deleting the records and therefore changing the enumeration, that last parameter is set to `true` instead of the `false` value that was previously used.

It's true that this sample isn't practical, but it illustrates that deleting a record is a simple matter requiring only the `recordID`.

Pop quiz

1. What class is used to open a `RecordStore`?
    a. `RecordStore`
    b. `RecordStoreFactory`
    c. `Database`

2. What is the only data type that can be used with an RMS record?
    a. `Stream`
    b. `byte[]`
    c. `File`

3. What method is used to retrieve the data of a record from the `RecordStore`?
    a. `nextRecord`
    b. `getData`
    c. `read`

The BlackBerry way: Persistent Store

As we said before, RMS is the storage method provided with Java. Like most of the Java SDK there are BlackBerry-specific alternatives available and, in general, these should be used unless you are trying to create a true **MIDlet**. When it comes to database storage the BlackBerry-specific alternative is called the Persistent Store.

- **Easier to code:** Using the `PersistentStore` approach is generally easier than RMS because `PersistentStore` provides a generic serialization mechanism allowing you to store complex objects in it. This means that the special code you made for the `load` and `save` methods are not needed. There are several factors that should be considered before choosing to use either `PersistentStore` or RMS

- **Must implement Persistable interface:** In order to store custom data classes in `PersistentStore` they must implement the `Persistable` interface. Implementing this interface serves as a flag to the `PersistentStore` object that the class is intended to be stored in the database. Implementing this interface doesn't require any real work but is still a requirement.

- **Can be controlled with policies:** Access to the `PersistentStore` data can be controlled by the BlackBerry administrator through the **BlackBerry Enterprise Server (BES)**. This level of control is something that administrators love and a strong selling point into businesses. Unfortunately, that means for you, as a developer, may not be able to access the `PersistentStore` and you will need to account for it.

- **Share with other code-signed applications:** Unlike RMS, where an application has very limited sharing options, Persistent Stores can be granted access on a much more granular level. Generally, sharing data in a `PersistentStore` is not a common occurrence, but this might be something very important to you for your project. If this is the case, using the `PersistentStore` is going to be your best choice.

- **Faster to search:** The `PersistentStore` is geared to storing key/value pairs of data with an interface that acts like a hash table. Therefore, accessing a single object, as long as you have the proper key, is a very fast operation and is generally going to be faster than iterating through records in the `RecordStore`.

PersistentStore and PersistentObject

The `PersistentStore` and `PersistentObject` classes work hand-in-hand to get access to data in the `PersistentStore`. All of the methods in the `PersistentStore` class are static, which means that you won't ever create an instance of the `PersistentStore` class. Instead, the `PersistentStore` class primarily exists so that you can get a `PersistentObject`, which in turn allows you to get your data.

A `PersistentObject` represents the object being stored in the `PersistentStore`. It is a wrapper class that handles the serialization and storage of the data for you. As a wrapper it is possible for a `PersistentObject` to actually reference no object or to have a null value. This is the case when a new `PersistentObject` is created.

You can store as many instances of `PersistentObject` in the `PersistentStore` as you want, limited by device memory of course. Each object in the `PersistentStore` must be given a unique key value by you and this key value is used to reference the object at a later date. As each object requires a unique key and that key must be defined in advance, it may seem difficult to add an arbitrary number of records. Rest assured, this isn't an issue! In fact, most applications use only a single `PersistentObject`.

The secret to this is through the use of data structures to store complex data. Most applications will create objects to hold many pieces of data in a single object. Furthermore, arrays, lists, or other complex data structures can be used to hold many similar objects creating even more complex structures. An entire complex structure can be put into a `PersistentObject` as a whole unit. So you see, with the right object design up front there isn't a need for more than one `PersistentObject` most of the time.

That's not to say that you must use just one `PersistentObject`, of course. There are a lot of good reasons to use more than one as well. It should be clear though, that we shouldn't use a `PersistentObject` for each `JournalEntry` however.

Using the `PersistentStore` offers a huge advantage over RMS—in that you can store any object in the `PersistentStore`, even your own complex objects with complex data structures. Furthermore, you don't need to create the serialization code like we had to when using RMS.

Time for action – preparing the JournalEntry class

The one requirement for storing your own custom classes in the `PersistentStore` is that the class (and any other classes that it might contain) must implement the `Persistable` interface. So let's do that now. Replace the `JournalEntry` class declaration with the following one and you will be set up to store the `JournalEntry` objects in the `PersistentStore`.

```
public class JournalEntry implements Persistable
```

What just happened?

Implementing the `Persistable` interface couldn't be any easier! The interface itself has no methods in it so there is no code to write besides creating the `implements` specification itself. How easy is that?

You have to do this only for your own custom classes. Primitive data types as well as some common data structures, such as `Vector`, are already handled automatically. However, if your data structure is complex, you will need to add the interface declaration to each class which is included as well as the main class that contains them all.

Now, just because you CAN store practically any object in the `PersistentStore` doesn't mean you should. Unlike RMS, the only limits on the size of the `PersistableStore` are the device memory itself, but this is still a limited resource so you should take some care to not store unnecessary data. You could, for instance, create custom derived classes for the fields you use on the screen and then insert the entire screen in the `PersistentStore`. I wouldn't recommend it, however.

Now that you've prepared the `JournalEntry` class to be stored you can get on with the code needed to open the `PersistentObject`. Creating and getting a `PersistentObject` is done in one action, much like creating and opening a `RecordStore` is done with RMS. When you call the `getPersistentObject` method the `PersistentStore` will create a new object (if one does not already exist) and return it to you automatically. Each `PersistentObject` is identified by a `long integer`, which is commonly called a key.

A `PersistentStore` key can be any number, but they are generally generated by hashing a long string that is specific and meaningful to your application, such as the package name or some minor variation of it. This string should be easier to remember than a randomized series of numbers, and by hashing it you can generate a key that is very unlikely to be guessed or duplicated. It's not guaranteed to be unique though.

So let's get started by generating the key that you will be using and then get the `PersistentObject` using that key.

Time for action – getting a PersistentObject

1. Create the key that will be used to access the `PersistentStore` by typing the package name into the `JournalMainScreen` constructor.

    com.rimdev.demos.JournalPS

2. Eclipse will flag it in as a syntax error, but don't worry about it. Select the string that you just typed in and then right-click on the selected text and select the **Convert String to Long** menu item.

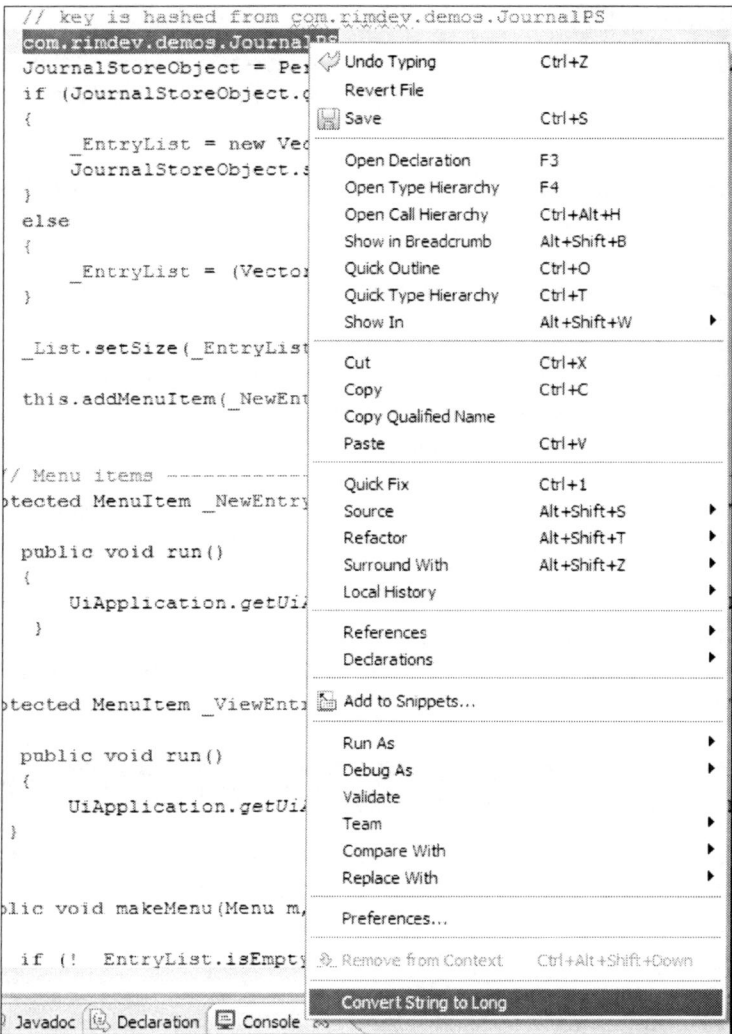

3. After the menu is selected the hash value will replace the selected text in the source file, `0xa216041d6596a51cL`.

4. Because you already have the key value in the source file you need to add the rest of the code, incorporating the hash value into the call to `getPersistentObject` as a parameter.

   ```
   // key is hashed from com.rimdev.demos.JournalPS
   JournalStoreObject = PersistentStore.getPersistentObject(
   0xa216041d6596a51cL);
   ```

Storing Data

What just happened?

These simple steps illustrate the most common technique for generating the key values used for persistent objects. Fortunately, Eclipse provides a menu item to make this task nearly trivial, it's just not obvious or easy to find.

Once you generate the key, using it to get a PersistentObject is a straightforward call to getPersistentObject and passing that key in. Remember, getPersistentObject will return a PersistentObject even if one did not previously exist, so just getting a PersistentObject does not necessarily mean that you have data in it. You still have to access the data inside of a PersistentObject.

In order to get data from a PersistentObject we need to call the getContents method. The getContents method will return NULL if the PersistentObject has no data stored in it, which is what can happen when the PersistentObject is first created. If the PersistentObject has had data previously stored in it, then the getContents method will return a generic object reference of that data. In order to use the data you will have to cast the reference to one of the proper type, that is to say the same type that was put into the PersistentObject.

In your case, you will be placing the entire Vector _EntryList into the PersistentObject so that all of the JournalEntries are stored and retrieved at once. So let's add the code to do that.

Time for action – accessing the PersistentObject data

1. Add the following code to the JournalEntryMainScreen constructor under the call to getPersistentObject that we just added.

```
if (JournalStoreObject.getContents() == null)
{
   _EntryList = new Vector();
}
else
{
   _EntryList = (Vector)JournalStoreObject.getContents();
}
```

What just happened?

This last baby step is where you actually get the data from the `PersistentObject` that you had previously got. The most important things to notice here is that you have to check to see if the contents of the `PersistentObject` are set to `NULL`. If they are, then you simply create a new `Vector` in the typical fashion. If not though, the `_EntryList` member is set to the contents of the `PersistentObject` after being cast to the proper type first.

This code replaces the enumeration and looping that you did for RMS in order to load each entry in the list. Because you are loading the entire `Vector`, and not just individual `JournalEntry` objects, there is no need to loop through the contents of the `PersistentObject`, it does that for you automatically.

The last thing to consider is storing the data in a `PersistentObject`. This too is very simple and requires relatively little code.

Storing data in a `PersistentObject` is a two-step process that mimics a database transaction. First, you must set the contents of the `PersistentObject` by using the `setContents` method. Later, when you are ready to save the data, a final call to the `commit` method will actually serialize the data and put it into the `PersistentStore`. Any data which had previously been stored for the given key will be overwritten with the new data.

That's all there is to it—just two calls to `setContents` and `commit`. Let's add these calls to the application and finish up this application.

Time for action – accessing the PersistentObject data

1. Modify the code you just added to add the call to `setContents` in the `if` statement to match the following code.

   ```
   if (JournalStoreObject.getContents() == null)
   {
     _EntryList = new Vector();
     JournalStoreObject.setContents(_EntryList);
   }
   else
   {
     _EntryList = (Vector)JournalStoreObject.getContents();
   }
   ```

2. Next, add the call to `commit` to the `onClose` method.

   ```
   JournalStoreObject.commit();
   ```

Storing Data

What just happened?

These two calls are all that is needed to save your data to the `PersistentStore`. The call to the `commit` method was placed into the `onClose` method because we want to save the data when the application exits, but it doesn't have to be. You may have a good reason to call the `commit` method in the middle of your application for some reason and there is no problem in doing so.

The call to `setContents` also requires a little explanation. Notice that the call to the `setContents` method is made only in one of the two branches of the `if` statement. If the contents of the `PersistentObject` are NULL you do two things—create a new `Vector` and then set that `Vector` as the contents of the `PersistentObject`. Remember, this branch is taken only if there was no `PersistentObject` previously.

The other branch is taken if there was data already in the `PersistentObject`, which means the contents have already been set. In fact, this branch does the opposite by creating the `Vector` from the `PersistentObject` contents. Instead of setting the contents to be the data created by the program you're setting the program data to the contents of the `PersistentStore`. Because the contents have already been set you don't need to do it again and therefore, don't need the call to `setContents` here.

Even though this example is not multithreaded, many applications use multiple threads to accomplish tasks in the background—one of which might be to save data to a `PersistentObject`. Because the `PersistentObject` is potentially an object that can be accessed from multiple threads it is a good idea to enclose calls to `PersistentObject` methods with a synchronized block, similar to the following example.

```
synchronized(JournalStoreObject)
{
   JournalStoreObject.commit();
}
```

An application typically won't delete a `PersistentObject` through code, but it is possible of course for those times when you do need to delete it. In order to delete a `PersistentObject` you need the same long key that you used to retrieve a `PersistentObject`. If you wanted to delete the `PersistentStore` of `JournalPS` then you would use the following line of code.

```
PersistentStore.destroyPersistentObject(0xa216041d6596a51cL);
```

For the most part, though, you don't need to worry about deleting the instances of `PersistentObject` that your application creates. This is because the operating system will automatically delete them for you if your application is ever uninstalled.

If your application uses a custom class (such as the `JournalEntry` class) to store data then the operating system will automatically remove any `PersistentObject` that your application creates. However, if you your application uses and stores only basic types (for instance, if your application did its own serialization or stored only string values) then the operating system won't delete the `PersistentObject` that your application creates. This is a very subtle point to understand and one that should be planned for. In general, applications will want to use custom classes to store data and will want to have that data removed when the application is uninstalled. If this isn't the case, then you should plan accordingly.

Pop quiz

1. What class is used to get a PersistentObject?
    a. `PersistentStore`
    b. `PersistentObject`
    c. `Database`

2. What important piece of information is needed to access a `PersistentStore`?
    a. The store name
    b. The store key
    c. The store password

3. What method is used to read the data from a `PersistentObject`?
    a. `Tread`
    b. `getData`
    c. `getContents`

Sometimes, during the development process, things can change a lot and you may suddenly find out that you have to change the structure of the objects being stored in the `PersistentStore`. You can program around the change by keeping multiple versions of your data structure classes around, changing the `PersistentObject` key or even forcibly deleting the `PersistentObject` in code. If you have versions that have been released you have little choice, but if it's still in development and has not been released then this work will simply be thrown away once the transition has been bridged. It is often just better to reset the simulator file system and delete any data that has been stored there.

Storing Data

There are two ways to do delete the file system data in the simulator. The first, and easiest, is through the BlackBerry menu in Eclipse. The penultimate menu item is the **Erase Simulator File** submenu that includes several options to delete various portions of the simulator memory. The best way to reset the simulator is to use the **Erase File System** menu item. The same thing can be done by manually deleting the .DMP files in the directory where the simulator has been installed. I think you will agree, though, that using the menu is better.

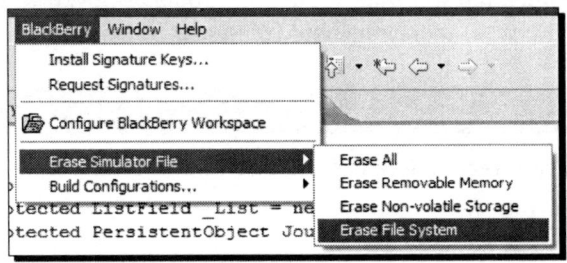

Accessing removable storage

There is one more way that we can use to store data for an application. Most of the recent handheld models have the ability to use removable storage, such as a micro SD card. Some models even include some non-removable flash memory storage. These storage modules are truly file systems and can be accessed by a BlackBerry application as well as by a desktop system when connected to the handheld. The capacity of flash memory components has been increasing rapidly and can be used to add additional storage that is many times greater than the internal memory of a handheld.

Removable storage is particularly well-suited for situations where the application data needs to be shared with a desktop system or is too large to be stored practically in the internal memory of a handheld. However, they present their own set of challenges as well. For instance, even though a handheld can support a micro SD card one might not be inserted into the handheld at that moment. Also, removable media can be removed at any time so it is possible to have the card removed while your application is running.

RMS and `PersistentStore` have many limitations, but you can be certain that they will be there. You can't make that assumption when accessing removable media. These are just some of the considerations that make working with flash memory storage special and different.

Connector and FileConnection

Working with SD Cards starts with a complicated and powerful class called `Connector`, which is a generic factory for creating connections to all kinds of resources, whether they are file, network, USB, or serial. At this point we're focusing only on how to access the file system, so we won't cover any of the other uses for the `Connector` class.

The `Connector` class follows a pattern called a `Factory`. This class has only one purpose, and that is to make objects which themselves perform the actions and do the work. In this case there are a variety of `open` methods that all require a name of some kind and return a `Connection` object of some kind.

The `name` parameter that the `Connector` class wants is actually a **Universal Resource Locator (URL)**. A **URL** is a long string with all of the connection information in it describing what should be connected and how the connection should be made. It can also be called a **connection string**. You are probably already familiar with URLs from simply browsing the Internet, but in this case, URLs are used for much more. The first part of a URL specifies what kind of connection is supposed to be made. For files, a URL starts off with `file://` instead of `http://`, like you would use to access an Internet website. What follows afterward is the path to a specific file or directory, so that a file connection string might look like `file:///SDCard/BlackBerry/MyApp/AppData1.dat`. Connection strings can vary greatly, depending on the type of connection being made.

Even though, it's not the best application for it, we can demonstrate accessing the flash memory storage using the Journal application once again. This version will look similar to the RMS version that you made before because this version borrows heavily from it for serialization of the data. In the section on RMS I compared working with RMS to saving the data to a file, and in this case, we really are saving the data to a file.

So let's get started with this version of the Journal application. Once again, we will start with a `JournalSD` project in the *Chapter 7, Storing Data*

Time for action – storing data to a file

1. Add the data member declaration to the class about the constructor.

   ```
   protected String _URL = "file:///SDCard/BlackBerry/Journal.data";
   protected String _SDCardURL = "file:///SDCard";
   protected String _SaveDirURL = "file:///SDCard/BlackBerry";
   ```

2. You need to add a helper method to the `Screen` class. Insert the following `CheckPathExists` method into the class.

   ```
   protected boolean CheckPathExists(String path)
   {
   ```

Storing Data

```java
      boolean return_value = false;
      try
      {
        FileConnection fileConn =
          (FileConnection) Connector.open(path);
        if (fileConn != null)
        {
          if (fileConn.exists())
          {
            return_value = true;
          }
        }
          fileConn.close();
      }
      catch (IOException e)
      {
        // TODO Auto-generated catch block
        e.printStackTrace();
      }
      return return_value;
    }
```

3. Then, you need to update the `JournalEntry` class with a `save` method. Add this code to the `JournalEntry` class.

```java
public void save (DataOutputStream outputStream) throws
IOException
{
  // Add the Entry Date as a long integer.
  outputStream.writeLong(getEntryDate().getTime());
  // Then add the entry itself
  outputStream.writeUTF(getEntry());
}
```

4. Add the following code to the `onClose` method making sure to replace or comment out any code already there.

```java
if (CheckPathExists(_SDCardURL))
{
  try
  {
    FileConnection _JournalFile = (FileConnection)
      Connector.open(_BlackBerryURL,Connector.READ_WRITE);
```

```
          if (!_JournalFile.exists())
          {
            _JournalFile.create();
          }
           _JournalFile.close();
      }
      catch (IOException e)
      {
        // TODO Auto-generated catch block
          e.printStackTrace();
      }
      SaveData(_URL);
    }
    else
    {
       Dialog.alert("No SDCard present. Save failed.");
    }
    return super.onClose();
```

5. Lastly, add the `SaveData` method to the `JournalMainScreen` class.

```
protected void SaveData(String path)
{
  try
  {
   FileConnection _JournalFile = (FileConnection)
      Connector.open(path,Connector.READ_WRITE);
    if (_JournalFile != null)
    {
      if (!_JournalFile.exists())
      {
        _JournalFile.create();
      }
        DataOutputStream ostream =
          _JournalFile.openDataOutputStream();
        ostream.writeInt(_EntryList.size());

        Enumeration e = _EntryList.elements();
        for(e; e.hasMoreElements();)
        {
          JournalEntry Entry = (JournalEntry) e.nextElement();
          Entry.save(ostream);
```

Storing Data

```
        }
        ostream.flush();
        ostream.close();
      }
      _JournalFile.close();
    }
    catch (IOException e)
    {
      // TODO Auto-generated catch block
      e.printStackTrace();
    }
  }
}
```

What just happened?

The first part of this code section is to simply add the file connection string that we will be using as a class member and the primary reason for doing this is just to eliminate the possibility of typos. The connection string itself probably needs a little explanation though.

As we said initially, the connection string begins with the connection type indicator of `file://` and is followed by the path of the file. In the code, you will see that there are three slashes in the connection string. This is not only intentional, but is actually required. The third slash is actually part of the path, which begins with a slash. That many slashes tend to blend in together, but just understand that there are three slashes there and that it is not a typo.

The next part of the path is really a virtual path that the operating system uses to identify which flash memory segment to put the file in. Some devices have both removable and non-removable flash memory areas in the handheld. There are two specific virtual paths that are allowed—`/store` and `/SDCard`. If you look at the documentation for the `FileConnection` class you may notice an example using `/CFCard`. This is not a valid path, but is used in the documentation just as an example.

Once you get past the virtual directory the path is a simple path as you might be used to from working with other file systems. Each element in the path is a directory and they are separated with forward slashes (not backslashes) until the final element, which is the filename. In this, the connection string specifies a file called `Journal.dat` that resides in the BlackBerry directory of the SD Card storage.

This sample hardcodes the filename, which is generally a bad thing to do. Here we have three URL strings, each with a different component of the path added to it. This is just to make it easier to do the testing, which is necessary when we get to the code that performs the loading and saving of the data.

The helper method `CheckPathExists` is added and will be used a number of times throughout this section. As with file-based operations on a desktop system, you need to make sure that the file or path exists before trying to access it. You will need to do this a lot so the helper method helps to make the code cleaner and easier to read. The method does only two simple steps, but it also wraps up the error handling and shutdown code.

The first step is to actually open the connection using the URL that was passed in. If you've made a mistake and the URL is invalid, calling the `open` method can throw an exception. One of the most common mistakes people make is to use the wrong slash in the connection string, supply an incorrect virtual directory (that is, store or SDCard), or to not include the starting slash in the path. Otherwise, as long as the path is valid, calling `open` will succeed even if the file or directories in the path do not exist.

```
FileConnection fileConn = (FileConnection) Connector.open(path);
```

Because the `open` method will fail only if the connection string is invalid, you always have to check to see if the directory or file exists before accessing it. You can do that with the `exists()` method. Notice also that the `FileConnection` object is closed afterward. It is always a good practice to close a connection when you are done with it, even if the object will automatically close when it is destroyed by the Java garbage collector.

```
if (fileConn != null)
{
  if (fileConn.exists())
  {
    return_value = true;
  }
}
fileConn.close();
```

The actual `save` method that you added to the `JournalEntry` is rather small compared to the `save` method for either the RMS version of this application. This is largely because most of the setup is being done in the `Screen` class and because the `FileConnection` object works on a stream object directly and not a generic byte array, like RMS does.

Because you have to operate on the save file as one whole operation and not as individual records, the `onClose` method is doing a lot more work. A large part of that work is simply ensuring that the file can be saved on the SD card successfully. The first part of this is testing to see if the device has an SD Card and displaying an appropriate message if so. The next is testing to see if a "BlackBerry" directory already exists. This directory is considered a standard and should already exist, but it doesn't hurt to make either. Because you want to create the directory if it doesn't already exist though, you aren't using the `CheckPathExists` method. This code is doing the same thing though, except calling the `create` method to create the directory if it doesn't exist. Once you are sure that it is safe to start saving the data the `SaveData` method is called, and this is where the real work is done.

Storing Data

The first part of `SaveData` is nearly identical to what you just looked at in the `onClose` method because, again, you are testing to see if the file already exists and creating it if not. Notice that the parameter to the `open` method contains another parameter this time, the `READ_WRITE` flag. Because you are going to be writing to this file, you need to make sure to request write permissions.

Just opening the file doesn't let you start putting data into it though. To do that you need to get the `OutputStream` for the object.

```
DataOutputStream ostream = _JournalFile.openDataOutputStream();
```

The `openDataOutputStream` method shortcuts some of the setup you needed to do in the `JournalRMS` version by skipping the need to open the file and create the `ByteArrayOutputStream` altogether. For this reason the `JournalEntry` save and read methods are slightly different in this version than they are in the `JournalRMS` version, but functionally they serialize records the same.

Another big difference is that the file system does not have the concept of records. As a result of this you are, in essence, storing all of the entries in one giant record and therefore you need more information, specifically you need the number of entries in the list. After opening the file, you want to first write into the file the number of entries in the list and then save each entry afterward.

```
ostream.writeInt(_EntryList.size());
```

Each record is saved in the same way that you've done before—by enumerating the list of records and calling the `save` method on each one. Of course, you need to close the streams and file connections afterward as well. Closing the file before the stream is closed is allowed but will cause the file to remain open until the stream is.

Now, with half of the work done, it's time to read that data back in. When it comes to reading data from a file, the process is very much the same. The biggest difference is that you must also allow for the case where file doesn't exist to begin with. Let's take a look at that code now.

Time for action – reading data from a file

1. Again, you need a `load` method for each `JournalEntry` so add this `load` method to the `JournalEntry` class.

    ```
    public void load (DataInputStream inputStream)
    {
      try
      {
        setEntryDate(new Date(inputStream.readLong()));
    ```

```
      setEntry(inputStream.readUTF());
    }
    catch (IOException e)
    {
      e.printStackTrace();
    }
}
```

2. You will also need a `LoadData` method in the `JournalMainScreen` to handle the load of the file as a whole.

```
protected void LoadData(String path)
{
  // TODO: Load Data
  try
  {
    FileConnection _JournalFile =
      (FileConnection) Connector.open(path);
    if (_JournalFile != null)
    {
      JournalEntry newEntry;
      DataInputStream istream =
        _JournalFile.openDataInputStream();
      int count = istream.readInt();
      for (int i=0; i<count; i++)
      {
        newEntry = new JournalEntry();
        newEntry.load(istream);
        EntryList.addElement(newEntry);
      }
        istream.close();
    }
      _JournalFile.close();
  }
  catch (IOException e)
   {
     // TODO Auto-generated catch block
     e.printStackTrace();
   }
}
```

Storing Data

3. Finally, you need to add this code to the constructor so that you load the data when the screen is created.

```
if (CheckPathExists(_SDCardURL))
{
  if (CheckPathExists(_URL))
  {
     LoadData(_URL);
  }
}
```

What just happened?

Loading the data back in isn't any more or less complicated than saving it out, you just have to make sure to do it in reverse order. The first code you added here adds the `load` method to the `JournalEntry` class so that each object can get the data it needs when loading.

The `LoadData` method that you added to the `JournalMainScreen` class is also very similar to the `SaveData` method you covered previously and follows the same basic steps. Besides using a `DataInputStream` instead of a `DataOutputStream` the `LoadData` method also loops a little differently compared to the `SaveData` method. Because you don't have a list to enumerate, the `LoadData` method first reads in how many entries there are in the file and then uses a standard `for` loop to create and read data for each `JournalEntry` object. Once the objects are created properly they are also added to the list.

The last chunk of code you added to the constructor simply makes a few calls to the `CheckPathExists` helper method to make sure that the file is there before attempting to load it. These checks aren't strictly necessary, however. If they were not made and you simply called `LoadData`, the `open` method would succeed and the `openDataInputStream` method would throw an exception. Even the code to make sure that the SDCard path is valid could have been omitted because simply making sure that the filename exists is enough. Having a separate check for the SDCard allows you to display an intelligent message warning the user, although this sample doesn't actually do that.

The `JournalEntry` sample functions the same regardless of which method you use to save the data. You did these samples as three separate applications, but there isn't any reason why you couldn't implement them all and allow the user control over where and how they save that data.

Pop quiz

1. What class is used to get the `FileConnection` object?

    a. `FileConnection`

    b. `Connection`

    c. `Connector`

2. What method is used to save data in a file?

    a. `open`

    b. `openDataOutputStream`

    c. `save`

3. What method should always be called when done working with a `FileConnection`?

    a. `closeAll`

    b. `closeConnection`

    c. `close`

Have a go hero – allowing the user to specify the filename

In all of these examples the filename and location were hardcoded just to make it easier to demonstrate, but I wouldn't recommend doing that in a commercial application. Instead, you should allow the user to specify the filename and path that should be used when loading and saving the data.

There are a lot of ways by which this can be accomplished. You could, for instance, add an `EditField` for the path location to the main screen and move the `load` and `save` operations to a menu item. You could make a `Preferences` screen to collect this and other information to make the application easier to use. Regardless of the method used there will be a lot of changes needed. Here are a few things to consider when making these changes.

You will probably want to use one of the `EditField` classes to collect the filename and/or location. You can use the `FilenameTextFilter` to help ensure that the value entered is a valid path. Of course, this isn't a substitute for testing the path so tokenizing the filename to make sure the path exists is also important.

If you don't want to collect the information over and over, then you should store the location somewhere for future use. Doing this in a `PersistentStore` is probably your best choice.

Many desktop users are used to an "Explorer" type of screen that shows the file structure of the storage area organized in a tree. You could create another screen which implements a "browse" type of feature as well. The SDK doesn't include this kind of dialog in the SDK. It is a pretty complicated task though, but could be developed into a reusable component for other projects too.

Summary

This chapter has been all about storing data in one of the two BlackBerry databases that are available. After reading the chapter you should understand why the term database isn't very accurate. We covered each of the approaches in detail and provided some solid examples of using them within an application. We also covered the removable storage options that are available in case neither of the record based options work out.

After reading this chapter you should know:

- The pros and cons for each record-based approach and be able to pick which best meets your needs
- Understand the file-based storage capabilities and when this might be the best way to store data
- How to put and get data from so that your program can persist data even when it's no longer running
- Reset the simulator and the data in it

Persisting data is just one of many essential aspects of programming. It is also important for understanding the next chapter. One of most common tasks for BlackBerry applications is to interface with and leverage the **Personal Information Management (PIM)** applications and data. The next chapter will cover how you can interface with these important tools that exist on every BlackBerry device and in doing so, make your own application more compelling.

8
Interfacing with Applications

Now that we've covered some of the basics of application development it's time to expand our horizons a bit and look at interfacing with other BlackBerry applications. You can create many great applications that don't do anything more complex than interfacing with the user and storing data. Sometimes though, developing an interesting application means doing something more or something special with the existing applications on the device. When you think about development from this point of view, there are suddenly a lot more applications that can be created than before.

The BlackBerry handhelds come pre-loaded with many great programs to help make a person more productive. While messages may be the most common reason a person will purchase a BlackBerry, the other **Personal Information Management (PIM)** applications often quickly become essential as well.

As a developer, you cannot ignore the other applications on the handheld. The more integrated an application can be with these standard applications, the better the user experience will generally be. Our `TipCalc` application is very specialized, and one of the few that works well without integrating with other applications. More often than not though, any applications that you create will benefit from some level of integration.

Not only can you interface with these applications by adding or editing content in them, you can also listen for events that allow you to react to things that happen. Some of the applications even allow you to add menu items and other "active content" to them. That's a lot to talk about, so we'll just focus on some of the most common tasks to get you started in this chapter.

Interfacing with Applications

Introducing PIM

The first area that we will take a look at is the Personal Information Management, or PIM applications and data. **PIM applications** are a rather generic name for a group of tools that manage your personal information, especially as it relates to your handheld. This could be stretched to include a lot of things, but it generally means your messages, contacts, and scheduling information that help you to manage your life. In BlackBerry terms it means the **Messages**, **Address Book**, **Calendar**, **Tasks**, and **Notes**.

Access to the PIM data in the BlackBerry SDK is provided through the **JSR-75 specification**, which is a Java standard. Like many of the Java standards in the BlackBerry SDK, there are also BlackBerry-specific extensions available that expand the basic classes with new BlackBerry-specific functionality.

Like many of the other standards we find in Java, JSR-75 implements a factory pattern where one class, in this case the PIM class, is used to create objects for the other more specific types of PIM data. The PIM class can basically do only one thing and that is to retrieve a `PIMList` object that contains a bunch of specialized `PIMItem` objects.

Why is all so generic?

All of these PIM classes may seem very generic and you would be absolutely correct. They are generic and they are supposed to be that way. PIM data is a very generic concept so the implementation is very generic as well. Also, because it is a Java standard, it needs to be flexible enough to accommodate any system that it might be implemented on.

A perfect example of this kind of flexibility is the **BlackBerry PIN** field. The **BlackBerry PIN** is an entry in your address book and therefore, it should be included in the PIM data that you get. However, a **PIN** is a BlackBerry-specific concept and no other device out there will use it. You can't really expect the Java standard to include specialized fields for every possible piece of data that some device may have or want to include. The answer to this is to present PIM data in a key-value pairing so that it is flexible enough to handle every possible scenario.

A **key-value** pairing is a somewhat technical term to describe the pattern for storing values based on a static key. Or, more simply, if you know the proper key you can access the value. The flexible part is that the PIM object storing all of the values does not need to know about each specific value or provide any special mechanism for accessing each specific value. All access is done through generic methods, which also require the key.

The difficulty in using this kind of approach is that the keys must be common knowledge. In addition, simple numeric keys do not support self-documenting code or even easily readable code. Keys that are string values offer a lot of advantages—in that the keys are much more readable, but the possibility for mistakes is very great because you don't have the compiler to help ensure that only correct keys are used.

PIMLists

As we said early on, the `PIM` class is used primarily to retrieve a `PIMList` object for a specific kind of PIM item, that is, address book contact, calendar event, and so on. For each of these types, there is also a specialized class that you can use instead of the generic `PIMList` class. Classes such as `ContactList`, `EventList`, and `ToDoList` offer a specialized version of the more generic `PIMList` class. These specialized classes are also part of the Java standard and should be preferred because they offer a few more methods which are specific to that kind of data.

There are BlackBerry-specific versions of these classes as well. Therefore, the `BlackBerryContactList` class is the BlackBerry-specific version of the `ContactList`, which is in turn a specialized version of `PIMList` for contact data. Generally speaking, you will want to use the BlackBerry-specific versions of `PIMList` classes when making your applications.

PIMItems

A `PIMItem` is the generic representation for any piece of PIM data. Just like there are specific versions of the `PIMList`, there are also specific versions of the `PIMItem` class for each kind of `PIMItem`. `Contact`, `Event`, and `ToDo` are all specific versions of a `PIMItem` for that kind of PIM data. As you might expect, there are BlackBerry-specific versions as well. `BlackBerryContact`, `BlackBerryEvent`, and `BlackBerryToDo` all exist to extend and further specialize the standard Java classes.

These specialized classes aren't as specialized or easy to use as one might expect though. Providing a method called `getFirstName` might be really useful, but unfortunately, you will find nothing of the sort. The specialized classes offer few methods for accessing data. Instead, they provide static values for the keys used to set and retrieve data from the `PIMItem` class. Remember, earlier we noted that one drawback to using this kind of key-value pairing was that keys were sometimes not clear and that you could not expect help from the compiler. By providing each key value in the specialized class, both of these goals are accomplished. The name of the key value now provides a readable name and the compiler will flag an error if there is a typo or problem with the constant value being used.

Interfacing with Applications

Another aspect of `PIMItem` is that each value that an item has a specific type associated with it as well. Some of these are obvious, such as the start date of an event using a `Date` type. Some of them, such as the **Name** field of a **Contact** that requires an array, are not. Some fields can be given a subtype as well, such as the **Phone** field. With the subtype you can specify what kind of phone number it is: home, work, or mobile. Furthermore, some of the fields can have multiple occurrences while others cannot. A good example of this is the **Email** field in a **Contact**. A contact is allowed to have up to three e-mail addresses, but there is no subtype associated with them like there is with phone numbers. The bottom line to all this is that the `PIM` items have a defined structure to them and they won't allow just any value to be put into a field. The documentation plays a big role here in understanding this because there are no field-specific methods to provide some additional assistance in the proper way to access each field.

Laying the ground work

Still, this is all rather abstract because you haven't seen any real code samples yet, so let's get into some code! For this chapter, you will build an application that someone will use to request some time off from their manager. This is definitely one of those applications that just can't be done without interfacing with other applications on the handheld! To make getting started a little easier we will take the starter `TimeOff` application from the code bundle and add to it throughout this chapter.

The first task to undertake is one to help make testing and debugging easier. Remember, you will be working on the simulator, which is essentially a brand new device and which can be often reset. That means you don't have any of your contacts there! You will need some contacts later, so to get started let's add a menu item to the application that will create a few contacts that you can later use to test with.

Time for action – creating test contacts

1. Modify the `_AddTestAddressesAction` menu item in the `TimeOff` project to look like the following completed code.

```
protected MenuItem _AddTestAddressesAction = new MenuItem(
        "Add Test Data", 800000, 50)
{
 public void run()
 {
  PIM pimInstance = PIM.getInstance();
  try
  {
    // TODO: Create test contacts
    BlackBerryContactList contacts =
```

```
      (BlackBerryContactList)pimInstance.openPIMList(
        PIM.CONTACT_LIST, PIM.READ_WRITE);
    BlackBerryContact newContact1 =
      (BlackBerryContact)contacts.createContact();
    BlackBerryContact newContact2 =
      (BlackBerryContact)contacts.createContact();

    String[] names = new
      String[contacts.stringArraySize(BlackBerryContact.NAME)];
    names[BlackBerryContact.NAME_FAMILY] = "Smith";
    names[BlackBerryContact.NAME_GIVEN] = "John";
    if (contacts.isSupportedArrayElement(Contact.NAME,
        Contact.NAME_SUFFIX))
    {
       names[BlackBerryContact.NAME_SUFFIX]="Jr";
    }
  newContact1.addStringArray(
    BlackBerryContact.NAME,
    BlackBerryContact.ATTR_NONE,
    names);
        names[Contact.NAME_FAMILY] = "Doe";
        names[Contact.NAME_GIVEN] = "John";
    if (contacts.isSupportedArrayElement(Contact.NAME,
        Contact.NAME_PREFIX))
    {
      names[Contact.NAME_PREFIX] = "Dr.";
    }
    newContact2.addStringArray(Contact.NAME, Contact.ATTR_NONE,
                             names);
              //TODO: Add Phone numbers

              //TODO: Add Email Addresses

              //TODO: Add Addresses

    newContact1.commit();
    newContact2.commit();
  }
  catch (PIMException e)
  {
    // TODO Auto-generated catch block
    e.printStackTrace();
  }
 }
};
```

Interfacing with Applications

2. Then add this line to the constructor to make the menu item available when you run the application.

```
this.addMenuItem(_AddTestAddressesAction);
```

What just happened?

This is the first of several baby steps as you work towards the goal of creating some test contacts in the address book in the simulator. As the address book in the simulator doesn't have any entries to begin with, and can be erased frequently, doing this provides you with a way to quickly and easily create or recreate the contacts you will use later on for testing other parts of this application. It also happens to be a great way to demonstrate how to add contacts.

This first baby step does only a few things. First, it gets a `PIMList` object for contacts and then creates two new contacts. After this it sets the name of each one and finally commits the records into the address book. These steps make sense at a high level, but let's take a look at the details.

The first step is to get an instance to the `PIM` object, which is done through a static method in the `PIM` class called `getInstance`.

```
PIM pimInstance = PIM.getInstance();
```

Once you have an instance of `PIM`, the next step is to get a list of contact items using the `openPIMList` method on the instance you just retrieved. This same method is used to get a list of any kind of `PIM` item so you must specify the type of data to get as one of the parameters. The `PIM` class offers constant values for every kind of `PIM` item, so in this case, use the constant `PIM.CONTACT_LIST`. As you plan to add new contacts, the next parameter needs to be the constant `PIM.READ_WRITE` so that you have `write` permissions. It's always good practice to request the minimum amount of permissions that you need, so if your application doesn't change or add data to the list you should simply use the `PIM.READ` permission.

As we touched on earlier, this method returns a generic `PIMList` type so you also have to cast it to the appropriate specialized type. If a list type of `CONTACT_LIST` has been specified, you can cast the resulting `PIMList` to either of the available specialized classes—`ContactList` or `BlackBerryContactList`. As long as your application is a BlackBerry-specific application, there is no good reason to use the less specialized class of `ContactList`. Instead, you should always use `BlackBerryContactList`.

```
BlackBerryContactList contacts =
   (BlackBerryContactList)pimInstance.openPIMList(PIM.CONTACT_LIST, PIM.
   READ_WRITE);
```

The next step is to create a couple of new contacts that you will start to populate. This is done through the `createContact` method available on the `ContactList` class. Again, you need to cast the resulting objects to the proper type. The `createContact` method returns a contact, but again you've chosen to use the more specialized version of `BlackBerryContact` instead. Because this is all being executed on a BlackBerry handheld, you can always cast a contact to a `BlackBerryContact` safely. The same is true for each of the Java specialized classes and their corresponding BlackBerry specialized class.

```
BlackBerryContact newContact1 =  (BlackBerryContact) contacts.
                                  createContact();
BlackBerryContact newContact1 =  (BlackBerryContact) contacts.
                                  createContact();
```

The next segment of code sets the `name` attribute of the newly created contacts. Notice that this is done through an array of `String` objects instead of individual methods. This isn't something that is done to be more efficient, it is done this way because it must be; there is no other way.

We mentioned before about each field in a `PIMItem` having a type associated with it. Most of the field types are basic `String` or `Date` type fields, but `NAME` is more complicated than most of the other fields. The `NAME` field is defined as a `StringArray` because there are many parts to a name and you want to be able to set each part separately. There aren't very many fields of this type used, but this is probably one of the most important. You can only set the `NAME` field as a whole unit, so if only one part of the name needs to be changed the entire name field must be replaced.

To work with the name, you must first create a string array of the proper size. There is no constant value for this as it may vary with the SDK version. Instead, you must first get the size by using the `stringArraySize` method on the `ContactList` and then construct a new array by using the returned value.

```
String[] names = new String[contacts.stringArraySize(BlackBerryConta
ct.NAME)];
```

Once you have an array of the proper size each part of the name is set by indexing the array by using the `NAME` constant from the `Contact` class.

```
names[BlackBerryContact.NAME_FAMILY] = "Smith";
names[BlackBerryContact.NAME_GIVEN] = "John";
```

Interfacing with Applications

In this example, you also want to add another name part but are not sure whether the field is supported in this system. Not all fields are supported and not all of the name subfields are supported either. You can test to see whether a field or a subfield is supported by using the `isSupportedField` or `isSupportedArrayElement` methods in the `ContactList` class. In this case, you test to see if the suffix is supported, and then set the suffix if so.

```
if (contacts.isSupportedArrayElement(Contact.NAME,
                                     Contact.NAME_SUFFIX))
{
   names[BlackBerryContact.NAME_SUFFIX]="Jr";
}
```

This step is very important if you want to use the same code for multiple platforms. Each system can support the fields it chooses. In this case, the suffix is NOT supported and if you were to step through this code in the debugger, you would see that the code to set the suffix is skipped over. Later on, when you test this application, you will also see that the suffix was not added to the contact.

Other platforms may implement it differently. You could just assume each of the name subfields are supported and set the field without testing to see if it is supported. In the BlackBerry SDK, unsupported fields are just quietly ignored. This can lead to confusion wondering why a field doesn't appear in the **Address Book** application, but it won't cause an error.

The next step is to actually add the NAME field to the contact. Up until this time you've simply been building an array in memory with all of the proper values.

```
newContact1.addStringArray(
    BlackBerryContact.NAME,
    BlackBerryContact.ATTR_NONE,
    names);
```

Notice that the method `addStringArray` doesn't give any indication about what field is being added, but only what type of data is being added. All of the `PIMItem` methods are like this. Remember, this class is designed to be generic. The first parameter is the field indicator, which is one of the many constants that are defined in the `Contact` class. In this case, we use the `BlackBerryContact` class. Because `BlackBerryContact` derived from `Contact`, all of the constant values are accessible. The `BlackBerryContact` class does define some constants that are BlackBerry-specific, such as PIN. For this field you must reference the constant value from `BlackBerryContact` because the Java standard `Contact` class does not define it. Partly for this reason, I suggest always referencing constant values from `BlackBerryContact` because all of the constant values will be available through this class.

The method `addStringArray` was chosen because that is the type of data that you are adding. The NAME field is defined as a string array and so you must use the `addStringArray` method because it corresponds to the data type of the field.

Once you finish with the first contact, the code starts building the NAME string array to add a second contact. For demonstration sake, all of the constant values that are referenced are done so using the Contact class instead of the BlackBerryContact class.

```
names[Contact.NAME_FAMILY] = "Doe";
names[Contact.NAME_GIVEN] = "John";
if (contacts.isSupportedArrayElement(Contact.NAME,
                                     Contact.NAME_PREFIX))
{
  names[Contact.NAME_PREFIX] = "Dr.";
}
newContact2.addStringArray(Contact.NAME, Contact.ATTR_NONE, names);
```

Also, notice that the second contact applies a prefix to the name and tests to see if it is supported in the same way as you did for the suffix when adding the previous contact. However, the prefix is supported and if you were to step through this method in the debugger, you would see that the prefix is being set properly.

The last step you have to do is to commit the data that has been added to the contact.

```
newContact1.commit();
newContact2.commit();
```

Simply creating a new contact is not enough; you must commit the changes in it by using the commit method. Creating a contact and then never committing it will not have any effect on the **Address Book** application. It simply won't be shown in the list. That's the whole point of this exercise, so you have to make sure and commit the changes once they are all done.

At this point, if you were to run the application and select the menu, you would see two new contacts added to the **Address Book** application in the simulator. They would show up as **Dr. John Doe** and **John Smith**. There would be only names with these contacts because that is all that you've added so far.

In the example code that you just stepped through there was one mistake that could have proven to be very serious. Did you catch it? You are reusing the names array to set the names of both contacts. This is actually risky, but it happens to work out in this case. If the SUFFIX field had been supported then your **Dr. John Doe** would have actually been **Dr. John Doe Jr.** because the array was not reset before it was used again. If you had changed the order around, **John Smith** would have been **Dr. John Smith**. This might have lead to a bug that could have been tough to track down, so keep it in mind.

Expanding your test contacts

Being able to create a contact is nice, but you really need for them to have more information than just a name in order to be useful. So, for the next step, add some telephone numbers to the contacts. If you are familiar with the **Address Book** application already, and you should be, then you know that a contact can have multiple phone numbers—each with a different role or locations. After having seen how the `NAME` field is handled, you may well assume that the telephone field, named `TEL`, would operate in the same manner; as a `StringArray` type.

You would be wrong though.

When it comes to the `TEL` field each field is a simple `String` and is given an additional attribute defining which kind of phone number it is. Let's take a look at this with the following code.

Time for action – adding telephone numbers

1. Add the following code to the `run` method of the `AddTestContacts` menu item.

```
//TODO: Add Phone numbers
newContact1.addString(BlackBerryContact.TEL,
   BlackBerryContact.ATTR_MOBILE, "555-555-1212");
newContact2.addString(Contact.TEL,Contact.ATTR_HOME,
               "555-555-1234");
newContact2.addString(Contact.TEL,Contact.ATTR_FAX,
               "555-555-9999");
newContact2.addString(Contact.TEL,
     Contact.ATTR_MOBILE,"555-555-1313");
// This is bad!
newContact2.addString(Contact.TEL,Contact.ATTR_FAX,
               "555-555-1414");
```

What just happened?

Working with phone numbers may look very straightforward, but there are many pitfalls to look out for here as well. Each phone number is added using the `addString` method, which should look similar to the `addStringArray` method that you just worked with. Again, the proper method to add the field is the one that matches the fields' type and has nothing to do with the name of the field or its function.

Also, like the previous example, the first parameter to the method is the constant value defining which field is being added, which in this case is TEL. Following the field indicator though is the important part, called the `field` attribute. The attributes are used as a way of providing additional information about a field. In this case, that information defines what kind of phone number is being added.

Every add method requires an `attribute` field, but this doesn't always make sense for some fields. When this is the case, the attribute ATTR_NONE should be used. The phone number field though requires an attribute. Attempting to use ATTR_NONE will in fact be treated the same as ATTR_HOME.

```
newContact1.addString(BlackBerryContact.TEL,
    BlackBerryContact.ATTR_MOBILE, "555-555-1212");
```

Now that you've covered the basics, this line to add a mobile telephone number to John Doe should be self explanatory.

```
newContact2.addString(Contact.TEL,Contact.ATTR_HOME,"555-555-1234");
newContact2.addString(Contact.TEL,Contact.ATTR_FAX,"555-555-9999");
newContact2.addString(Contact.TEL,Contact.ATTR_MOBILE,"555-555-1313");
```

Now, as John Smith is a doctor, he will have many more ways to be reached, but you can see that this also presents no problems for the Contact class. Again, this example uses the Contact class to reference the constant values instead of the BlackBerryContact class.

This is fine, but there are some phone attributes which are not available from the Contact class. The Java standard Contact only provides for six telephone types, but the BlackBerry **Address Book** application will allow eight. So what is the difference? The Home2 and Work2 numbers are specific to BlackBerry. The constants for these attributes can be found only in the BlackBerryContact class.

As long as you use one, and only one, of each attribute, you will be in good shape, but things get really messy when you try to add a number with the same attribute again.

```
// This is bad!
newContact2.addString(Contact.TEL,Contact.ATTR_FAX,"555-555-1414");
```

Interfacing with Applications

You may expect that adding a number with the same attribute would simply replace any existing value, but this is not the case. Instead, the system will add the number into the "next available slot". The results can be quite confusing because in this case, the number will be placed into the PAGER attribute because FAX is already populated. If the PAGER already had a value, then it would be added to some other field that didn't have a value.

```
Dr. John Doe
  Email: JDoe@test.com
  Email: JohnDoe@test.com
  Email: Admin@test.com
   Home: 555-555-1234
 Mobile: 555-555-1313
  Pager: 555-555-1414
    Fax: 555-555-9999
```

Adding another phone number with the same attribute as an existing number yields unpredictable results.

The corollary to this is that if you are editing a contact in your application you can't just blindly add the TEL fields. You must first either remove the old field by using the removeValue method, or change the value by using the setString method.

Either way, things are going to be a lot more complicated. You would think that there would be methods for getting, setting, or removing values that match those for adding values, but this is not the case either. There are getString, setString, and removeValue methods, but all of the methods rely on an index value and not the attribute that was originally supplied. This just reinforces the idea that attributes are simply meant to provide additional information about the field and nothing more.

So, if you wanted to change one of the TEL fields you first need to find the field with the proper attribute out of the list of TEL fields. Remember that this field is not an array though, so even though there may be up to eight values, there may be as few as 0 and the order in which they are stored apparently has nothing to do with their attribute. The following code fragment should serve as an example of how to update the ATTR_HOME phone number.

```
// The proper way to change a value
int count = newContact2.countValues(Contact.TEL);
for (int i = 0; i < count; i++)
{
  if ((newContact2.getAttributes(Contact.TEL, i) & Contact.ATTR_HOME)
      == Contact.ATTR_HOME)
  {
```

```
            newContact2.setString(Contact.TEL, i, Contact.ATTR_HOME,
                        "555-555-4321");
    }
}
```

To start off, you can get the number of values in the field by calling the `countValues` method. Once you know how many are there, a simple `for` loop is used to test each one. In order to see if a value has the `ATTR_HOME` attribute, you first get all of the attributes of the value by calling the `getAttributes` method. Some attributes can be combined using a bitwise OR, so to check for a specific attribute you must test with the bitwise AND, which effectively removes just the desired attribute from any other combined attributes. Once you know that a value has the `ATTR_HOME` attribute, you can call `setString` by using the index value from the loop to change the value.

Like I said, it's a lot more complicated and as a result, I think it is safe to suggest that you not do it unless you really need to. There will always be special cases where such a thing is desired, but in general, a user should be in charge of their contacts and not your application. Besides, there is no way to stop a user from changing or deleting a contact that has been programmatically added.

Expanding even more

After tackling the relatively complicated fields of NAME and TEL, the EMAIL field should be a lot easier. Making sure that your contacts have an e-mail address is the whole point of this task because these will be used later on when testing another feature. Knowing that the **Address Book** application allows you to have up to three e-mail addresses, how would you think they are implemented in the PIM? Is it implemented as a `String` with multiple values (such as the TEL field), or as a `StringArray` (such as the NAME field)? If you chose a `String` with multiple values, you chose correctly!

The **EMAIL** field actually fits well with this concept of a `String` field with multiple values. Unlike the TEL fields, there are no attributes that are attached to each of the e-mail addresses, so adding one simply adds it to the list and there is nothing more to be concerned about. So let's look at some code already!

Time for action – adding e-mail addresses

1. Add the following code to the `run` method of _AddTestAddressesAction_ under the proper comment line.

    ```
    //TODO: Add Email Addresses
    newContact1.addString(Contact.EMAIL,Contact.ATTR_NONE,
                    "John@Test.com");
    ```

Interfacing with Applications

```
newContact2.addString(Contact.EMAIL,Contact.ATTR_NONE,
                    "JDoe@test.com");
newContact2.addString(Contact.EMAIL,Contact.ATTR_NONE,
                    "JohnDoe@test.com");
newContact2.addString(Contact.EMAIL,Contact.ATTR_NONE,
                    "Admin@test.com");
```

What just happened?

Wow, that code segment looks really easy. The lines are all practically the same! Each line specifies the field as `EMAIL` and the attributes as `ATTR_NONE`, so there isn't much more to talk about except for the "what-ifs".

Much like the `TEL`, things get a little trickier if you want to edit the contact in your application, but not as tricky as they are with the **PHONE** field. The addresses are stored in the same order that you added them to the field so you can use this fact to your advantage when editing. Because there are no attributes for the various e-mail addresses, it is best to remember the index of each value when you read them out. In this way, when you need to change the value you can use the `setString` method and provide the index of field.

Alternatively, you can remove one of the `EMAIL` values and add a new one, but this will also change the order of the values in the field. Values that are added are always placed at the end of the list.

The biggest thing to watch out for here is that you don't add a fourth `EMAIL` value to the field. This will cause an exception to be thrown that the application will have to handle. In the case of this application, it just quietly fails and neither of the contacts are added.

You can also put bad data into the **Address Book** application by adding values with bad data. For instance, the **Email Address** field in the **Address Book** application has special validation logic to ensure that the value is actually a valid e-mail. If you leave out the `@`, for instance, the user would see an error and not be allowed to commit the data. All of those safeguards don't exist when working directly with the PIM. This goes for phone numbers as well as for any other formatted values. It is one more reason that you must be very careful about when working with the PIM directly.

Finishing the test contacts

We have done enough work to solve the initial problem of getting some contacts with e-mail addresses into the **Address Book**. However, there is one more area of the contact left to tackle—the address itself. The `ADDR` field is a combination of the `NAME` and `PHONE` fields in that each address is a `StringArray`, but there are multiple addresses which each have an attribute specifying what kind of address it is. Sounds confusing? It is by far the most complex piece of PIM data. Seeing code always helps me, so let's dive into the code and tackle it head on.

Time for action – adding e-mail addresses

1. Add the final code segment under the appropriate comment in the `run` method of `_AddTestAddressesAction`.

```
//TODO: Add Addresses
String[] Address1 = new String[contacts.stringArraySize(BlackBerry
Contact.ADDR)];
String[] Address2 = new String[contacts.stringArraySize(BlackBerry
Contact.ADDR)];
Address1[BlackBerryContact.ADDR_STREET] = "123 Main St.";
Address1[BlackBerryContact.ADDR_EXTRA] = "Apt. 4";
Address1[BlackBerryContact.ADDR_LOCALITY] = "AnyTown";
Address1[BlackBerryContact.ADDR_REGION] = "AnyState";
Address1[BlackBerryContact.ADDR_COUNTRY] = "USA";
Address1[BlackBerryContact.ADDR_POSTALCODE] = "12345";
newContact1.addStringArray(BlackBerryContact.ADDR,
                BlackBerryContact.ATTR_HOME,Address1);

Address1[BlackBerryContact.ADDR_STREET] = "345 Main St.";
Address1[BlackBerryContact.ADDR_LOCALITY] = "AnyTown";
Address1[BlackBerryContact.ADDR_REGION] = "AnyState";
Address1[BlackBerryContact.ADDR_COUNTRY] = "USA";
Address1[BlackBerryContact.ADDR_POSTALCODE] = "12345";

Address2[BlackBerryContact.ADDR_STREET] = "20 N Oak St.";
Address2[BlackBerryContact.ADDR_LOCALITY] = "AnyTown";
Address2[BlackBerryContact.ADDR_REGION] = "AnyState";
Address2[BlackBerryContact.ADDR_COUNTRY] = "USA";
Address2[BlackBerryContact.ADDR_EXTRA] = "Suite 200";
Address1[BlackBerryContact.ADDR_POSTALCODE] = "12345";
newContact2.addStringArray(BlackBerryContact.ADDR,
```

Interfacing with Applications

```
                            BlackBerryContact.ATTR_HOME,Address1);
newContact2.addStringArray(BlackBerryContact.ADDR,
                            BlackBerryContact.ATTR_WORK,Address2);
```

What just happened?

This code should be pretty similar to the code that you saw for the `NAME` field. The first step is to simply create an array of `String` objects of the proper size and once again relying on the `stringArraySize` method to give that proper value. The only real difference here is that the field specified in the code is the `ADDR` field.

```
String[] Address1 = new String[contacts.stringArraySize(BlackBerryCon
tact.ADDR)];
```

Once you have an array of the right size, setting the data for each part of the address is just a matter of referencing the right index within the array by using the constants already defined. The names of the constant values for the ADDR field are so generic that they are confusing.

```
Address1[BlackBerryContact.ADDR_STREET] = "123 Main St.";
Address1[BlackBerryContact.ADDR_EXTRA] = "Apt. 4";
Address1[BlackBerryContact.ADDR_LOCALITY] = "AnyTown";
Address1[BlackBerryContact.ADDR_REGION] = "AnyState";
Address1[BlackBerryContact.ADDR_COUNTRY] = "USA";
Address1[BlackBerryContact.ADDR_POSTALCODE] = "12345";
```

Maybe, other parts of the world think in terms of "locality" and "region", but I somehow doubt it. As if those weren't bad enough, the name `ADDR_EXTRA` just gives no help at all towards understanding its use. This is just one of those things that you have to remember when working with addresses in a contact though.

Once the address is fully populated, adding it to the field is the same as adding a `TEL` field in that you also have to specify one of the two supported attributes, either `ATTR_HOME` or `ATTR_WORK`.

```
newContact1.addStringArray(BlackBerryContact.ADDR,
                            BlackBerryContact.ATTR_HOME,Address1);
```

The whole point to this is that an address can have more than one address in the contact record and the second contact in the example code has been set up in this way. Because the values for the `ADDR` field are based on their attribute, the order in which they are added is not important. However, the index is still important when it comes to updating or deleting a value.

The `ADDR` field also follows the same quirks that the `TEL` field does. If you add a second address with the `ATTR_HOME` attribute, the attribute will get silently reassigned to `ATTR_WORK` if one doesn't already exist. If there are already two addresses in the contact, then an exception will be thrown so it is important to utilize the methods for checking the field before adding new values.

Adding new address values isn't that bad, but changing one is the worst of both worlds. If you recall from working with the `NAME` field, you cannot change just one element of the `StringArray`. You have to replace the entire `StringArray` by calling the `setStringArray` method.

This quirk is somewhat annoying, but now adds the fact that there is more than one value in the list and it can get pretty complex. In order to get the address you want, you have to find it in the same way that you did for the `TEL` field. The home address will not be in the same index position all the time so you must look at each address in the list (there are only two at most) and test the attribute to see if it has the attribute you want.

Pop quiz

1. What class do you use to get a list of PIM items?
    a. `PimItem`
    b. `PimList`
    c. `PIM`

2. When adding a value to a `PIMItem`, how do you choose the proper method to use?
    a. Use the method whose name matches the value name, that is, `setFirstName()`
    b. Use the method whose name matches the data type of the value, that is, `setString()`
    c. Use the `setValue()` method

3. For values that are an array, how do you change the value of one element in the array?
    a. Use the `setStringArrayElement()` method.
    b. Use the `setArrayValue()` method.
    c. You can't set a single element in an array. You must replace the entire array with a new array of values.

Interfacing with Applications

Embedding the address book into your application

Now that you have some test data in the address book it's time to use it. The purpose of the `TimeOff` application is to provide a way for an employee in the field to request time off. In order to do this, the application will collect an e-mail address, beginning and ending dates, and a reason for the request through four fields on the screen. When the request is submitted through the menu item the application uses these pieces of information to compose an e-mail message that will be sent to the manager by using the e-mail address provided.

As we already have a field for the e-mail address, wouldn't it be nice to be able to allow the user to pick the e-mail address to use from the address book instead of requiring them to re-enter it by hand?

You already went over how to get the `ContactList` from the `PIM` object. You could create a screen and list all of the contacts on the screen, but this could be quite a long list that would take up a lot of processing time and memory. There are some other techniques you could use to display only a limited list, but even if you went through all of that work you still would be lacking several key pieces of functionality such as searching or even adding a new contact on the fly. In short, you would almost be reimplementing the `AddressBook` application! Wouldn't it be better to just reuse the address book?

Good news, you can do that! The `AddressBook` application has exposed an interface that lets you leverage it, so you don't have to solve all of those problems a second time. In addition to saving a ton of work, it also helps to provide a consistent user interface that will be familiar and easy to use.

Time for action – embedding the address book

1. You first start by overriding the `makeMenu` method. With this method you can display the menu to access the **Address Book** application only when the e-mail field is selected.

   ```
   if (this.getFieldWithFocus() == _To &&
       context != Menu.INSTANCE_CONTEXT_SELECTION)
   {
       m.add(_AddressBookAction);
   }
   ```

2. Then, we need to implement the Run method of the _AddressBookAction menu item.

   ```
   PIM pim = PIM.getInstance();
   try
   {
   ```

```
      BlackBerryContactList contacts =
        (BlackBerryContactList)pim.openPIMList(PIM.CONTACT_LIST,
          PIM.READ_WRITE);
      BlackBerryContact selected = (BlackBerryContact) contacts.
choose();
      if (selected != null)
      {
       int EmailAddressCount = selected.countValues(Contact.EMAIL);
       // check to make sure that there is an Email address for
          this contact.
        if ( EmailAddressCount > 0)
        {
          String selectedEmail;
          // If there is more than just one email, display a
            dialog to choose
          if (EmailAddressCount > 1)
          {
            String[] Addresses = new String[EmailAddressCount];
            int[] Values = new int[EmailAddressCount];
            for (int i = 0; i < EmailAddressCount; i++)
            {
              Addresses[i] = selected.getString(Contact.EMAIL, i);
              Values[i] = i;
            }
            Dialog dlg = new Dialog("Select which address to use.",
             Addresses, Values, 0,
             Bitmap.getPredefinedBitmap(Bitmap.QUESTION));
            int selectedAddr = dlg.doModal();
            selectedEmail = Addresses[selectedAddr];
          }
          else
          {
            selectedEmail = selected.getString(Contact.EMAIL, 0);
          }

          TimeOffMainScreen theScreen =
            (TimeOffMainScreen)UiApplication.getUiApplication()
              .getActiveScreen();
          theScreen._To.setText(selectedEmail);
        }
       }
      }
      catch (PIMException e)
```

```
    {
      // TODO Auto-generated catch block
      e.printStackTrace();
    }
```

What just happened?

The first part of this is all about making the menu item appear when the users want it to be shown, and not when they don't. It makes sense that when the **Email** field has focus, the menu will be shown in the list. When any of the other fields are selected, the user probably doesn't care about selecting an e-mail address from the **Address Book** application and so the menu should be hidden. By adding a little bit of logic to the already understood `makeMenu` method you can see how you can improve the user experience simply by choosing to hide or show menu items when it is appropriate.

The standard BlackBerry applications do this often and effectively in every application on the handheld. It is an established pattern that you as a developer should give conscious thought to and follow.

The next step of this is much more involved with several parts. The first part is just about setting up the `PIM` object and getting the `ContactList` (which we've done in the previous section). The real magic happens with this simple line of code:

```
BlackBerryContact selected = (BlackBerryContact) contacts.choose();
```

The `choose` method is rather nondescript and plain, but this simple method is the exposed functionality that will display the address book list and prompt the user to select a contact. All of the functionality of the `AddressBook` is available, including searching by typing a contact name and even adding or modifying an existing contact, and it's been optimized to be fast and memory efficient.

There are a number of menu items that are NOT present, such as those allowing you to compose messages or initiate calls. As you can see, a lot of thought went into this screen and you should all be thankful that the `choose` method is available and is able to be reused. It's not perfect though, and there are several limitations. For instance, you can't provide any parameters at all to the method so you can't specify that you want addresses only with an e-mail address to be shown, for instance.

Any contact may be selected, and as a result you must handle any situations where the selected contact does not have the information that you desire. In this case, you are interested in collecting only an e-mail address from the contact so you must check to make sure that it has one.

```
    int EmailAddressCount = selected.countValues(Contact.EMAIL);
    // check to make sure that there is an Email address for this contact.
```

```
if (EmailAddressCount > 0)
{
...

}
else
{
   Dialog.alert("This contact has no Email Addresses.");
}
```

Once you are sure that the contact has at least one e-mail address you need to further examine how many addresses the contact does have. Remember that a contact can have up to three e-mail addresses. If there is just one, then it is very easy to know which one to use. However, if a contact has more than one then the user needs to choose which of them should be used.

```
String selectedEmail;
// If there is more than just one email, display a dialog to choose
if (EmailAddressCount > 1)
{
...
}
else
{
   selectedEmail = selected.getString(Contact.EMAIL, 0);
}
```

If there is more than one e-mail address in the selected contact you need to present a dialog box listing all of the addresses available and allow the user to choose the correct one. You haven't seen this form of a dialog before, so let's cover it now.

One of the standard forms of the dialog class is one that just forces the user to select a value from a list of values. This constructor for the form of dialog requires two parameters—an array of objects and an array of Integer values. Therefore, the first step to creating this dialog is to create arrays that contain the same number of elements as the number of e-mail addresses in the contact. The `integer` value can be any value that makes sense to your application, but in this case you really just want the index position of the selected address in the list.

```
String[] Addresses = new String[EmailAddressCount];
int[] Values = new int[EmailAddressCount];
for (int i = 0; i < EmailAddressCount; i++)
{
  Addresses[i] = selected.getString(Contact.EMAIL, i);
  Values[i] = i;
}
```

Interfacing with Applications

Once these arrays are created, the dialog can be displayed. The doModal method is used to display the dialog in a modal style, which just means that the application will wait until the dialog has been dismissed before continuing. Alternatively, there is a `show` method that will display a modeless dialog, which just means that the application will not wait for a response before continuing to run.

```
Dialog dlg = new Dialog("Select which address to use.",
    Addresses,Values,0,Bitmap.
    getPredefinedBitmap(Bitmap.QUESTION));
int selectedAddr = dlg.doModal();
selectedEmail = Addresses[selectedAddr];
```

The value returned by the `doModal` call is one of the values supplied in the `Values` array—the value that corresponds to the index of the selected item returned. In this example, if the second item in the dialog was selected the return value of `doModal` would be 1.

Once you have an e-mail address, the last action is to set the text of the _To field to be that address. Remember, earlier we mentioned that if you insert contacts directly you will bypass all of the formatting and validation that would otherwise normally happen. The same holds true here—inserting an e-mail address by using the `setText` method will bypass any validation and formatting that would normally happen with the `EmailAddressTextField`.

Adding the event to your calendar

The next step would be to actually submit the request. There are actually two different things that we want to happen when a user submits the request. The first is that, we will assume that the request will be approved and go ahead and add the time off to your calendar as a new event. Second, we will need to compose and send the e-mail request. This second part we will cover in more detail later. For now, let's stay focused on the PIM data and add an event.

Working with the calendar is very similar to working with contacts. Items in the calendar are generically called **events** and are also included in the umbrella of PIM items. As a result, the process begins with the PIM class once again. The similarity continues with the Java standard `Event` class and the BlackBerry-specific `BlackBerryEvent` class.

With that understanding, let's get started looking at some code.

Time for action – adding an event to the calendar

1. Add the following code to the `addEvent` method.

```
PIM pim = PIM.getInstance();
EventList events;
try {
    events = (EventList)pim.openPIMList(PIM.EVENT_LIST,
            PIM.READ_WRITE);
    BlackBerryEvent newEvent =
      (BlackBerryEvent) events.createEvent();
    newEvent.addString(BlackBerryEvent.SUMMARY,
        BlackBerryEvent.ATTR_NONE, "Requested time off.");
    newEvent.addString(BlackBerryEvent.LOCATION,
        BlackBerryEvent.ATTR_NONE,   "Special place");
    newEvent.addDate(BlackBerryEvent.START,
        BlackBerryEvent.ATTR_NONE, _StartDate.getDate());
    newEvent.addDate(BlackBerryEvent.END,
        BlackBerryEvent.ATTR_NONE, _EndDate.getDate());
    newEvent.addString(BlackBerryEvent.NOTE,
        BlackBerryEvent.ATTR_NONE, _Comments.getText());
    newEvent.addBoolean(BlackBerryEvent.ALLDAY,
        BlackBerryEvent.ATTR_NONE, true);
    newEvent.addInt(BlackBerryEvent.FREE_BUSY,
        BlackBerryEvent.ATTR_NONE, BlackBerryEvent.FB_BUSY);
    newEvent.commit();

BlackBerryEvent reminder = (BlackBerryEvent) events.createEvent();
reminder.addString(BlackBerryEvent.SUMMARY,
    BlackBerryEvent.ATTR_NONE,  "Check on request");
reminder.addDate(BlackBerryEvent.START, BlackBerryEvent.ATTR_NONE,
                new Date().getTime()+86400000);
reminder.addDate(BlackBerryEvent.END, BlackBerryEvent.ATTR_NONE,
                new Date().getTime()+86400000);

RepeatRule repeat = new RepeatRule();
repeat.setInt(RepeatRule.FREQUENCY,RepeatRule.DAILY);
repeat.setInt(RepeatRule.INTERVAL, 1);
```

Interfacing with Applications

```
            reminder.setRepeat(repeat);
            reminder.commit();
        }
        catch (PIMException e) {
            // TODO Auto-generated catch block
            e.printStackTrace();
        }
```

What just happened?

The menu item **Submit request** uses two helper methods to do the work of submitting the request. The menu item and these methods are already stubbed out in the starter code so this section is devoted to implementing the second step of the submit process—adding an event to the calendar.

To get started, use the same general steps that you did when working with the contacts. Calling the same `openPIMList` method with a different parameter, `PIM.EVENT_LIST`, gives you a list of events instead of a list of contacts. The `createEvent` method on this list is used to establish a new `Event` object to start populating.

```
        PIM pim = PIM.getInstance();
        EventList events;
        try {
            events = (EventList)pim.openPIMList(PIM.EVENT_LIST, PIM.READ_WRITE);
            BlackBerryEvent newEvent = (BlackBerryEvent) events.createEvent();
```

The next step is to add each piece of data to the event. Unlike the contact, events do not have complicated data types at all. There is only one field with multiple values and none of the fields use a `StringArray` type. They are all basic types like you've seen before. You do see several new types such as `Date` and `Boolean`, but setting and getting values from these is not any different then setting or getting `String` values; just use the right method for the field.

Also, like contact, most of the field indicator constants are available in the `Event` class, but there are a few that are available only through the `BlackBerryEvent` class. For this reason, I still recommend using the `BlackBerryEvent` for all field identifier constants.

The code starts off by setting some constant values to the SUMMARY and LOCATION fields. On a BlackBerry, these are the first two fields on the screen where a new event is entered in the **Calendar** application. The SUMMARY field is labeled as **Subject** in the calendar application. It didn't make sense to prompt for these values in `TimeOff` request (does your boss really need to know where you sister's wedding will be?), so they are just set to some static values. Presumably, the user can change them later. After that, the start and end dates are set to the dates which have been entered into the fields on the screen. The **NOTE** field follows and is populated with the **Comments** field from the entry screen.

```
newEvent.addString(BlackBerryEvent.SUMMARY, BlackBerryEvent.ATTR_NONE,
            "Requested time off.");
newEvent.addString(BlackBerryEvent.LOCATION, BlackBerryEvent.ATTR_NONE,
            "Special place");
newEvent.addDate(BlackBerryEvent.START, BlackBerryEvent.ATTR_NONE,
            _StartDate.getDate());
newEvent.addDate(BlackBerryEvent.END, BlackBerryEvent.ATTR_NONE,
            _EndDate.getDate());
newEvent.addString(BlackBerryEvent.NOTE, BlackBerryEvent.ATTR_NONE,
            _Comments.getText());
```

The last thing you do is to set two other fields that make the whole thing a little more polished, the All Day indicator and the Free or Busy flag. When the All Day indicator is set to true the time portions of the START and END date time values are ignored because the event will take the entire day. The start time is effectively midnight of the start day and the end time is the next midnight after the end day. Because the TimeOff application doesn't even allow a time portion to be entered, you can just hardcode the ALLDAY field to be true. The FREE_BUSY field uses special constants that are defined in BlackBerryEvent to determine the status. These constants all begin with FB_ to define the status. As you are asking for the entire day off, you will set the FREE_BUSY field to FB_BUSY.

```
newEvent.addBoolean(BlackBerryEvent.ALLDAY, BlackBerryEvent.ATTR_NONE,
true);
newEvent.addInt(BlackBerryEvent.FREE_BUSY, BlackBerryEvent.ATTR_NONE,
            BlackBerryEvent.FB_BUSY);
```

After setting all of the fields up for your new event, the last step is to commit (just like you did when adding the contacts).

```
newEvent.commit();
```

Recurring events

Events do have one thing that is different than contacts and which can be rather confusing—a recurring event. A **recurring event** is an event that is set up once and shows up many times in your calendar at regular intervals. An example might be a regular Monday morning conference call at work. You don't really want to enter that event into your calendar every week, but you do want it to show up on your calendar so that other people don't try to set up another meeting at the same time.

The event you just requested time off for doesn't need to be a recurring event. Let's create another event to remind you to check for approval of your request in order to demonstrate this aspect of the Calendar. The initial steps to create the event are the same as before. You won't supply as much information because this is just a reminder.

```
BlackBerryEvent reminder = (BlackBerryEvent) events.createEvent();
reminder.addString(BlackBerryEvent.SUMMARY, BlackBerryEvent.ATTR_NONE,
            "Check on request");
reminder.addDate(BlackBerryEvent.START, BlackBerryEvent.ATTR_NONE,
            new Date().getTime()+86400000);
reminder.addDate(BlackBerryEvent.END, BlackBerryEvent.ATTR_NONE,
            new Date().getTime()+86400000);
```

The special math for the START and END fields is there to create the event 24 hours from now. The long integer value that represents date and time is actually the number of milliseconds from January 1, 1970 (commonly called the epoch for Unix time). The really big number being added to it actually the number of milliseconds in 24 hours (24 hrs * 60 minutes/hour * 60 seconds/min * 1000 milliseconds/second).

That bit of code only sets up one event for the next day. The real work of a recurring event is done by the RepeatRule class—the class that holds the logic for how an event is to repeat.

Your example of a reminder repeating each day is very simplistic. You might need a rule that describes an event that repeats every seven days instead of everyday. Or how about events that happen on the third Tuesday of the month? With just these few examples you can see that there can be some very complicated rules about how an event repeats.

```
RepeatRule repeat = new RepeatRule();
repeat.setInt(RepeatRule.FREQUENCY,RepeatRule.DAILY);
repeat.setInt(RepeatRule.INTERVAL, 1);
repeat.setDate(RepeatRule.END, new Date().getTime()+(86400000 * 7));
```

This format should look very familiar now because it follows the same pattern that all of the PIM items do. It is not, however, derived from PIMItem itself. As a result, you should never use any of the constant values that are defined in BlackBerryEvent or any other PIMItem with a RepeatRule. All of the constants that are needed will be defined with the RepeatingRule class itself.

There are two basic parts of a RepeatRule though, and those are the frequency with which something repeats and the interval of time between events. In this case, you set the FREQUENCY field to the constant RepeatRule.DAILY because the time between events is counted in days. The INTERVAL field is set to 1 because we want this event to happen again after just one day. These two values together indicate that the event should repeat every day. How would you represent a biweekly meeting? The FREQUENCY would be set to WEEKLY and the INTERVAL would be set to 2. There are a great many possibilities, but this example should get you started understanding how the two fields work together.

The third line in your RepeatRule sets up the date that the event should stop repeating. In this case, the last day to prompt the user is seven days from the current time. This is an arbitrary number for the sake of this example, but the thought is that if the user's request hasn't been resolved in 7 days then you should stop checking on it.

Once the `RepeatRule` is set up, you still need to apply the rule to the event by calling the `setRepeat` method. Afterward, the only thing left to do is to commit the event to the **Calendar** application.

```
reminder.setRepeat(repeat);
reminder.commit();
```

There is so much more that you can do with a `RepeatRule`. In addition to some of the more complex repeating patterns, you can add dates which are to be excluded from the `RepeatRule` as well. Generally, these aren't used often, so let's move on to the next step of this application.

Pop quiz

1. What is the base data type for items from the **Calendar** application?
   a. `EventItem`
   b. `CalendarItem`
   c. `BlackBerryCalendarItem`

2. What class is used to define events that occur more than once?
   a. `Recurrance`
   b. `RepeatRule`
   c. `RepeatingEventItem`

3. What two values are used to define how often an event repeats?
   a. `TIMESPAN` and `OCCURANCE`
   b. `INTERVAL` and `FREQUENCY`
   c. `OCCURANCE` and `INTERVAL`

Sending e-mail

The last step that you need to do to finish up the `TimeOff` application is to actually send the message out making the request. Using the messaging system like this is just scratching the surface of what can be done when working with the messaging APIs.

This example will send a message as a regular text e-mail to one recipient. The BlackBerry claim to fame is messaging though, and the API to work with Messages is extensive. Not only can you send plain messages like this, but you can send more complicated messages like multi-part messages with attachments.

Interfacing with Applications

Time for action – sending an e-mail from an application

1. It's time to make this application actually do what it is meant to do—send that email! Add the following code to the `sendRequest` method in the `TimeOff` application.

```
StringBuffer msgBody = new StringBuffer();
msgBody.append("A new TimeOff application request has been
submitted \nFrom:");
msgBody.append(Integer.toHexString(DeviceInfo.getDeviceId()));
msgBody.append("\nStarting: ");
msgBody.append(DateFormat.getInstance(DateFormat.DATE_DEFAULT).
            formatLocal(_StartDate.getDate()));
msgBody.append("\nEnding: ",;
msgBody.append(DateFormat.getInstance(DateFormat.DATE_DEFAULT).
            formatLocal(_EndDate.getDate()));
msgBody.append("\nComments: ");
msgBody.append(_Comments.getText());

Message newMsg = new Message();
try {
   Address recipient = null;
   recipient = new Address(Address.EMAIL_ADDR, _To.getText());
   newMsg.addRecipient(Message.RecipientType.TO, recipient);
   newMsg.setSubject("Time off Request");
   newMsg.setContent(msgBody.toString());
   Transport.send(newMsg);
}
catch (MessagingException e)
  {
    // TODO Auto-generated catch block
    e.printStackTrace();
  }
```

What just happened?

The first part of this method is simply creating the body of the message that will be sent. The most interesting part of this code is using the `DeviceInfo` class to get the device ID, also called a PIN number. You needed some way to identify who the e-mail is from, and the device ID serves this purpose well. Yes, the sender's e-mail will be in the message itself, but this works well too. The PIN number is typically represented in hexadecimal so you must convert it by using the `toHexString` method.

```
StringBuffer msgBody = new StringBuffer();
```

```
msgBody.append("A new TimeOff application requestion has been
submitted.\nFrom:");
msgBody.append(Integer.toHexString(DeviceInfo.getDeviceId()));
msgBody.append("\nStarting: ");
msgBody.append(DateFormat.getInstance(DateFormat.DATE_DEFAULT).
                formatLocal(_StartDate.getDate()));
msgBody.append("\nEnding: ");
msgBody.append(DateFormat.getInstance(DateFormat.DATE_DEFAULT).
                formatLocal(_EndDate.getDate()));
msgBody.append("\nComments: ");
msgBody.append(_Comments.getText());
```

The next section is devoted to actually creating and sending the message. You might expect this to be very complex, but it's almost embarrassing how simple this code is.

The first step is to create a `Message` object to work with. There are actually three different `Message` classes available through the BlackBerry API. They all exist in different namespaces and serve different purposes, so this part can be confusing. The `Message` class that you need here is in the `net.rim.blackberry.api.mail.Message` package. This `Message` class is used with e-mail and PIN messages. Fortunately, creating this object is very straightforward.

```
Message newMsg = new Message();
```

The next step is to populate the `Message` object with the recipient. At this point, you should have a valid address in the _To field of the application. You would want to perform basic testing before using the address in a real application, but for now you will just use whatever is in the field. The message doesn't want to use just a string value for the recipient though, you need to construct an `Address` object before adding it to the message.

This class doesn't do any validation either. Instead, its primary purpose is to provide an address along with a "readable name" for it. In this case, you simply specify a readable name of "TimeOff Recipient". If you chose an address from one of your test contacts instead of manually typing one in, the Message application will match on the address and use the name from the Address Book instead of this readable name provided.

The last step is to add the `Address` object to the message by using the `addRecipient` method. This method also requires an identifier constant to indicate what kind of recipient it is. Notice that the `Message` class has a `RecipientType` inner class, which in turn contains the constant definitions. This is just another way of organizing the constant values into groups that make sense together. The `PIM` classes don't do this and as a result, the constant values are harder to use. The `Message` class has several inner classes like this.

```
Address recipient = null;
recipient = new Address(_To.getText(), "TimeOff Recipient");
newMsg.addRecipient(Message.RecipientType.TO, recipient);
```

Interfacing with Applications

After setting the recipient of the message, you set the main text of the message in the subject and body. The important thing to note here is that the `setContent` method can accept a simple string (like you have in this example) or a more complex object called a `Multipart`. A `Multipart` is used any time there is more than one piece to a message, such as when a message has an attachment.

```
newMsg.setSubject("Time off Request");
newMsg.setContent(msgBody.toString());
```

After the message has been fully constructed, you can finally send it. Here, you see a new class called `Transport`—a class that handles all of the messy stuff when it comes to integrating with the rest of the system. The `send` method is as simple as it can be and yet handles so much.

```
Transport.send(newMsg);
```

At this point, the message is part of the **Messages** application and is handled from there just as if the user had typed it up. You can see the message as a sent message by going to the **Messages** application. It will handle queuing up the message to be sent, retries, failures, and the transmission of the message itself. The `TimeOff` application simply returns and continues executing without having to worry about any of the technical details of what it takes to actually send the message.

Pop quiz

1. What class is used to set the recipient address when sending a message?
    a. `EmailAddress`
    b. `Email`
    c. `Address`

2. What method is used to actually send the message?
    a. `Messages.send()`
    b. `Email.send()`
    c. `Transport.send()`

Chapter 8

Have a go hero – sending a different kind of message

There is still one kind of `PIMItem` that we haven't discussed at all, and that is a `ToDo` item from the **Tasks** application. This `PIMItem` type doesn't have any complicated value types like contacts nor does it have any usual aspects like recurring events. It is pretty straightforward once you understand the other concepts from these other `PIMItem` types.

Take this opportunity to explore the `ToDo` class and expand the `TimeOff` application to also add a `ToDo` item to check on the status as well as the reminder events that have already been added.

Summary

Interfacing with other applications on the handheld is the best way to make the applications you write more user-friendly and more likely to be used. The BlackBerry SDK offers many ways by which applications can leverage, extend, or integrate with the existing suite of applications that come with a new device. In this chapter, we primarily focused on accessing the PIM data. We also dabbled a little into how to use the messaging systems to send an e-mail message. There is much more that can be done to make applications that don't just work with the operating system, but which can even become embedded into the operating system so that the use may never know they are a separate application.

In this chapter, we covered:

- What we mean by PIM data.
- How to access a particular list of PIM data.
- How to create new PIM items and how to assign values to their fields.
- How to send an e-mail message.

Interfacing with the PIM data and messaging applications are some of the most common things an application developer will do when creating a new application. Another area that is becoming more and more important is accessing networks through the built-in channels, and in particular, accessing the Internet. This is the area we will be focusing on in the next chapter.

9
Networking

At this point, we've seen most of the most common tasks that might be presented to an application developer save for one. That is of course, the task of communicating with servers through a network connection. This task is by far the most complicated task we've attempted yet, and doing it well is probably the most complicated thing you can do in with the BlackBerry SDK.

The reward is worth the work however. Many of the top applications available on the BlackBerry AppWorld store are networked applications. Networked applications have the distinct advantage of being able to deliver new content without requiring the user to reinstall the application. Our world is constantly becoming more connected and applications that can help users with that task are in high demand.

There are two main things that we will go over in this chapter about networking: **the transport** and **the message**. It's important to understand that these two components are somewhat independent of each other. Still, many resources on this topic don't distinguish between them well and it is easy to get matters confused and think of them as being the same thing.

The first item, the transport, really focuses on the physicality of what path or route the second item, the message, will take. The message, then of course, focuses on what is being sent to the server and what that message means. The transport is HOW it is sent and the message is WHAT will be sent.

Some transports are better suited for use with some kinds of messages, but in general, any message can be sent using any transport. The difficulty and confusion comes when we try to look at all of the combinations that are possible. Furthermore, some transports are not available in some situations and these can depend on many factors such as the wireless carrier, and even the specific plan of a user

Threading

Another thing that makes working with networking difficult is that you must also use **threading**. Networking just can't be done without threading, but this also makes the applications more complicated and difficult. Network traffic is the epitome of a "long running task" by even desktop computer standards. Mobile devices and mobile networks are much slower than desktops! Therefore, you should always utilize a thread when doing anything that relates to sending or receiving of data over a network. Unfortunately, this means more complicated code, but there is just no avoiding it.

An in-depth discussion of threading is beyond this book. In general, threading is a way to branch the flow of execution and, in essence, performing two actions at the same time. Every piece of code that is executed is done so in a thread. We've never had to mention it before though because the samples that we've created haven't needed more than one execution path. The only exception to this is in the Chapter 5 when we demonstrated the `GaugeField`; that sample used a thread, but at the same time we glossed over the details.

By branching the flow of execution we can have one thread sending or receiving data through a network connection while the other is allowing the user to continue to use the application, display menus, or enter data. If a thread were not used, the user would not be able to do anything else in the application while the network communication is happening. It would be unresponsive to menu clicks or even redraw the screen properly so the user would probably believe the application was broken or had crashed. This obviously isn't good, which is why the recommendation is to never do network communication unless it is done in a thread.

If you are unfamiliar with threads, the sample application we make here won't make much sense. It would be best to get this understanding and then return to networking later.

Connector class

Another critical part of the networking toolkit is the `Connector` class. This class has only a few static members and acts as a factory for all of the `Connection` types. The networking that we will be doing is of course one of these, but there are, in fact, many kinds of connections that can be made through the `Connector` class. This class is very flexible because the `open` method takes only one parameter—a connection string.

It may seem funny but the `Connector` class doesn't actually initiate a connection. It simply creates an object that represents the connection. The `Connection` object does the actual work of opening the connection sometime later when it needs to do so. Therefore, the `Connector` won't fail unless the connection string is invalid in some way.

A connection string is also called a URL but it is more than just an address like you might think of when web browsing. It can also contain all of the instructions and options that the `Connection` class might need in order to establish the connection. Certainly an address is part of that, but the options may be just as important and are likely to vary greatly depending on what kind of connection is being made.

When a connection string has options they are given as a name/value pair and are separated by a semicolon. An example of a connection string with an option that we will see and use later is `http://www.someserver.com;deviceside=true`. The `Connector` class puts no limits on the number of options a connection string might have. In the right circumstances, a connection string can get very long and complex.

HTTP basics

The BlackBerry SDK does provide good support for networking, but the support is primitive. Not only are there a myriad of ways to connect to a server in order to make a request, and that we as developers are left to account for them all, but we must also have a fairly detailed understanding of the underlying protocol.

In this case, we will be creating an `HttpConnection` object so we also need to have a basic understanding of the `HTTP` protocol. The only thing that most people really know about `HTTP` is that it is something you put in front of the website addresses in a browser.

The extremely simplistic answer is that `HTTP` is a protocol designed for requesting files from one computer by another computer. The name, Hyper Text Transfer Protocol, comes from the idea that a document would have HyperText links embedded into it, which a user can use to gather more information about a topic. When this happens, one computer would request the linked document from the other so that the user can see it. In order to make this happen, both computers have to understand what each other are saying and so the protocol, `HTTP`, was created to make this possible. The protocol has grown over time to do more than just get documents, but the basic idea is still the way it is primarily used, even today.

In order to support more than just document retrieval the protocol has a series of commands, or methods that are supported. The basic operations of `GET` and `POST` are by far the most common uses. HTTP v 1.1 added a few more commands such as `PUT`, `DELETE`, and a few others that are still not widely used.

The protocol requires a request/response pattern in which the sender issues a request, to get a file for instance, and the receiver then issues a response with the requested data if there were no errors. There is also a header in both the request and response where additional parameters can be placed. These parameters might give an indication about what type of document it is, how large it is, or the event authentication information if the document is secured.

Networking

This all makes sense when you look at it from this a low level like this. The point, however, is that we do need to know about it in order to make an application that uses it. Only the basic operations of GET and POST will be used here, but the important thing is that we have to build the request. Therefore, we need to know what pieces we will need to go into it and when to use them.

HTTP GET requests

So now that we have some of the basic information out of the way, let's start with a simple page fetch from a website. This is just a baby step of course, but we need to start somewhere.

The biggest part of this will involve simply setting up the thread to service the connection and then setting up the connection. The code isn't too difficult, but there are a lot of things that can go wrong as well.

Time for action - HTTP Basics

1. Let's get started with a new project named HTTPBasics. Create a BlackBerry project in Eclipse and create a standard UiApplication derived class and a MainScreen derived class.

2. At this point you need only one field added to the screen—a RichTextField called _Output. Add a constructor for the screen and then add that field to the screen in the constructor.

3. You need one more class in this application, a thread to handle the processing of the request. One more time, create a new class derived from Thread called ServiceRequestThread.

4. Now that the skeleton is in place, start adding some code. The first step will be to set up the thread with the data that you will need in order to make the request. Add these data members and the following constructor to the ServiceRequestThread class.

```
protected String _URL;
protected HTTPBasicsMainScreen _Dest = null;

public ServiceRequestThread(String URL, HTTPBasicsMainScreen
screen)
{
   super();
   _Dest = screen;
   _URL = URL;
}
```

Chapter 9

5. We will need more code in the thread, but we will come back to that in a bit. Instead, add a menu item to the `HTTPBasicsMainScreen` class so that you can start the request.

```
protected MenuItem _GetDataAction = new MenuItem("GetData" ,
100000, 10)
{
  public void run()
  {
    String URL = "http://www.google.com;deviceside=true";
    ServiceRequestThread svc = new ServiceRequestThread(URL,
                    (HTTPBasicsMainScreen)
  UiApplication.getUiApplication().getActiveScreen());
  svc.start();
    }
};
```

6. Don't forget to add the new menu item to the menu by adding this code in the constructor of the screen.

```
addMenuItem(_GetDataAction);
```

7. Another thing you need in the screen is a method to make sure the screen is updated safely.

```
public void updateDestination(final String text)
{
  UiApplication.getUiApplication().invokeLater(new Runnable()
  {
    public void run()
    {
      _Output.setText(text);
    }
  });
}
```

8. The last step is to implement the actual request and network call by implementing the `run` method of the `ServiceRequestThread`.

```
public void run()
{
  try
  {
    HttpConnection conn = (HttpConnection)
    Connector.open(_URL, Connector.READ_WRITE);
```

[239]

Networking

```
      conn.setRequestMethod(HttpConnection.GET);
      int responseCode = conn.getResponseCode();
      if (responseCode == HttpConnection.HTTP_OK)
       {
         InputStream data = conn.openInputStream();
         StringBuffer raw = new StringBuffer();
         byte[] buf = new byte[4096];
         int nRead = data.read(buf);
         while (nRead > 0)
         {
          raw.append(new String(buf,0,nRead));
          nRead = data.read(buf);
         }
           _Dest.updateDestination(raw.toString());
       }
       else
       {
        _Dest.updateDestination("responseCode="+
            Integer.toString(responseCode));
       }
    }
    catch (IOException e)
    {
      // TODO Auto-generated catch block
      e.printStackTrace();
      _Dest.updateDestination("Exception:"+e.toString());
    }
}
```

9. If you run the application and click on the **Get Data** menu item, the screen will soon fill up with raw HTML from the `Google.com` home page!

HTTP Basics

Output: <!doctype html><html><head><meta http-equiv="content-type" content="text/html; charset=ISO-8859-1"><title>Google</title><script>window.google={kEI:"INuFS72HC52KeNH2hcoL",kEXPI:"23868",kCSI:{e:"23868",ei:"INuFS72HC52KeNH2hcoL",expi:"23868"},ml:function(){},kHL:"en",time:function(){return

[240]

What just happened?

Wow, that was exciting, wasn't it? It's not much to look at, but this simple application is a great example for demonstrating the basics of networking. The first few steps were all about setting up and getting started, but I didn't give you much help there. How did it feel? That basic setup has been done with every project we've made so far and will likely be the first steps of nearly every project in the future. I don't know why the "new BlackBerry project" template doesn't do all that boilerplating for you, but it doesn't.

We got into some code in Step 4 with setting up the `Thread` object. This is just basic stuff so we could add the code to create and start the thread in the menu in Step 5. Although this just shows that even though the thread runs separately from the rest of the application doesn't mean it can exist in a vacuum. We had to have some information to start the request, that is, the URL, and we had to have some way to get the results back out to the main application. This part was simply about making sure that information was collected.

In Steps 5 and 6 we created the menu item that will start the thread and added it to the application. For this sample, the connection string was simply hardcoded in the menu, but the thread is set up to be dynamic and allow the URL to be passed in as a parameter.

As we've said before, the URL is more than just a web address and this URL includes that parameter we mentioned earlier. First, let me explain that `www.google.com` was chosen simply because the web page loads fast and it isn't very large. Can you imagine trying to load a page with a lot more content?

Secondly, that parameter is used to force the device to initiate a TCP/IP direct connection. While there may be concern about using TCP/IP direct in a production application, this is just the simulator and we shouldn't face any problems using it. We could have left the parameter off completely and the result would still be the same. Each device has a default set that makes sense for the device, and for the simulator, the default is a TCP/IP direct connection.

Step 7 is where we added an odd looking little method to update the `_Output` field with the text that is being passed into the method. Why is this needed? Remember that this application is a multithreaded application. Updating user interface fields from another thread is dangerous! This is often said in another way; it is not thread-safe. There are other things going on in the other thread and when we try to set the text from the `ServiceRequestThread`, those things might conflict and cause problems. This is particularly important when something could happen that would cause the screen to be redrawn, such as in this case.

The `invokeLater` method is used as a way for one thread to ask another thread to run some code when there is a chance. The calling thread (the `ServiceRequestThread`) doesn't have any control over WHEN the code runs. The receiving thread, which in this case is the main application thread, will decide when to execute the code.

Networking

The last step in this code is where the real fun stuff happens. Everything up until this point is supporting code so we can make the request and do something useful with the response.

This first line is where we set up the connection and use the `Connector` class that was mentioned previously. The `Connector` class will always return a `Connection` class, but we really need an `HttpConnection` object and so, it is cast to the proper type. We can safely cast it because we know for certain the URL will begin with `http://`, which is what tells the `Connector` to make an HttpConnection object. Also, remember that the `Connector` doesn't actually open the connection, so as long as the URL is valid we should be fine. The second parameter specifies the permissions requested of the new connection. Even though we won't be writing at this stage we're still going to ask for `Read` and `Write` permissions for later on.

```
HttpConnection conn = (HttpConnection)Connector.open(_URL, Connector.READ_WRITE);
```

The call to the `setRequestMethod` is how we specify which HTTP command is to be sent to the destination address. Like we've seen a number of times earlier in the SDK, the valid values have been defined in the `HttpConnection` class to make things clear and easy to understand.

```
conn.setRequestMethod(HttpConnection.GET);
```

If we were making a more complicated request then there may be other parameters and values to be set before calling `getResponseCode`. However, for the simple fetch that we are doing here, there is nothing else required and we can issue the request. It should be plain to see that we make that request with a call to the `getRespsonseCode` method.

What? No, that's not clear at all!

Well, it does sort of make sense. How can you get a response code if the request hasn't been sent? The bottom line here though is that there isn't a single method that will make the request. Any method which requires the request to be sent will actually cause it to happen. It's an on-demand methodology that has its benefits, but clarity isn't one of them.

The whole purpose of getting the response code though was to get and check the return value to know if the request was successful or not. The HTTP protocol uses a defined set of numbers to indicate various success or failure conditions. A large number of them are defined as constants in the `HttpConnection` class. For the most part though, you will only be concerned about whether it worked or not and we check for this with the `HTTP_OK` constant. There are other constant values that can mean success as well, and so again, this is where the framework leaves the details to us to handle at a low level. Generally, any response code in the range of 200 to 300 means success of some kind, but this is where a detailed understanding of HTTP comes in useful.

```
if (responseCode == HttpConnection.HTTP_OK)
```

Once we know the request has succeeded, we can start to get the data that has been returned. In this case, it is done by reading 4k of data at a time and building up a `StringBuffer` object with the data. You can use a `ByteArrayInputStream` or other technique if you prefer.

```
InputStream data = conn.openInputStream();
StringBuffer raw = new StringBuffer();
byte[] buf = new byte[4096];
int nRead = data.read(buf);
while (nRead > 0)
{
   raw.append(new String(buf,0,nRead));
   nRead = data.read(buf);
}
```

The last step is to simply update the screen by using the helper method we created, called `updateDestination`. Generally, you won't be displaying the raw HTML in the screen like this though and you would process the data somehow. We'll get to an example of that later in the chapter.

```
Dest.updateDestination(raw.toString());
```

Pop quiz

1. What method is used to determine if the request succeeded?
    a. `isSuccess`
    b. `HttpConnection.HTTP_OK`
    c. `getResponseCode`

2. Which command is used to issue an `HTTP` request?
    a. `HTTPConnection.GET`
    b. `HTTPConnection.REQUEST`
    c. `HTTPConnection.SEND`

3. All networking communication should be done within a thread.
    a. TRUE
    b. FALSE

Have a go hero – but what if it didn't work?

In spite of laying out good plans and even using already tested code, sometimes things just don't work. Debugging this kind of situation can be very hard! For me, I always assume that there is some kind of bug in the code first, but when dealing with networking code we have to look at the environment as well. If this sample didn't work you are in luck because you know that it can't be the code that is wrong.

Remember that even though we are running this in the simulator, that simulator is running on your computer, which is a part of your network. The simulator doesn't try to simulate the network traffic. No, it actually issues the request on your computer so that the request can be completed for real. This means that the simulator is connecting to the network and sending data to the host just like the device will do. This also means that if there is some networking issue on the computer you are running the simulator on, it will interfere with the application being run on the simulator in the same way. Do you have a firewall running? Is your networking configured correctly? There are a 101 possibilities as to why the simulator might be failing—all of them dealing with the computer it's running on.

Now, you may try to run the browser in the simulator as a test to make sure that the simulator is working right. Sadly, this isn't going to work without running an additional program on your desktop. We'll use this program later, but for now, just understand that the simulator browser application isn't a good way to test things out.

The best way to test things out is through your standard desktop browser. Can you address the host or service you are trying to connect to? If you can't do it through your desktop browser then the simulator isn't going to work either.

HTTP POST requests

The other method that is available in HTTP is the POST method. Using an HTTP POST is the most common way to send data to a server and it is supported with the HttpConnection (which we just used). The server will send some data back as well, so a POST command isn't just a one way message. Consider it to be a POST immediately followed by another GET, all rolled into one command.

Historically, an HTTP POST is used to submit a form on a web page once the user is done filling it out and has clicked a **Submit** button. You can certainly use a BlackBerry application to do an HTTP POST to interact with forms like a user would do, but this isn't the best approach.

Because the forms are meant to look good, be displayed on the screen and interact with a user there is a lot of other stuff that comes along with the HTML than just the form. There will be HTML tags related to the layout of fields on the form, there may be color or image tags, or even JavaScript, all of which a BlackBerry application just doesn't need to be concerned with. For these reasons, you shouldn't interact with HTML pages unless there is no other choice.

The clear alternative is to utilize a web service of some kind to trade information with a server. With a web service there isn't any other data related to formatting or presentation, and so the amount of data being transmitted is significantly less than utilizing web pages like a user might use. These can also use the HTTP POST method.

For simple web services, the process for making a request is exactly the same as the process of submitting a form like a user might do. The biggest difference is in the response data—a web service response should be much more concise.

In order to pass the data with an HTTP POST command we must get familiar with a new class—the URLEncodedPostData class. This class has two important purposes. First, it stores the data that will be sent with the request to the server as a list of name-value pairs. There is no data type information to go along with these parameters either; they are all just string values.

The second purpose is to encode the data into a URL encoded format. Why is that needed? The URL encoded format isn't complicated or special; it just makes sure that the data provided with the parameters can be sent to the server. The HTTP specification uses a lot of characters for special purposes within the protocol, and so those characters aren't allowed to be in the data being sent through HTTP. Some things, such as spaces, are ignored while others such as a greater-than-sign are given special meaning. We can't just do without these characters so we must encode them in some way so that they can be passed with the request.

Time for action – calling a web service

1. The first step is to get the CopyCat service working. This service is written in .NET and is built with Microsoft Visual Studio 2008 and can be found in the code bundle of this book. Not everyone will have access to this tool so feel free to create a web service using your favorite tool. The thing we are interested in at this point is a web method named CopyMe that accepts a string parameter named Value and returns a string. In fact, the implementation of CopyMe is exceedingly simple as it just returns the same string that was passed into it.

2. As you actually need to send data to a server now, you need to start by adding an edit field to the application that prompts for the data to send. Add an EditField as a data member to the application.

   ```
   protected EditField _CopyString = new EditField();
   ```

3. Next, add the field to the screen by adding this code into the constructor.

   ```
   _CopyString.setLabel("Copy Source: ");
   _CopyString.setMaxSize(50);
   _add(CopyString);
   ```

Networking

4. We'll come back to the `Screen` class later. At this point, we need to modify the `ServiceRequestThread` class to add a data member and a method to set it.

```
protected URLEncodedPostData _PostData = null;
public void setPOSTData(URLEncodedPostData data)
{
    _PostData = data;
}
```

5. Once you have the `_PostData` object, you need to use it. In the `run` method, replace the `setRequestMethod` call with this `if` statement.

```
if (_PostData != null)
{
   conn.setRequestMethod(HttpConnection.POST);
   conn.setRequestProperty("Content-type",
       "application/x-www-form-urlencoded");
   conn.setRequestProperty("Content-Length",
       Integer.toString(_PostData.size()));

   OutputStream strmOut = conn.openOutputStream();
   strmOut.write(_PostData.getBytes());

   strmOut.close();
}
else
{
   conn.setRequestMethod(HttpConnection.GET);
}
```

6. Now that the `ServiceRequestThread` class is changed you can come back to `HttpBasicsMainScreen` and add a new menu item that you will use to trigger a request. You will likely need to change the address in the connection string or, at the very least, the port number of the service. Make sure that the URL is correct for referencing the web service and that the service is currently running.

```
protected MenuItem _PostDataAction = new MenuItem("PostData" ,
100000, 10)
{
  public void run()
  {
    URLEncodedPostData oPostData = new URLEncodedPostData(
           URLEncodedPostData.DEFAULT_CHARSET, false);
    oPostData.append("Value",_CopyString.getText());
```

[246]

```
            String URL = "http://localhost:2997/CopycatWebServiceCSharp/
                    Service.asmx/CopyMe;deviceside=true";
            ServiceRequestThread svc = new ServiceRequestThread(URL,
                                    (HTTPBasicsMainScreen)
            UiApplication.getUiApplication().getActiveScreen());
            svc.setPOSTData(oPostData);
            svc.start();
        }
    };
```

7. Lastly, you need to add the menu into the application by adding the next line to the constructor.

```
addMenuItem(_PostDataAction);
```

What just happened?

Step 1 of this section is simply about setting up a web service that you can test with. While I do provide some code, I also know that not everyone will be able to use the tool or be able to set up the service. This is why there are specific directions given in case you need to create your own. We could have tried to rely on one of the public web services such as at www.webservicex.net, but the services can change, break, or be removed all together and the example wouldn't be valid any more. Therefore, it's better to utilize a service that you control. If you choose to use the provided code, great! If you prefer to write your own, that's great too!

The other steps are mostly housekeeping steps until you get to steps 4 and 5, which modify the `ServiceRequestThread` class. As we pointed out earlier, the `URLEncodedPostData` class is used to collect the parameters that are passed with the `HTTP POST` request. This thread is designed to be generic, therefore it can't populate the parameters. Instead, the `setPOSTData` method is there to allow the class that starts the thread to supply a pre-populated `URLEncodedPostData` class that will be used later when the request is actually processed.

```
protected URLEncodedPostData _PostData = null;
public void setPOSTData(URLEncodedPostData data)
{
    _PostData = data;
}
```

Networking

The `run` method is also changed slightly to check and see if there are any POST parameters supplied. If so, then the request type is set to use a POST method and the parameters are added to the output stream. Also, there are a couple of properties that are set to support the additional POST data. The `Content-type` property is used to let the receiving computer know more about the data that is included within the request. In this case, you are specifying that the data has been URL encoded by using the `application/x-www-form-urlencoded` value. This value isn't an arbitrary value, but a specific value that the server already knows about. In addition to setting the content type, you also set the size of the data being sent with the request.

Once the supporting attributes are set you get a stream that will be used to add the parameter data in with the request by using the `openOutputStream` method. The actual data is written by using the stream's `write` method before being closed.

All of this work is necessary because of the extra data that needs to go with an HTTP POST command. If the `_PostData` object isn't set, then we skip all of this work and issue an HTTP GET command instead.

```
if (_PostData != null)
{
  conn.setRequestMethod(HttpConnection.POST);
  conn.setRequestProperty("Content-type",
      "application/x-www-form-urlencoded");
  conn.setRequestProperty("Content-Length",
     Integer.toString(_PostData.size()));

  OutputStream strmOut = conn.openOutputStream();
  strmOut.write(_PostData.getBytes());

  strmOut.close();
}
else
{
  conn.setRequestMethod(HttpConnection.GET);
}
```

Once the thread is taken care of, you go back to the screen and add the menu that will be used to issue the request. The request is largely the same as the request that is used fetch a web page, but this adds the step of creating and populating the `URLEncodedPostData` object. When populating this object keep in mind that the parameters that you add must be named the same as those in the web service definition. In this case, the web service declares the input parameter to be named `Value` so you must use that same name when adding the parameter to the `PostData`.

```
URLEncodedPostData oPostData = new
```

```
    URLEncodedPostData(URLEncodedPostData.DEFAULT_CHARSET, false);
oPostData.append("Value",_CopyString.getText());
```

The final step is to give the completed `URLEncodedPostData` object to the thread that will be handling the request by using the `setPostData` method that we created earlier.

Once you run the application you can see that the `CopyMe` service is doing exactly what it is supposed to do, which is to simply return the input parameter as the output of the web service. But, if that's the case, why is there all of this extra stuff around it?

> **HTTP Basics**
> Copy Source: testing
> Output: <?xml version="1.0" encoding="utf-8"?>
> <string xmlns="http://tempuri.org/">testing</string>

Web services return data wrapped in XML using a protocol called **SOAP** that can get very large and complicated when dealing with custom structures or complex objects. This is about as simple as we can get. You can see that the real data we are after is buried in the middle of a lot of XML data. Sooner or later, you will need to parse that XML in order to get to the meaningful data that you care about.

Pop quiz

1. What must be done to any data sent with an `HTTP` request?
    a. It must be converted into a byte array
    b. It must be a string type
    c. It must be URL encoded
2. What properties must be set passing additional data with an `HTTP` request?
    a. The content length property
    b. The content type property
    c. Both content length and content type
3. When adding parameter data, what name should be used?
    a. The name that is defined in the web service definition
    b. The name is irrelevant; any name will work.
    c. The name should be in the form of `param` with a sequential number afterward

Networking

There are a few different approaches to parsing the data as well. You can try to do the string matching and manipulations yourself. If the data you are working with is both small and static, then this might be the easiest approach. However, if the data is at all complicated, then this approach gets real messy real quick. It's better to rely on a tool that has already been tested.

The BlackBerry SDK provides an implementation of a **Simple API for XML (SAX)** parser that we will use to retrieve data from the returned pages. As the name implies, this tool is simple to use and simple in capabilities, which can mean that if you want to do something complex, it may no longer be simple! In technical speak, a **SAX parser** is a non-validating parser that uses a callback mechanism to notify the application each time it encounters a new attribute or element.

When we say it is a non-validating parser it means that the parser does not have any knowledge about how the XML should be formatted and it doesn't try to validate whether the XML is formatted properly or not. As long as the XML structure is technically valid the parser will parse it without issue. If certain nodes are supposed to be nested, if a node is supposed to be of a particular type, or only supposed to occur once the SAX parser will not enforce any of these rules.

Generally, you don't need to worry much about validating the structure of the XML when consuming the string from a service; you can usually trust that the service will provide well structured output. Because of this, a SAX parser usually works out just fine.

In order to utilize the SAX parser you must create a specific `Handler` class for each kind of XML response that you want to parse. This class is derived from a class called `DefaultHandler` and is how the parser makes callbacks to notify the application of various events that are encountered when parsing the XML. For example, a method called `StartElement` is there and can be overridden to do some processing each time a new element tag is encountered.

So with that bit of overview in place, let's expend the `HttpBasics` class to process the results of the `CopyMe` web method call.

Time for action – parsing the response

1. You've already seen the output for a call to the `CopyMe` service. Even so, when creating a custom `Handler` for a specific response it's a good idea to have a copy of the raw XML response handy to compare with and view. The first step in implementing a parser is to create that custom `Handler` class.

2. Create a new class in the existing `HttpBasics` namespace and call it `CopyMeHandler`.

Chapter 9

3. Insert the following code into the class stub that is created.

   ```
   private String currentElement;
   public String copymeResponse;

   public void startElement(String uri, String localName,
                           String qName, Attributes attributes)
   {
     currentElement = localName;
   }

   public void characters(char[] ch, int start, int length)
   {
     if ( currentElement.equals( "string" ) )
     {
        copymeResponse = new String( ch, start, length );
     }
   }
   ```

4. Now, you need to modify the `updateDestination` method of the `HttpBasicsMainScreen`. Previously, it displayed the raw output into the `_Output` field. Now, however, you need to parse the output and display only the results. Comment out the existing contents of the `run` method.

5. Then insert the following code into the `run` method.

   ```
   SAXParserImpl parser = new SAXParserImpl();
   CopyMeHandler handler = new CopyMeHandler();
   ByteArrayInputStream inputStream = new ByteArrayInputStream(
                                     text.getBytes());
   try
   {
     parser.parse( inputStream, handler );
   }
   catch ( Exception e )
   {
     _Output.setText( "Unable to parse response." );
     return;
   }
   _Output.setText( handler.copymeResponse );
   ```

Networking

What just happened?

Now when you click on the **Post Data** menu and call the `CopyMe` service, the data that is shown in the output window is the text that has been returned by the web service response. As the text is the same as what was in the **Copy Source** field, it isn't too interesting, but it's a lot better than the raw XML response. Now, let's take a closer look at what you've changed and how it works.

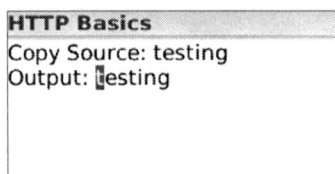

The first step that you took was to create a new handler for the `CopyMe` service that will be used with the SAX parser. This new handler is about as simple as one can get because there is just one element being returned, not including the XML header element.

This new class utilizes only two of the methods that are available—the `startElement` and `characters` methods.

As the name suggests, the `startElement` method is called each time a new element is encountered in the XML. This method provides only a little detail, including the name of the new element. Also notice what it doesn't provide, and that is any information about the parenting or position of this node in relation to others in the file. All you need to do in this method is to save the name of the node in a member variable before the processing continues.

```
public void startElement(String uri, String localName, String qName,
                    Attributes attributes)
{
    currentElement = localName;
}
```

The other method that you overrode in this class is called `characters`. This method is called after parsing the inner text of an element, that is the text between the start and end tags, which is not otherwise within a tag. If the element name that we are currently processing is called "string", then the inner text will contain the value of the string that has been returned by the web service. We capture this value in another member variable so that it can be retrieved later.

Again, notice that this method does contain any other contextual information about the element containing the text. This is why you need to override the `startElement` method and keep track of which element you are currently processing. Because you know that there is only one element named "string" in the XML this simple logic works. However, for large and complex XML files, a lot more complex logic will be needed.

```
public void characters(char[] ch, int start, int length)
{
   if ( currentElement.equals( "string" ) )
   {
      copymeResponse = new String( ch, start, length );
   }
}
```

The `DefaultHandler` class provides a lot of possible override points that you can take advantage of to perform more complex processing of XML. Remember though, that this is a *Simple* API for XML so you really can't get too complex. Still, methods such as `startDocument`, `endElement`, and `error` can be used to cover most scenarios.

The `startElement` method though is probably one of the most important methods in this class. In addition to the element name you are also provided with an array of attributes that are attached to the element. Most of the time, the data you are looking for will be found in the inner text or one of the attributes of an element.

The last step is to change the behavior of the `updateDestination` method so that response is parsed out by using the SAX Parser and only the real response data will be put into the `_Output` field.

Initial setup is simple by creating the `SAXParser` and the `Handler` objects. Notice that we're actually creating a `SAXParserImpl` object and not a `SAXParser` object. This is because the `SAXParser` class is an abstract class, and by definition, cannot be instantiated. This was done so that other implementations of the SAX Parser could be created if there was a special condition that wasn't handled otherwise. I don't know what that might be, but the capability is there if needed.

As part of the setup, you also need to create a stream that the parser can consume. It's kind of silly because the data comes in from a stream in the thread and is converted into a string as it is read in. Then, in this step, you convert the string back into a stream so that it can be parsed.

```
SAXParserImpl parser = new SAXParserImpl();
CopyMeHandler handler = new CopyMeHandler();
ByteArrayInputStream inputStream = new ByteArrayInputStream(text.getBytes());
```

The actual parsing must be in done in an exception block in case there are catastrophic problems. In this case, we simply set the output to indicate there is an error in the catch block. The call to the `parse` method is where the actual work of parsing the output is done. The `parse` method then makes calls to the methods you have implemented in the `CopyMeHandler` and which ultimately retrieves the value from the XML.

```
try
{
   parser.parse( inputStream, handler );
```

```
}
catch ( Exception e )
{
   _Output.setText( "Unable to parse response.");
}
```

Lastly, if there are no problems parsing the response we set the `_Output` field to the real response text and not just the raw XML. Remember, the response text was added to the `copymeResponse` data member as part of the `characters` method in the `handler` class. Now that the parsing is completed, that member should contain the value.

```
_Output.setText( handler.copymeResponse );
```

So far you've seen how to call a basic web service by using a basic HTTP POST command and have introduced the SAX parser as a way to parse data from the response. These examples have so far been very simple; trivial really. Web services can be much more complicated so the question is, how well does this technique scale?

You can use an HTTP POST command to call web services as long as the data being passed to a web service is a string. The return data can be as complex as you want it, because it all gets serialized into XML anyway. It's the sending part that will only work if the data is a string.

If you must work with more complex data types then you must use SOAP requests instead of an HTTP POST request. There are alternatives that enable this, but I consider them to be beyond the scope of this book. One possibility is to use the **kSOAP2 library**—an open source project hosted at SourceForge (http://ksoap2.sourceforge.net/). Another is the Sun Java Wireless Toolkit for CLDC (http://java.sun.com/products/sjwtoolkit/). Even though the toolkit has been rolled into the Java ME SDK 3.0 you can still download the 2.0 libraries and use them with the BlackBerry SDK, which supports only Java ME 2.0. Using this toolkit will actually create service stubs that handle the SOAP envelope creating and parsing for you so you wouldn't need the SAX parser to get data out. Instead, data would be nicely wrapped up in a class much like you would experience when using a web service in Visual Studio.

There is another approach that is recommended if you have control over both the client and server-side communication. If you have control over both sides you have a lot more flexibility. One thing that you always want to think about with network communications is how much data is being transmitted over the network. Web services with SOAP and XML are great as standards go, but they can also be very verbose and cause a lot of traffic to be generated. If you control both sides of communication you can eliminate a lot of this extra traffic by transferring XML snippets, or even JSON formatted data instead of a full SOAP packet.

This would mean that your services wouldn't be easily reusable by other platforms, but the performance and simplicity of your mobile client-side are significantly better. Consider the very simple example that we did with the `CopyMe` service. If you exchanged a single XML snippet or JSON formatted string then the code to call the web service is exactly the same! Your data can be as complex as you need it to be but your network communication code isn't.

Now that we've covered the details in the code for sending data, let's take a look at the transport possibilities that are available.

The transport—so many possibilities

On top of having to understand threading, HTTP, and XML you must now also be aware of network details about how data will be sent and then choose the right transport for the application. Each transport has strengths and weaknesses such that there is no single right way to send data over the network. Additionally, as a developer, you have to determine which transports are available and then choose which one is the best choice to use for sending data.

There are six types of transports that are available on a BlackBerry. Each of them can be specified through one or more connection string directives and all can be used to carry HTTP data.

Any transport can be used to send data, but each one has its own set of concerns and restrictions. The default connection type depends on how your device is configured, but generally, the default is a good place to start. However, you should also understand each connection type as well.

Direct TCP/IP

All of the examples that we've done so far have used the **Direct TCP/IP** transport. This is because this transport is the easiest to understand and implement. Using this transport you ignore any servers or gateways that might be provided by other parties and make the connection by using standard TCP/IP networking right from the handheld. There is no additional security or encryption and you can only access servers that are available publicly on the Internet.

However, because there are no servers or gateways to get in the way, making this connection should be the easiest to use. For most carriers, direct TCP/IP traffic is considered normal data and part of your data plan. There are some carriers that do not though.

You can force a connection to be made using Direct TCP/IP by specifying `deviceside=true` in the connection string.

MDS/BES

These two acronyms stand for **Mobile Data Services** and **BlackBerry Enterprise Server**. The BES is a server that is typically installed inside the data center of a large organization and provides the tight integration with your corporate e-mail system. If you have a company-issued BlackBerry and you get company e-mail on it, then chances are good that your company has a BES installed. The MDS is a component of the BES and is used to route network traffic through the same secure channel that is used to transfer messages. You can't really have a BES without with an MDS server as well, so while they are separate components, for this example, it means the same thing. If your device is configured to use a BES then the MDS/BES transport will be the default transport.

When using the MDS connection to route network traffic you are using the same encrypted and secure channel that e-mail messages travel on. This secure channel can be very appealing if the data being transferred needs to be protected. Also, as the MDS is a component inside your corporate data center, you can also use this transport to access other services inside your company network such as application servers or an intranet. This transport is the only transport that can be used to access internal servers.

Not everyone has a handheld that works like this. If you purchased your handheld from a carrier directly, or if you use it to receive messages from a public service such as Yahoo mail or Gmail, then you probably are using **BlackBerry Internet Service** (**BIS**) instead of BES. BIS is provided by carriers directly and therefore, does not provide all of the same advantages. The BIS server also has an MDS component to it so using this transport will be encrypted and secure to the destination but, in this case, the destination is the carrier's network center.

You can force a connection to use the MDS transport by specifying `deviceside=false` in the connection string. In order to debug an application that uses the MDS transport you must also be running the MDS simulator. That will be covered in the next section in more detail.

BIS-B

The **BIS-B** transport is mentioned here only for the sake of completeness. It is the same transport that is used by your carrier's version of the browser on your handheld and every carrier is required to support it. In order to use this transport though, you must be a BlackBerry Alliance partner, which costs a lot of money and requires some high-level agreements with Research In Motion. In short, it isn't something done by a beginner. If these requirements are not a hurdle, then using BIS-B is the best approach, but otherwise, you have to use one of these other types.

Wi-Fi

Some handhelds have Wi-Fi capabilities and can connect to Wi-Fi hotspots. This feature is highly desirable for applications which do a lot of network communications because data sent through Wi-Fi is faster and cheaper than data sent over the carrier's network.

The downside is that there are a lot of uncertainties about what the capabilities are of the Wi-Fi hotspot that you are using. It might be a public Wi-Fi that is not protected and all of the data being sent or received is therefore unencrypted and insecure. It might be a hotspot provided by your company that is secure and has access to the internal networks of your company; you just don't know and there is no way to find out.

Because of this uncertainty and the inability to gather this information, Wi-Fi should be used only when the data needs are high and when there are no concerns for security of the data. Things such as streaming audio or video are well-suited for this.

You can force a connection to be made using Wi-Fi hotspot by adding `interface=wifi` to the connection string. You can use the `interface` parameter along with the `deviceside` parameter in the connection string together. This will succeed only if the destination (`if deviceside=true`) or the MDS Server (`if deviceside=false`) can be reached successfully through the Wi-Fi hotspot.

WAP

WAP stands for **Wireless Application Protocol** and there are actually two versions of WAP to be concerned about. Using the WAP transport causes the network traffic to be routed through a WAP gateway that is part of your carrier's network.

WAP 1.X

Version 1.0 and 1.1 are likely to be the most common transports available on BlackBerry handhelds, but it does not support all of the connection types such as `https`. Furthermore, a host of carrier-specific values must be added to the connection string. These include gateway address, port, and sometimes even username and password information. There is no way to get these values programmatically either. You must know them in advance or prompt the user for them, and chances are that the user doesn't know them. Even if you get all of this right, the carrier still might not allow it. WAP is really intended to be used with WML so the WAP gateway at the carrier may try to filter out content that is not WML. Because of these issues, this transport is generally avoided.

WAP 2.0

WAP 2.0 simplifies things greatly. It still might not be provisioned on the device, but this can be detected through programming. The WAP 2.0 connection information is stored in a **service book.** This solves the problem of requiring the user to enter a lot of data that they probably don't know anyway. It is also required to allow non-WML content through it so that shouldn't be an issue either.

Using WAP 2.0 requires a little code to find the right service book and then the connection string must include `ConnectionUID=<uid>` as part of the connection string. The `<uid>` is a value similar to a GUID and must be found by querying the service book. The specific value will be different for each user.

Debugging with the MDS simulator

The MDS simulator is an important piece of the debugging puzzle. So far, you have used only the Direct TCP/IP transport in the examples that you've done. While this is the easiest to do during development and testing, it is not necessarily the best transport to use in production. It's good to use in testing because there are fewer components involved and therefore, fewer points of failure. If you can't get it to work by using Direct TCP/IP in the simulator, you most likely won't be able to get it to work using any other transports.

If you recall, using the MDS transport provides an encrypted and secure tunnel for the networking communication to travel through between your handheld to your server in your office. The MDS simulator provides that same secured tunnel between the simulator and your local machine so that you can test applications that use that tunnel.

The browser application on the simulator uses the MDS transport, which is why you can't use the browser on the simulator to test out your connectivity and which is why you haven't been able to use the browser so far. Once you start the MDS simulator though, you can use the browser application just fine.

The MDS Simulator is not started automatically though, so you need to do one of two things to start using it—you can either launch the simulator manually or you can modify debugging configurations in Eclipse so that it is configured to start automatically.

The MDS simulator does come with the SDK that is installed with Eclipse, but there is no icon on the start menu to launch it. In order to launch it by hand you must navigate to the install path and double-click a file called `run.bat` located in the MDS directory of your `install` directory. If you choose the default options when you installed the Eclipse Full Package, then that directory will be `C:\Program Files\Eclipse\plugins\net.rim.eide.componentpack4.5.0_4.5.0.16\components\MDS`.

The second option is to modify the debug configurations in Eclipse. To do this, open the configuration manager dialog by navigating to **Run | Debug Configurations**. When the dialog is shown select the **Simulator** tab.

The selected profile should be **Default Simulator** in the drop list and all of the options in the property page are disabled.

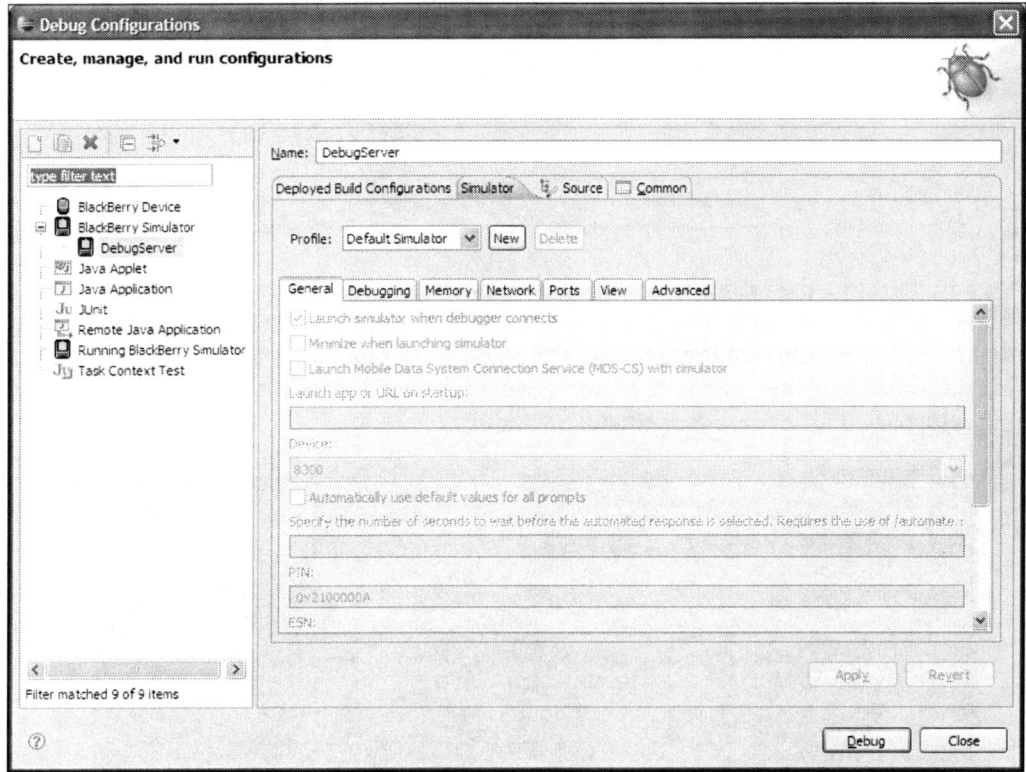

Networking

In order to enable the MDS simulator you must first select another profile from the profile list. Once another profile has been selected the fields in the dialog are enabled and you can place a checkmark into the field labeled **Launch Mobile Data Systems Connection Service (MDS-CS) with simulator**. Finally, click on **Close** to apply the changes. Alternatively, you can hit the **Debug** button to immediately start debugging the application. Changing the profile to another device will also change the simulator to appear like the other device selected. This can sometimes be undesirable, but often, it has little consequence.

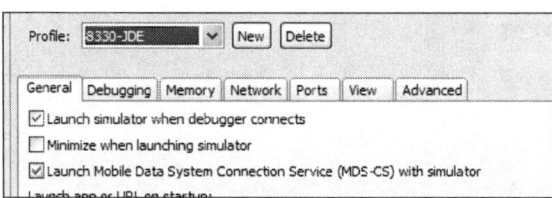

Either way, you start the MDS simulator; when it starts up you will see a boring black box with lots and lots of text in it. This is because the MDS simulator is a console program and doesn't have a user interface that you can or should be interacting with. You can look at the output and sometimes see errors or trace network activity, but for the most part, whatever output is displayed is not very meaningful or useful.

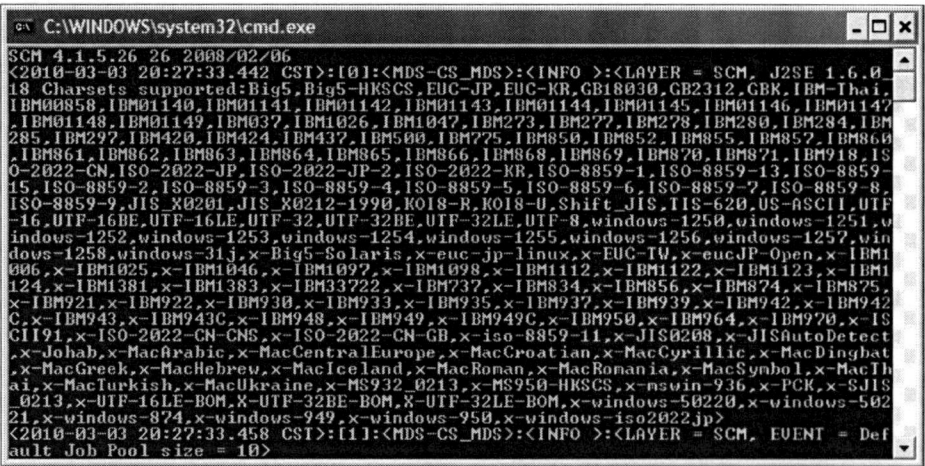

There is one thing in particular that is both useful and important if you happen to see it. In and amongst the initial spew of output that happens when starting the MDS, you may find an error message indicating the port 8080 is in use.

```
Feb 21, 2010 3:45:50 PM org.apache.coyote.http11.Http11BaseProtocol init
SEVERE: Error initializing endpoint
java.net.BindException: Address already in use: JVM_Bind:8080
```

```
        at org.apache.tomcat.util.net.PoolTcpEndpoint.
initEndpoint(PoolTcpEndpoint.java:298)
        at org.apache.coyote.http11.Http11BaseProtocol.
init(Http11BaseProtocol.java:139)
        at org.apache.catalina.connector.Connector.initialize(Connector.
java:1017)
        at org.apache.catalina.startup.Embedded.start(Embedded.java:827)
        at net.rim.application.ipproxyservice.TomcatThread.
startTomcat(Unknown Source)
        at net.rim.application.ipproxyservice.TomcatThread.run(Unknown
Source)
```

The MDS simulator must use port 8080 in order to operate. This port is used fairly commonly by other applications so chances are pretty good that another application might already be using that port. If this is the case, you must stop the other application and restart the MDS simulator. The MDS simulator won't abort if the port is already in use either, so unless you look for it, you might believe the MDS simulator is operating normally when it is not.

The port that the simulator uses is not something that you can just change through a configuration either. There is no configuration option available to change the port. The device simulator will be expecting to make a connection to port 8080 as well, and so these values are just hardcoded into both applications.

Once you are sure that the MDS simulator is running properly, you can pretty much forget about it. If you configured Eclipse to start the MDS simulator when debugging, then it will also terminate the MDS simulator when you are done debugging. If you started it manually, you will have to terminate it manually as well. This is done by closing the command prompt window or by pressing the *Ctrl + C* in the window.

If you started the MDS simulator manually you can leave it running through multiple debugging sessions. There is no real need to terminate it after each one. As the simulator runs, you will see regular activity in the output window, even if you aren't using it at that moment. However, when you make connections through the simulator by using the MDS transport you will see a lot of activity in the window as it works to process the request. What does it all mean? I don't really know, but it's there for the intrepid adventurer wanting to study it.

I think it's probably very common to have development environments for both the BlackBerry as well as whatever server-side software you plan to use on the same computer and to try to debug them both at the same time. Surprisingly, this may not be the best scenario, especially if you plan to use the MDS simulator.

Remember that the MDS Simulator is truly just a scaled down version of the MDS component, which is part of the BlackBerry Enterprise Server. Also remember that when using the MDS transport, the connection isn't made on the handheld itself. Instead, the MDS component makes the connection for you and then passes any data that came from the connection back to you.

Because of this, the MDS component and, by association, the MDS simulator specifically forbids connections to `localhost` or its numeric equivalent `127.0.0.1`. This would, in effect, open a connection back to the server that is running the MDS component instead of the handheld as one might expect. There isn't any good reason to do that, in fact it is considered a security risk so the MDS server just forbids any connections to that address.

As a result, if you want to debug your server on the same workstation that you have the MDS simulator running on you must use the external address of that computer. Most of the time, you don't know the address as it is given to your workstation dynamically by the router. You can find it by running the command-line application `ipconfig.exe`.

Using the external IP of your computer can introduce a new layer of routing issues though, which can make setting up a development environment very frustrating. Sometimes, the computer or the network just doesn't know how to route traffic back to the computer properly when the external address is used. There are a lot of possible reasons that are beyond the scope of this book, but just be warned, sometimes it just doesn't work like you might expect.

Testing for availability of transports

A big part of the decision for which transport to use comes down to being able to test to see which transports are available. You can't test for every possibility, but you can certainly test for certain aspects, such as whether the device supports Wi-Fi or whether the application is currently running on the simulator or not.

One common technique that seems to work well is to only prompt the user for an address and to remove any other connection string options the user might have added. Then, after some testing to determine which transports are available, add the appropriate connection string options and create the connection. This takes the responsibility of knowing anything about the network transports off the user and makes the whole experience much smoother for the user.

There are several classes that can be used to gather bits of information about what capabilities are present on the device. Some of these classes have changed over time, so there may be differences when working with other versions of the SDK. For our purposes here though, we will focus only on version 4.5.

With that in mind, let's add one more feature to the HttpBasics application—a small diagnostics screen. It is worth noting that Research In Motion provides a much more extensive tool called the **Network Diagnostic Tool**, which can be found at http://www.blackberry.com/knowledgecenterpublic/livelink.exe/fetch/2000/348583/800451/800563/What_Is_-_Network_Diagnostic_Tool.html?nodeid=1450596&vernum=0.

Time for action – testing for availability

1. Create a new class in the HTTPBasics project called DiagMainScreen, which is derived from the MainScreen class.

2. Add this constructor to the class

```
public DiagMainScreen()
{
  if (DeviceInfo.isSimulator())
  {
    add(new LabelField ("This is running in the simulator."));
  }

  if(WLANInfo.getWLANState() == WLANInfo.WLAN_STATE_CONNECTED)
  {
   add(new LabelField ("There is a WiFi connection available."));
  }
  if(CoverageInfo.isCoverageSufficient(
      CoverageInfo.COVERAGE_DIRECT)
   {
     add(new LabelField ("Direct TCP/IP Connections are available 
                       (Including WAP)."));
   }
   if(CoverageInfo.isCoverageSufficient(CoverageInfo.COVERAGE_MDS))
   {
     add(new LabelField ("Connections via MDS are available."));
   }
   ServiceBook sb = ServiceBook.getSB();
   ServiceRecord[] records = sb.findRecordsByCid("WPTCP");

   for (int i = 0; i < records.length; i++)
   {
     String uid = records[i].getUid().toLowerCase();
     if ( uid.indexOf("wifi") == -1 && uid.indexOf("mms") == -1
```

```
      {
         add(new LabelField ("A WAP 2.0 connection is available
                              using UID=" + records[i].getUid()));
      }
   }
}
```

3. Add a menu item to show the new screen to `HttpBasicsMainScreen`.

```
protected MenuItem _DisplayDiagAction = new MenuItem(
              "Display Diagnostics", 90000, 10)
{
   public void run()
   {
      UiApplication.getUiApplication().pushScreen(
              new DiagMainScreen());
   }
};
```

4. Lastly, add the menu item to the application by adding the following line to the constructor of the `HttpBasicsMainScreen` class.

```
addMenuItem(_DisplayDiagAction);
```

What just happened?

This small screen demonstrates the kind of checks you can do to determine what capabilities are available on a handheld. These are the most general conditions which should be checked, but there may be other more specific cases that you run into for your specific application, such as having multiple service books available for WAP 2.0.

There are only a few checks that you can make and unfortunately, they aren't all in one class. Some of them aren't even available in older versions, such as the `WLANInfo` class, which didn't appear until version 4.5.

The first, and most basic, test is to see if the application is running in the simulator. The `DeviceInfo` class will show this and much more information about the hardware aspects of the device that the application is running on. Methods such as `hasCamera()` and `isInHolster()` can be essential for some tasks. You can also get the OS software version from this class as well, which can be an important piece of information when debugging problems with a user's handheld.

```
if (DeviceInfo.isSimulator())
{
   add(new LabelField ("This is running in the simulator."));
}
```

The next simple test is one to check whether there is a Wi-Fi connection or not. The `WLANInfo` class can provide information about whether the Wi-Fi is currently connected to an access point or not. If there is a connection, you can also get additional information about the access point it is connected to, such as what kind of 802.11 connection is being used, A, B, or G, and so on. There is no way to tell if the device is Wi-Fi capable, but is simply not currently connected however.

```
if (WLANInfo.getWLANState() == WLANInfo.WLAN_STATE_CONNECTED)
{
    add(new LabelField ("There is a WiFi connection available."));
}
```

The `CoverageInfo` class is used to gather information about the cellular network that the device uses. For this situation we're particularly interested in the `isCoverageSufficient` method. Things get a bit muddied with this class though because the WAP and TCP/IP direct transports are both lumped into the COVERAGE_DIRECT grouping. A separate constant, COVERAGE_MDS, is used to determine if the MDS transport is available though, and this makes it easy to use.

```
if (CoverageInfo.isCoverageSufficient(CoverageInfo.COVERAGE_DIRECT))
{
    add(new LabelField ("Direct TCP/IP Connections are available
                        (Including WAP)."));
}
```

The last section of code is there to find the service book entry to use with the WAP 2.0 transport. Remember, earlier we said that in order to use the WAP 2.0 transport you need to append the `ConnectionUID=<uid>` parameter to the connection string. The `<uid>` value in that string is not a constant and is provided by your carrier in the form of a service book.

A **service book** is a collection of configuration records, called **service records**, which are provided by your carrier or your BES administrator and is what controls how your device can communicate with other servers on the network. You can have a great number of service records in the service book actually, each for a different situation

This small loop is used to query the service book for records that have the CID, or Content ID, of WPTCP. WPTCP is basically another name for WAP 2.0.

The first step is to get the service book itself, which is done using a static method in the `ServiceBook` class called `getSB`. Once you have an instance of the `ServiceBook` you can get only those records that have a Content ID of WPTCP by calling `findRecordsByCid`. It is possible to simply get all of the service records with the `getRecords` method, but this would just mean more work for us.

```
ServiceBook sb = ServiceBook.getSB();
ServiceRecord[] records = sb.findRecordsByCid("WPTCP");
```

Networking

If there are no records with that CID then the array that is returned will be empty, but if there is at least one you need to examine it more closely to pick the best one. The conditional `if` statement inside the loop does some checking on the UID of the service record to see if it is one you are looking for. The **UID** is essentially a unique name identifier. There can be multiple WPTCP service records which facilitate communicating over other methods besides the carrier network. Specifically, there can be service records for use with Wi-Fi or **Multimedia Messaging Service (MMS)**. In general, we only want to be using the carrier network so service records with these words in the name are skipped over in this algorithm.

```
for (int i = 0; i < records.length; i++)
{
  String uid = records[i].getUid().toLowerCase();
  if ( uid.indexOf("wifi") == -1 && uid.indexOf("mms") == -1)
  {
    add(new LabelField ("A WAP 2.0 connection is available using UID="
                        + records[i].getUid()));
  }
}
```

Unfortunately, running this code in the simulator isn't very interesting because only the labels regarding the simulator and direct TCP/IP will be shown. The simulator doesn't have service books for WCTCP like a real device does. You can go through the BES association process on a simulator just like you can on your phone in order to configure the MDS connection. But this isn't done very often unless necessary because it truly configures the simulator as a device on your BES.

Moving beyond HTTP connections

After spending this much time on `HTTP` connections you may think that this is the only supported connection type available. Oh no, not so! If you want, there are many other connections available. Most people are only interested in `HTTP` though, but for those who are interested we'll briefly cover a few other types here.

A very near relative to `HTTP` is the secure version, `HTTPS`. In general, communicating with an `HTTPS` connection is the same as with an `HTTP` connection. The only real difference is that the address portion of the connection string specifies `https://` instead of `http://`. When this happens, the `Connector` class returns an `HttpsConnection` object instead of an `HttpConnection` object, but as the `HttpsConnection` is derived from `HttpConnection`, it will essentially function the same.

`HTTP` is just one of many protocols built on the low-level socket connection, which is the basis for TCP/IP. You can also do raw socket communication if you prefer. Using the raw sockets eliminates all of the help that an `HTTP` connection gives. There are no `GET` and `POST` methods, no content type, headers, or even parameters. It's all just raw bytes going over the network. You can't really do raw socket communication unless you can control both the client and server sides and there can be a lot more work involved, but the result can be a much more efficient use of network resources as well.

Making a socket connection follows the same basic procedure that we've covered so far by replacing the `http://` portion of the address in the connection string with `socket://`. With this in your connection string, the `Connector` will return a `SocketConnection` object, which provides little more than just input and output stream operations.

Not only can we make a variety of connections, but we can also open listening connections that can receive connections as well. Just like the server we've been connecting to this whole time, the BlackBerry can host its own services and respond to requests from other devices as well. Now, a BlackBerry isn't the best device for hosting services so use this feature with caution!

Opening a server connection is as simple as omitting the destination address from the connection string. So passing a connection string of `http://` to the connector would return an `HttpServerConnection` object—an object is very similar to the `HttpConnection` object with a few additional methods to support a server connection.

Similarly, specifying a socket connection string and omitting the host address will create a `SocketServerConnection` object. Of course, with a `SocketServerConnection` you must specify a port to listen on still.

The `HTTP` Connection is by far the most common connection type used. You will know if you need a more advanced connection, but for now, it is enough to simply know that all of these other kinds are available.

Pop quiz

1. What connection string parameter should be used to initiate a connection using the Wi-Fi modem?

    a. `useWiFi=true`

    b. `deviceside=true`

    c. `interface=WiFi`

Networking

2. What connection string parameter should be used to initiate an MDS connection?

   a. `deviceside=true`

   b. `deviceside=false`

   c. `interface=MDS`

3. Which transport is reserved for alliance partners?

   a. WAP 1.0

   b. MDS

   c. BIS-B

Summary

This chapter just scratched the surface really of how to do networked communications between a BlackBerry application and another server or service. There are so many options that it is easy to get confused as well. After reading this chapter though, you should be much better equipped to tackle the challenges that come with a networked application. There are a lot of options and details that were covered, but some real practical examples and suggestions were also given.

After completing this chapter, you should understand:

- The transport mechanism is separate and distinct from the data being transmitted
- The basics of `HTTP` and when to use a `GET` or `POST`
- How and why threading is critical to networked communications
- What each transport method means and how to specify a specific method using the connection string parameters
- Why using an `HTTP POST` with simple `String` parameters is often the best approach

At this point, we've covered many of the basics surrounding building applications with the BlackBerry SDK. The next chapter will work with some of the newer features such as interfacing with a GPS. We will also look at a few specific tips and tricks and some other advanced features that you may want to work with.

10
Advanced Topics

Although we've covered many important and common topics, there are still plenty of nuggets left to discover in the BlackBerry SDK, as well as some tips and tricks to share. In this chapter, we will get to cover a few concepts that don't really warrant a chapter by themselves, or which are only going to be useful to a select audience. It's actually so hard to choose what to include here because there are so many!

One of the really hot areas in mobile development right now is the area of location-based services. Nearly all mobile devices now include a **Global Positioning System (GPS)** receiver on them, so it only makes sense that applications try to leverage them to provide useful and meaningful content for the user. This next section will focus on how to interface with the GPS system on BlackBerry handhelds that do support them (not all do).

The next section will be devoted to a BlackBerry development concept called **alternate entry point** projects. Sometimes, you need an application that will do two related, but separate tasks. These tasks might be done using two different applications except that they need to share events or data as well. A good example might be the **Messages** application that handles both the receiving of messages and providing a user interface application so that we can read them. Alternate Entry Points are one way to accomplish this dual functionality.

Many industry analysts have been saying for some time now that location-based services will be the next "Killer App" in the mobile market. In a nutshell, a **location-based service** is an application or tool that does something useful and appropriate based on where you are at that moment. At the very core of this concept is the first word, Location. Knowing where you are in the world is essential to being able to offer a service which is appropriate at that moment.

A good example of this might be an application that can tell you which restaurants are nearby, complete with both personal or critic reviews and maybe even a coupon as well. This is a common example of what many people think an LBS application can and should look like, but accomplishing that task is not so easy. Technically it's easy, but socially, and business-wise, it isn't.

There are of course many other examples of how an application can leverage your location to provide a useful service. In this section, we'll build an application that will log your location and then offer direction and distance information, so you can find it again later. It could be useful for finding your car in a crowded parking lot, for example. In the spirit of the Brothers Grimm character who got lost and could not find the way back home, we'll call this application Hansel.

Introducing the Global Positioning System

It's been amazing how the use of GPS technology has grown over the past twenty years. What started out as a tightly controlled tool used primarily by the military has turned into a host of consumer products that have worked their way into our everyday lives. Nearly every new car comes with a GPS receiver for emergency purposes as well as a navigation aid built into the car. Most new cell phones are similarly equipped and yet, a majority of people don't really understand how it all works.

Most people know that GPS works using satellites, but not much more. This is true of course! There are actually 27 satellites that all work together. These satellites orbit the earth in a very precise pattern and on a precise timetable, such that a signal from at least four of them can be received at any time and at any location on the earth. It's a pretty amazing accomplishment!

A GPS receiver works using a technique called **triangulation**. It takes the signals from these four satellites and calculates how far away they are so that it can calculate the current location. The math is nasty enough that we don't need to know about it. What we do need to know is that a GPS receiver needs to be able to receive a signal from four different satellites in order to compute a coordinate.

The LocationProvider class

Much like networking began with the `Connector` class, getting a location starts with the `LocationProvider` class. The Location API is another Java standard, JSR-179 specifically; something we should keep in mind as we work with the class going forward. Like we've seen in the PIM classes, sometimes the Java standards don't line up very well with the capabilities on one particular device. In the case of location, it doesn't line up well at all and the result is a rather confusing mess.

The `LocationProvider` class is both a static factory class, like `Connector`, and an instance class that can be called to get a location. The bridge between these two forms is the `getInstance` method. This static method of `LocationProvider` is used to get an instance of the `LocationProvider` that will be used later on to actually get location data. The `getInstance` method takes only one parameter—a class called Criteria, which is used to determine how best to get coordinates.

Criteria

The `Criteria` class and its role with the `LocationProvider` is, I think, a classic example of over-engineering. The `Criteria` class is used to specify what criteria to use when getting a GPS location. The criteria provided will be used to determine the best way to get a GPS Location. There are several methods of getting GPS data, and there are pros and cons to each method, so the `Criteria` class is used to provide some hints to the operating system about how best to do that. The `Criteria` class collects four pieces of information to help the operating system make this decision. Those four pieces of information are:

- Whether a cost may be incurred
- Minimum accuracy of the horizontal coordinate
- Minimum accuracy of the vertical coordinate
- How much power may be consumed getting coordinates

We'll get into how you actually use this class a little bit later on.

Three ways to get GPS data

It might seem strange, but there are actually three ways by which you can get GPS data. How can that be if there is only one set of satellites providing that positioning data? Clearly, the answer is that there are actually other ways to get that data besides just relying on the satellites.

- **Cell site**: This technique is the fastest way to get a location, but it also has the worst accuracy. Plus, it's not available from every network carrier and there may be some cost associated in the form of data usage charges. This technique attempts to do the same thing that a GPS receiver does except that it gets the location information from three cell network towers instead of four satellites. The strength of the signal from each tower is used to approximate the current location, using the same technique of triangulation. However, it's not as accurate because there are a lot of other things which can cause the signal strength to change besides just distance. Trees, buildings, and even hills can potentially affect the signal strength, so coordinates generated by using this method tend to be the least accurate.

Advanced Topics

Using this method doesn't provide any speed, direction, or altitude information either. It is the fastest though, so if you don't really need an accurate location, this method may be best. One good example would be to use this approach to get a coordinate that will be used to determine your ZIP code. A **ZIP code** is a very large area, and if you aren't exactly right, it probably wouldn't make much difference.

- **Autonomous GPS**: Autonomous is the complete opposite of the cell site method. This method uses only the GPS satellites to compute the location and nothing else. Because the satellites are always moving, there is a pretty significant delay when starting to the GPS receiver, as it tests and determines which satellites are available and which are the best to use. This discovery process can take a long time, especially if there are obstacles overhead such as heavy clouds or thick foliage.

  The coordinates provided by the receiver are the most accurate they can be, but this also comes with a heavy cost in terms of power usage. Because the receiver is on, and actively listening for satellite information, the battery usage will be high. The other major consideration though is that there is no other communication with the cell network towers, so there can be no costs incurred or risks of some network not supporting the particular feature. In short, this method is the safest and most accurate, but you pay a price in terms of battery and start time.

- **Assisted GPS**: Assisted GPS is the *best of both worlds* approach between cell site and Autonomous GPS. This approach aims to shorten the discovery time when using Autonomous GPS by querying a cell network tower about which satellites are the best ones to be used. Once this is done, Assisted GPS operates just like Autonomous GPS.

Bringing it all together

Now that we've covered the three ways by which you can get a location, and the four pieces of data that can be provided to the `Criteria` class, do you see how easy it is to get the `LocationProvider` for the method that you want? No, neither do I.

The fact is that there just isn't a clear association between a set of criteria and a `LocationProvider`. The Criteria is **supposed** to be separate from the actual implementation of any system to get location information.

Personally, I want to know exactly what is going to happen when I write an application and fortunately, RIM has provided this information so we know what values to supply as criteria in order to get a specific `LocationProvider` for the method we want to use. Following is a list of the values to use when populating the `Criteria` object in order to get a `LocationProvider` that uses the corresponding method.

- **Cell site:**

   ```
   _CellCriteria.setHorizontalAccuracy(Criteria.NO_REQUIREMENT);
   _CellCriteria.setVerticalAccuracy(Criteria.NO_REQUIREMENT);
   _CellCriteria.setPreferredPowerConsumption(
           Criteria.POWER_USAGE_LOW);
   _CellCriteria.setCostAllowed(true);
   ```

- **Autonomous GPS:**

   ```
   _AutonomousGPSCriteria.setHorizontalAccuracy(50);
   _AutonomousGPSCriteria.setVerticalAccuracy(50);
   _AutonomousGPSCriteria.setPreferredPowerConsumption(
           Criteria.NO_REQUIREMENT);
   _AutonomousGPSCriteria.setCostAllowed(false);
   ```

- **Assisted GPS:**

   ```
   _AGPSCriteria.setHorizontalAccuracy(Criteria.NO_REQUIREMENT);
   _AGPSCriteria.setVerticalAccuracy(Criteria.NO_REQUIREMENT);
   _AGPSCriteria.setPreferredPowerConsumption(
           Criteria.POWER_USAGE_MEDIUM);
   _AGPSCriteria.setCostAllowed(true);
   ```

Version 5.0 of the SDK makes this process easier by providing a specialized `BlackBerryCriteria` class and predefining these modes into constants that be used to specify the mode in a clearer manner. These mode constants are in the new `GPSInfo` class that also defines several new static methods for testing the availability of modes and getting error codes. If this project was being made using version 5.0 of the SDK, the preceding code could be reduced to this code instead.

```
BlackBerryCriteria _CellCriteria = new BlackBerryCriteria(
                             GPSInfo.GPS_MODE_CELLSITE);
BlackBerryCriteria _ AutonomousGPSCriteria = new BlackBerryCriteria(
                             GPSInfo.GPS_MODE_AUTONOMOUS);
BlackBerryCriteria _ AGPSCriteria = new BlackBerryCriteria(
                             GPSInfo.GPS_MODE_ASSIST);
```

Getting coordinates

Now that we've covered some of the background material, let's get started on an application that will use the information! The ultimate goal will be to display the locations, but let's focus first on simply getting coordinates from the Location API successfully.

Advanced Topics

This application will display the current coordinates on the screen and update them in real time as new locations are received. When the application starts up though, it is not actively receiving GPS coordinates. It just starts to a screen with a `ChoiceField` to choose which method will be used to receive location coordinates. Clicking on the **Start Logging** menu will start the GPS and begin showing the coordinates. At this point, the **Start Logging** menu is no longer visible and instead a **Stop Logging** menu is shown, which will reset the application back to the starting point.

Plain GPS coordinates aren't too pretty, but once we get that far, we know that we're able to receive the coordinates successfully.

Time for action – acquiring a location

1. Create a new project, `Application` class, and `MainScreen` class (like we have done in the past). Remember, we decided early on that this application would be called `Hansel`.

2. This application will implement the `LocationListener` interface, so add that interface to the class declaration as well.

3. We need a number of data members which will be used in the application. Add the following code to the new MainScreen class.
    ```
    protected Criteria _CellCriteria = new Criteria();
    protected Criteria _AGPSCriteria = new Criteria();
    protected Criteria _AutonomousGPSCriteria = new Criteria();
    protected Criteria _AGPS_AutonomousGPSCriteria = new Criteria();

    protected ObjectChoiceField _AccuracyField;
    protected String[] AccuracyChoices = {"Cell Site", "AGPS",
                                          "Autonomous"};
    protected RichTextField _CurrentCoords;

    protected boolean _Started = false;
    protected LocationProvider _CurrentProvider = null;
    protected boolean _GPSSupport = false;
    ```

4. Next, you need to set up the screen with the fields that will be used in the constructor. Add the next code snippet to the body of the constructor for the screen.
    ```
    // Set up the Criteria objects for each type.
    _CellCriteria.setHorizontalAccuracy(Criteria.NO_REQUIREMENT);
    _CellCriteria.setVerticalAccuracy(Criteria.NO_REQUIREMENT);
    _CellCriteria.setPreferredPowerConsumption(Criteria.POWER_USAGE_LOW);
    _CellCriteria.setCostAllowed(true);
    ```

Chapter 10

```
_AGPSCriteria.setHorizontalAccuracy(Criteria.NO_REQUIREMENT);
_AGPSCriteria.setVerticalAccuracy(Criteria.NO_REQUIREMENT);
_AGPSCriteria.setPreferredPowerConsumption(
        Criteria.POWER_USAGE_MEDIUM);
_AGPSCriteria.setCostAllowed(true);

_AutonomousGPSCriteria.setHorizontalAccuracy(50);
_AutonomousGPSCriteria.setVerticalAccuracy(50);
_AutonomousGPSCriteria.setPreferredPowerConsumption(
        Criteria.NO_REQUIREMENT);
_AutonomousGPSCriteria.setCostAllowed(false);

setTitle(new LabelField ("Hansel"));
try
{
    if (LocationProvider.getInstance(null) != null)
    {
        _GPSSupport = true;
    }
}
catch (LocationException e)
{ }
if (_GPSSupport)
{
    _AccuracyField = new ObjectChoiceField("Accuracy",
                AccuracyChoices);
    _AccuracyField.setSelectedIndex(2);
    add(_AccuracyField);

    _CurrentCoords = new RichTextField();
    add(_CurrentCoords);
}
else
{
    add (new LabelField ("No GPS Support is available."));
}
```

5. The listener will need a method that can be called to update the screen. Add the code below to be used by the listener.

```
public void updateCoordinates(Location loc)
{
    String coords;
```

Advanced Topics

```
      QualifiedCoordinates qc = loc.getQualifiedCoordinates();
      coords = Double.toString(qc.getLongitude()) + " " +
                              Double.toString(qc.getLatitude());
      _CurrentCoords.setText(coords);
}
```

6. Next, you need to implement the `LocationListener` interface that you added to the class in Step 2. Add these methods to the class.

```
public void locationUpdated(LocationProvider arg0,
                            final Location arg1)
{
  Runnable r = new Runnable ()
  {
    public void run()
    {
       HanselMainScreen.this.updateCoordinates(arg1);
    }
  };
  HanselMainScreen.this.getApplication().invokeLater(r);
}
public void providerStateChanged(LocationProvider arg0, int arg1)
{}
```

7. After that, you need to create the menu objects that will be used. Remember, these menus will start and stop receiving updates to the GPS coordinates.

```
protected MenuItem _StartAction = new MenuItem("Start Logging" ,
                                  100000, 10)
{
  public void run()
  {
    Criteria selectedCriteria = null;
    switch (_AccuracyField.getSelectedIndex())
    {
      case 0:
         selectedCriteria = _CellCriteria;
         break;
      case 1:
         selectedCriteria = _AGPSCriteria;
         break;
      case 2:
         selectedCriteria = _AutonomousGPSCriteria;
```

```
                break;
        }
        try
        {
           _CurrentProvider = LocationProvider.
                         getInstance(selectedCriteria);
           _CurrentProvider.setLocationListener(HanselMainScreen.this,
                                    1, 1, 1);
        }
        catch (LocationException e)
        {
           // TODO Auto-generated catch block
           e.printStackTrace();
        }
        if (_CurrentProvider !=null)
        {
           _Started= true;
        }
     }
  };

  protected MenuItem _StopAction = new MenuItem("Stop Logging" ,
  100000, 10)
  {
    public void run()
    {
      _CurrentProvider.reset();
      _CurrentProvider.setLocationListener(null, 1, 1, 1);
      _CurrentProvider=null;
      _Started = false;

    }
  };
```

8. Now that you have menu items, add them to the menu by overriding the `makeMenu` method and add the next piece of code to it.

```
if (_GPSSupport)
{
  if (_Started)
  {
    m.add(_StopAction);
```

Advanced Topics

```
    }
    else
    {
       m.add(_StartAction);
    }
  }
  super.makeMenu(m, context);
```

What just happened?

Whew! That's a lot of code!

We started off by simply adding a bunch of data members to the new class. In addition to the normal fields, flags, and other typical data members, we also added an instance of the `Criteria` class for each method that we might want to use to get the GPS data. This clearly shows how to set the `Criteria` for each method.

We set the values for all of those data members along with setting up the screen elements in the constructor. One of the important steps in the constructor is to test whether the handheld actually supports a GPS. Just because the operating system or SDK can support a GPS doesn't mean that the handheld actually has one in it.

We do this with a simple test of getting a `LocationProvider` with no criteria at all specified by using the `getInstance` method with a `null` parameter. This will get the default `LocationProvider` for the system. Now, we aren't going to do anything with it, so what kind of provider we get is not important. Just getting one indicates that the handheld has GPS support available.

```
if (LocationProvider.getInstance(null) != null)
{
   _GPSSupport = true;
}
```

If the handheld has GPS support available, then you can add the normal fields to the screen. But, if the support isn't available then you add a simple `LabelField` to alert the user.

```
if (_GPSSupport)
{
  _AccuracyField = new ObjectChoiceField("Accuracy", AccuracyChoices);
  _AccuracyField.setSelectedIndex(2);
  add(_AccuracyField);

  _CurrentCoords = new RichTextField();
  add(_CurrentCoords);
}
```

```
        else
        {
           add (new LabelField ("No GPS Support is available."));
        }
```

Like many other systems in the SDK, the `Location` API also defines a `LocationListener` interface. By implementing this interface the application will to be notified of new changes, such as a new location. As we've seen before, updating the screen from the `Listener` methods is not thread safe, so you will need a method that can be used to safely update the screen from another thread.

This method will use the `Location` object that contains a lot of location information in addition to latitude and longitude coordinates. It includes speed, bearing, and other navigation data that would be useful in other applications. This application doesn't need it, so we just get the `QualifiedCoordinates` from the `getQualifiedCoordinates` method.

```
        public void updateCoordinates(Location loc)
        {
           String coords;
           QualifiedCoordinates qc = loc.getQualifiedCoordinates();
           coords = Double.toString(qc.getLongitude()) + " " +
           Double.toString(qc.getLatitude());
           _CurrentCoords.setText(coords);
        }
```

`QualifiedCoordinates` is closely related to the `Coordinates` class; it derives from the `Coordinates` class actually. In addition to the actual coordinates, a `QualifiedCoordinates` also contains other statistics about how accurate the coordinates are.

The coordinates themselves are double-precision floating point numbers. Each number represents the location in degrees of latitude or longitude. One degree of latitude is a very large distance, so to get a coordinate that is reasonably accurate, the number must include a lot of decimal places and be very precise. We're just going to take those numbers and convert them into `String` values so that we can show them on the screen.

The `LocationListener` interface requires only two methods to be implemented—`locationUpdated` and `providerStateChanged`. At this point, we are interested only in `locationUpdated`. This is where we get a real piece of data in the form of a `Location` object. The listener itself doesn't do anything interesting though and simply passes it on to the `updateCoordinates` method (we just looked at) by using a typical `invokeLater` method call.

```
        public void locationUpdated(LocationProvider arg0,
                                    final Location arg1)
        {
```

```
    Runnable r = new Runnable ()
    {
       public void run()
       {
          HanselMainScreen.this.updateCoordinates(arg1);
       }
    };
    HanselMainScreen.this.getApplication().invokeLater(r);
}
```

The next step is to add two menu items that will start and stop the GPS logging. Because we have the `ChoiceField` that lets the user choose which method to use, the first part of the `_StartAction` menu item is to get the proper `Criteria` object based on the user selection.

```
Criteria selectedCriteria = null;
switch (_AccuracyField.getSelectedIndex())
{
  case 0:
     selectedCriteria = _CellCriteria;
     break;
  case 1:
     selectedCriteria = _AGPSCriteria;
     break;
  case 2:
     selectedCriteria = _AutonomousGPSCriteria;
     break;
}
```

Once we have the right `Criteria`, it's time to get the proper `LocationProvider`. This is done again with the static `getInstance` method on the `LocationProvider` class and make sure to pass in the `Criteria` object that we just selected. We also want to set up a listener that will receive new coordinates and other updates on a regular basis. The next line calls `setLocationListener` on the `LocationProvider` that was just returned in the previous line.

The first parameter is the object that has implemented the `LocationListener` interface. Remember, in Step 2 we added that interface to the definition of this `Screen` class, so we need to supply the Java keyword `this`. However, because this is inside an anonymous class for the menu, the `true` value of `this` isn't the `Screen` class like we need. Fortunately, we can get the proper value from the `HanselMainScreen` class. The next few parameters include an update frequency (currently set to one second), then timeout, and maximum age. One second is a very fast update speed, so the timeout and maximum age fields are also set to one second. In a nutshell, we don't want to wait for a long time for a coordinate when another update is scheduled in another second.

```
try
{
 _CurrentProvider = LocationProvider.getInstance(selectedCriteria);
 _CurrentProvider.setLocationListener(HanselMainScreen.this, 1, 1, 1);
}
catch (LocationException e)
{
   // TODO Auto-generated catch block
   e.printStackTrace();
}
```

The `_StopAction` menu just resets the provider and listener back to their initial values. Passing a null value to `setLocationListener` removes the current listener and stops future updates.

The last step simply adds the new menu items to the menu in the `makeMenu` method. Even though two menus have been implemented, the code in `makeMenu` ensures only one is added to the menu. This is also a good example of how you can cause menu items to be shown only in certain situations and why you might want to do that. You could try to use the same menu item for both situations, but why bother? It's a lot cleaner to make each menu item self contained and then simply show the proper one at the right time. Once you were done making the application in the last section, I'm sure you went right out and ran it in the simulator to see what it did, right? Were you a little upset when it didn't work? Well, it did test an important feature of the application, the part that tested to see if we could get a `LocationProvider`!

The fact is that even though version 4.5 of the SDK does in fact support the `Location` API, the simulators that come with the 4.5 component package for Eclipse are of handhelds that don't have a GPS included. Now we can get and install a single simulator, but it wouldn't be set up with Eclipse and usable in the debugger so the easier thing to do is to install another version of the SDK in Eclipse. (We covered how to do this already in Chapter 3.) Version 4.6.1 of the Eclipse Component Package comes with the Curve 8900 and Bold 9000 simulators, both of which include GPS support. Let's install that one and then come back to test the application.

Advanced Topics

Now that you have a simulator capable of simulating a GPS, you can get to the main screen of the application and you can test the application a bit more. When it comes to choosing which method to use for acquiring the GPS, it doesn't really matter in the simulator. They are all going to come from the GPS simulator and not a real GPS receiver, so you can really pick any choice from the **Choice** field.

Once you start logging you will probably see just a single set of coordinates displayed there and possibly think something is wrong. This is where we need to look at the GPS simulator in order to get more interesting test data.

The GPS Simulator is available by selecting the **Simulate | GPS Location...** menu on the simulator window itself.

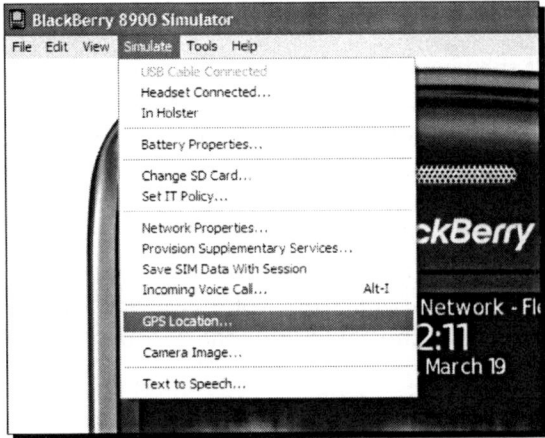

After selecting that menu, the GPS Location dialog will be displayed. This dialog is essentially divided into two parts. The top half allows you to select individual locations that have been entered in and saved with the simulator. Two locations have already been provided—Waterloo and Conestoga Lake Conservation.

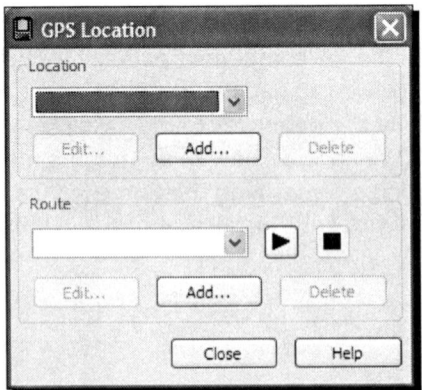

[282]

You can add your own location by using the **Add...** button and supplying some known coordinates to the dialog. The coordinates must be in the same format that the Location API uses, which is to say as two double precision numbers — the degrees of latitude and longitude. You can even provide an altitude.

The bottom half of the dialog is for managing routes that have been created. **Routes** are where the really interesting stuff is at. Routes are just a list of coordinate locations that are *played* like a recording to the GPS simulator. The net result is that the coordinate that you received in the application will be changing over time as the route is played.

When you click on the **Add** button in the Routes group box, you are presented with a small dialog asking how you want to get the data used in the route. Each method gets the coordinate data in a different way, so it's worth going over each one.

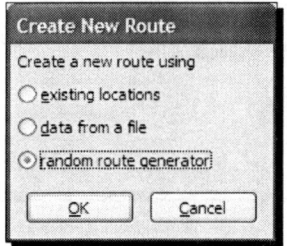

Choosing the existing **Locations** radio button shows the **Edit GPS Route** dialog. From this dialog, you can specify a starting and ending point for the route and then the speed at which to travel between them. Doing this doesn't actually generate a complete list of coordinates. Instead, when this route is *played,* the GPS simulator will compute new coordinates every second that matches the speed of travel that has been set. This dialog is also used to edit any existing routes that have been created using the other two methods.

Choosing the **data from a file** radio button displays a typical file open dialog that can be used to select a file with a **NMEA** extension containing the GPS coordinates exported from another system. The NMEA file format is actually based on a serial communication protocol developed by the National Maritime Electronics Association and is used to facilitate communications between a GPS and other devices. The data is loaded directly into a route that you can edit, just like we did in the previous example.

The last radio button on the **Create a New Route** dialog is the **random route generator** option. Selecting this option causes the **Generate Random Route** dialog to be shown:

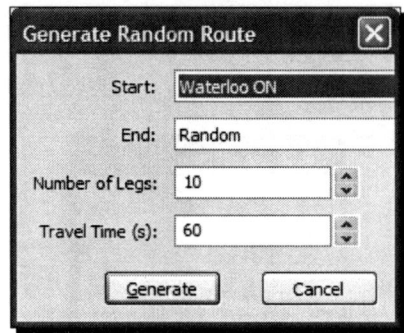

Generating a route in this manner also requires that you choose a starting and ending location. These can be existing locations already entered into the simulator, or they can be random as well. The resulting route will be between the start and end locations, but can be broken up into a number of legs. Although the legs do connect the start and end locations together, they do not necessarily form a straight line. Much like the road system, the course can alter at the location where legs connect. This can be used to generate a route that is most like that which a real user might take.

Once we have a route created one way or the other, you can start *playing* the route in the GPS Location simulator by pressing the button with a triangle on it, like the play button of a music or video player. This will make the GPS simulator change the simulated GPS coordinates at a regular rate so that your application will receive data that has some variety to it.

If you play a route in the GPS simulator and then display the application running in the Blackberry simulator, you should see that the coordinates are being updated on the screen each second

Expanding Hansel

This first step was a big step to prove that we can at least get some data from the `Location` API and into the application. Now, it's time to do something with that data and make a useful application.

Much like the Hansel from the fable, we all get lost every now and then. One very common use of a GPS coordinate is to mark a location of something interesting so that you can get back to it if you want. Fishermen often do this to mark spots of interest when it would otherwise be impossible to tell one spot from another on the open seas. This is also the heart of the treasure hunting game called **Geocaching**.

This next step will turn the Hansel application that we have built so far into an application that could be used for either of these purposes. Now what we have done so far isn't directly useful to this new purpose, so we'll be adding the new functionality on top of what we've already done. The two tasks don't really go well together, but it's better than deleting what we've already done.

When you are done, the new `Hansel` application will have the ability to record your current location, say where you parked the car for instance. Later, when you come out of the mall, airport, or wherever you were, the application can get a new set of coordinates and then tell you how far and in what direction to travel to get back to your car.

Time for action – expanding Hansel

1. The `HanselMainScreen` will need to be updated to include some new fields and menu items to support the new functionality. The first step is to add the data members to the `MainScreen` class. These are primarily the screen fields to display the new data. The listener will be described in more detail later.

   ```
   protected CalcDistanceLocationListener _CalcListener = null;
   protected RichTextField _EndLocation;
   protected RichTextField _StartLocation;
   protected RichTextField _Distance;
   protected RichTextField _Bearings;
   ```

2. You'll also need a couple of new menu items, so add these menu items to the `MainScreen` class.

   ```
   protected MenuItem _ResetAction = new MenuItem("Clear Start Location" , 100000,
                                                                     10)
   {
     public void run()
     {
   ```

```java
      if (_CalcListener != null)
      {
        _CalcListener.reset();
        _CalcListener = null;
        _Distance.setText("");
        _Bearings.setText("");
        _StartLocation.setText("");
        _EndLocation.setText("");
      }
    }
  };

  protected MenuItem _GetStartAction = new MenuItem("Get Start
                                        Location", 100000, 10)
  {
    public void run()
    {
      Criteria selectedCriteria = null;
      switch (_AccuracyField.getSelectedIndex())
      {
         case 0:
           selectedCriteria = _CellCriteria;
           break;
         case 1:
           selectedCriteria = _AGPSCriteria;
           break;
         case 2:
           selectedCriteria = _AutonomousGPSCriteria;
           break;
      }
      try
      {
        LocationProvider Provider = LocationProvider.getInstance(
                               selectedCriteria);
        _CalcListener = new CalcDistanceLocationListener(
                    HanselMainScreen.this, Provider);
        _CalcListener.getStartLocation();
      }
      catch (LocationException e)
      {
```

```
        // TODO Auto-generated catch block
        e.printStackTrace();
      }
    }
  }
};

protected MenuItem _FindStartAction = new MenuItem("Find Start
                                                   Location", 100000, 10)
{
  public void run()
  {
    if (_CalcListener != null)
    {
      _CalcListener.getEndLocation();
    }
  }
};
```

3. Additionally, these menu items will need to be added to the `makeMenu` method so that they can be displayed. Add them into the existing `if (GPSSupported)` block.

```
m.add(_ResetAction);
if (_CalcListener == null)
{
    m.add(_GetStartAction);
}
else
{
    m.add(_FindStartAction);
}
```

4. All of the rest of the new changes will go into a new class that will also implement the `LocationListener` interface. Create a new class called `CalcDistanceLocationListener` and make sure to add the `LocationListener` interface when adding the class.

5. Next, you need to add these members to the class. Some are data members, there is a constructor, and some other public methods.

```
protected HanselMainScreen _Screen = null;
protected LocationProvider _CurrentProvider = null;
protected Coordinates _StartLocationCoordinates = null;
```

Advanced Topics

```
      CalcDistanceLocationListener(HanselMainScreen screen,
      LocationProvider prov)
      {
        _Screen = screen;
        _CurrentProvider=prov;
      }

      public void reset()
      {
        _StartLocationCoordinates = null;
          if (_CurrentProvider != null)
          {
            _CurrentProvider.setLocationListener(null,10,10,10);
          }
      }


      public void getStartLocation()
      {
        _CurrentProvider.setLocationListener(this, 1, 1, 1);
      }


      public void getEndLocation()
      {
        _CurrentProvider.setLocationListener(this, 1, 1, 1);
      }
```

6. Lastly, you need to supply a body to the `locationUpdated` method that was created and stubbed in when the class was created because the `LocationListener` interface was specified.

```
      // stop listening
      _CurrentProvider.setLocationListener(null, 1, 1, 1);

      if (_StartLocationCoordinates == null)
      {
        QualifiedCoordinates QC = location.getQualifiedCoordinates();
        _StartLocationCoordinates = new Coordinates(
             QC.getLatitude(),QC.getLongitude(),QC.getAltitude());
        final String output= Double.toString(QC.getLatitude()) +
                          " "+Double.toString(QC.getLongitude());
        Runnable r = new Runnable ()
         {
```

```
      public void run()
      {
        _Screen._StartLocation.setText(output);
      }
    };
    _Screen.getApplication().invokeLater(r);
}
else
{
    Coordinates start = _StartLocationCoordinates;
    Coordinates end = location.getQualifiedCoordinates();

    double dist = start.distance(end);
    double bear = start.azimuthTo(end);

    String units = " Meters";
    if (dist > 1000.0)
    {
      // The distance greater than 1000 meters
      // turn it into Kilometers
      units = " Kilometers";
      dist = dist / 1000.0;
    }

    // round to two decimal places
    dist = ((double)((int)(dist*100.00)))/100.00;
    bear = ((double)((int)(bear*100.00)))/100.00;
    final String bearing = "Bearing: " +  Double.toString(bear) +
                        " degress from true north.";
    final String distance = "Distance is: "+Double.toString(dist) +
                         units;
    final String endoutput= Double.toString(end.getLatitude())+
                         " "+Double.toString(end.
    getLongitude());

    Runnable r = new Runnable ()
    {
      public void run()
      {
        _Screen._Distance.setText(distance);
        _Screen._Bearings.setText(bearing);
```

Advanced Topics

```
        _Screen._EndLocation.setText(endoutput);
    }
};
    _Screen.getApplication().invokeLater(r);
```

7. Now it's time to debug the application. Launch the debugger and open the application in the simulator.

8. This application will be using the two standard locations that are provided in the GPS simulator. First, open the GPS Simulator and select the **Waterloo, ON** location.

9. In the application, open the menu and select the **Get Start Location** menu item. The coordinates for Waterloo should appear on the screen in the field labeled **Start**.

10. Next, change the location to **Conestoga Lake Conservation** in the GPS Simulator dialog.

11. Back in the `Hansel` application, select the **Find Start Location** menu item.

12. At this point, the screen should look like the following screen showing the distance and bearing for how to get back to Waterloo from Lake Conestoga.

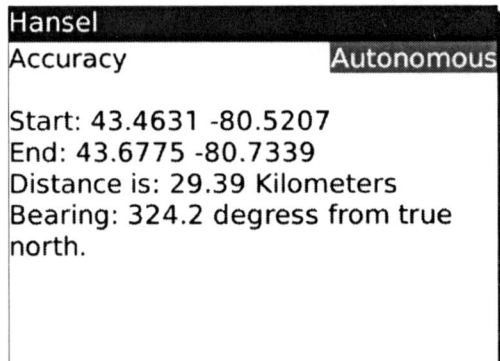

What just happened?

Most of the changes we made to the main screen aren't very interesting. The real fun happens inside the new class—the `CalcDistanceLocationListener`. Using a separate class for this listener demonstrates that you can have multiple listeners in an application, and that the main screen doesn't have to implement the listener. By putting the listener in another class you separate it from the screen, which may be an issue if there needs to be interaction between them. However, that separation can be a good thing too, allowing multiple screens to use the same listener or even to have multiple instances of the listener running at the same time.

Generally, each instance can have only one listener, and the same is true for the `LocationProvider`. Even if we call `LocationProvider.getInstance` multiple times, the same `LocationProvider` instance is returned each time. The net effect of this is that we can have only one `LocationListener` registered at a time. If you have the logging activated with the **Start Logging** menu item, click on the **Get Start Location** menu item, and the application will stop displaying coordinates to the screen.

As we look at the `CalcDistanceLocationListener`, we see there are three public methods that match up to the menu items we added to the screen. If we wanted to, the body of these methods could be put into the `run` method of each of the menu items, but as we said already, putting them into another class helps to separate it out.

The `getStartLocation` and the `getEndLocation` methods both simply set up a listener with a regular interval of one second. How can these two methods do the exact same thing? The real logic happens in the `locationUpdated` method! So let's start there.

The very first thing done in the `locationUpdated` method is to stop the listener from getting any more updates. We need only one coordinate to keep and store, so there isn't any point to getting more. Of course, this is mainly true because we are working in the simulator. GPS coordinates tend to jump around a bit and are rarely, if ever, the same from one sampling to the next. In a real world application it would be a good idea to collect ten or more coordinates, and then average them together.

```
// stop listening
_CurrentProvider.setLocationListener(null, 1, 1, 1);
```

The next step is to determine if we are getting an initial coordinate, (which I'm calling a start coordinate), or the final coordinate, (which I'm calling an end coordinate). The logic is simple: if we don't already have a start coordinate, then we must be getting a start coordinate. However, this is why the same method is used to get both start and end coordinates. We can't really do anything with an end coordinate without already having a start coordinate!

```
if (_StartLocationCoordinates == null)
{
…
}
```

If we've determined that this will be a start coordinate, the next bit of code simply stores the coordinate and updates the screen to show the new information. Again, we're separating the creation of the `Runnable` from the invocation of it. Many examples show them together, but it tends to be somewhat confusing. Separating them makes the code easier to read and understand, I think.

Advanced Topics

It is important to note that we're actually making a new `Coordinates` object to hold the starting location. Apparently, the SDK doesn't create a new `Location` object each time the `updateLocation` method is called. If you were to simply keep a reference to the `Location` or `QualifiedCoordinates`, the value inside those objects will change!

After storing the coordinates, the code constructs a string to display them and then updates the screen. We didn't need a new method in the `MainScreen` class though because we're doing only one action. The `_StartLocation` data member is marked as protected, so the listener class is allowed to access it, provided the string being used in the `Runnable` is also marked `final`. The `final` keyword is an indicator to the compiler that this object won't change after it has been created.

```
QualifiedCoordinates QC = location.getQualifiedCoordinates();
  _StartLocationCoordinates = new Coordinates(
                              QC.getLatitude(),QC.getLongitude(),QC.
  getAltitude());
final String output= Double.toString(QC.getLatitude()) +
                    " "+Double.toString(QC.getLongitude());
Runnable r = new Runnable ()
{
  public void run()
  {
      _Screen._StartLocation.setText(output);
  }
};
_Screen.getApplication().invokeLater(r);
```

Once you have a starting location, the application doesn't do anything until the user triggers the **Find Start Location** menu item. Because the `_StartLocationCoordinate` object exists and has a value, the code drops into the `else` block, where we will compute the distance information and update the screen again.

Computing the distance and bearing could have been a very daunting task, but fortunately, the SDK provides some very simple functions to do it for us. The `Coordinates` class has the methods, `distance` and `azimuthTo`, which are used with a second set of coordinates to get the distance and direction between them.

```
double dist = start.distance(end);
double bear = start.azimuthTo(end);
```

Once we have these values, we perform some cleanup on the values. The distance returned is in meters, but for very large distances, people would prefer to see them in kilometers. If there are more than 1,000 meters, then we should use kilometers.

```
String units = " Meters";
if (dist > 1000.0)
```

```
{
    // The distance greater than 1000 meters
    // turn it into Kilometers
    units = " Kilometers";
    dist = dist / 1000.0;
}
```

In addition to this change, most users don't want to see decimal numbers with a lot of digits of precision. Computers are very good at this, but people aren't. This bit of code rounds the values to two decimal places. It can be confusing to look at though.

Consider that casting a floating-point number to an `integer` data type essentially removes all of the fractional part of that number. We do want some of the fractional part though, so we first multiply the number by 100 in order to move the decimal place over two digits. After casting the result to an integer, we cast it back to the floating-point number and then divide by 100 to move the decimal place back over.

```
// round to two decimal places
dist = ((double)((int)(dist*100.00)))/100.00;
bear = ((double)((int)(bear*100.00)))/100.00;
```

The last bit of this code simply updates the screen again with the end coordinate, distance, and bearing. Now, this presentation isn't very user friendly. It would be much nicer to display an arrow or something on the screen because most people don't know what a bearing is, let alone know which way to go.

The `Location` class also has a method for `getCourse` to get the current bearing of the handheld, or the direction it has been going. The course is computed as the direction between the last coordinate and the current coordinate. Since this is a simulator, it would have been harder to use it, but if this application were to be really polished up, it would be a good idea to display the bearing to the user relative to their current course.

Pop quiz

1. What is the name of the static class used to get location data?

    a. `Location`

    b. `GPSData`

    c. `LocationProvider`

2. What is the difference between `QualifiedCoordinates` and `Coordinates`?

    a. `QualifiedCoordinates` have been verified to be correct

    b. `QualifiedCoordinates` contain information about the accuracy of that reading

    c. `QualifiedCoordinates` are more precise

3. What method is used to compute how far are two Coordinates from each other?
    a. `distance()`
    b. `Coordinate.getDistance()`
    c. `distanceTo()`

Now it's time to move on to something completely different! In the next section, we will look at how you can run multiple applications with one set of code through the use of alternate entry point projects.

Alternate entry points

We said very early on in this book that the static method called `main` was the entry point for a BlackBerry application, do you remember that? It's been so long ago and we've created so many projects using the same `UiApplication` structure that you might have forgotten. It's gotten so familiar that you don't even think about it anymore.

Well, now it's time to go back and look at things more closely and change how you think of that boring `main` method.

There is a special project type called an **alternate entry point project** that can be used to accomplish things that just can't be done otherwise. Using an alternate entry point project, you can use the same project and code to host more than one application. It is, in essence, saying that a second application should use the same program files as another existing project.

Alternate entry points don't change the fact that there is still one, and only one, static `main` method in the project. Instead, they rely on additional parameters being passed into the `main` method to identify which application is being activated. This will, of course, make the code in the `main` method more complicated, but the extra work is worth it.

Why would you want to use this strange type of application? You want to use this kind of project any time you really want to have two separate processes that will share some code or memory with the other. You can find a lot of good examples of this in the standard applications that are provided with a BlackBerry.

For instance, the **Calendar** application likely uses this technique. One project is used to add the calendar icon to the home screen and displays the screens to the user when they open the application. This application runs only when the user clicks the icon and then terminates once the user is done. But what causes the alerts to show up when the appointment time is reached? Obviously, this can happen even if the **Calendar** application isn't currently being displayed. This is another project, probably an alternate entry point project that has no user interface. This second application is set up to launch as soon as the device starts, and just quietly loops endlessly checking to see if an appointment time has arrived and then displaying an alert to the users.

There are many other possible applications as well. The **Messages** application probably uses the same technique to display the Messages application screens with one application and to send or receive messages using the background process. It even adds other applications which display screens, such as the **Compose Message** or **Saved Messages** applications.

Creating a focus icon

On many newer devices, each application will display a regular icon and also display a slightly different icon when selected by the cursor on the Home Screen. This is called a **focus icon**. The difference is often small and subtle, but enough that you notice these changes like the phone icon from the simulator that we've been running. Once the application icon is selected, the phone image tilts slightly, and the arrows move closer together.

You may have noticed that on the property pages of an image file, you can specify both the application icon, and the application focus icon. We've done this before to specify the application icon, but not the focus icon. The reason is simple, it doesn't work!

Well, that isn't exactly fair to say, because it does work if you are using an SDK version of 4.7 or greater. Of course, there isn't anything on this screen to let you know that, so you can very easily just check that checkbox and rightfully expect to see it work. Unfortunately, it doesn't.

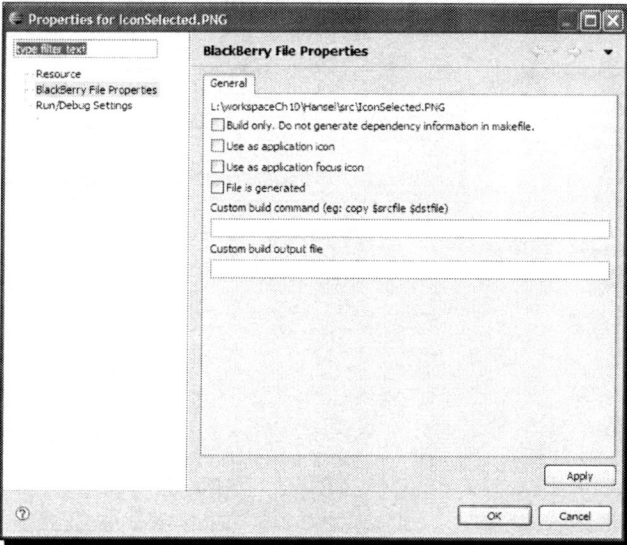

Advanced Topics

In order to achieve the same focus icon functionality, we need to create a new alternate entry point project and change the icon in code! So, let's get started and add this new project type.

 There are occasions where Eclipse doesn't seem to recognize changes made to the workspace. If this happens, you can usually close and restart Eclipse to fix the issue.

Time for action – creating an alternate entry point project

1. The first thing to do is add a new project, called `HanselIcon`, to the workspace. This follows the same steps that you had followed when creating a new project.

2. Right-click on the project to display the project's **Properties** dialog.

3. Select **BlackBerry Project Properties** from the list on the left-hand side of the dialog.

4. Select the **Application** tab from the tabs that are displayed on the right-hand side of the dialog.

5. Change the project type from the default **CLDC Application** to the **Alternate CLDC Application Entry Point** type. Under this drop list is another list of projects that this will be an alternate entry point for. If there is more than one project in the workspace, be sure to select the Hansel project here. If there is just one other project, this selection will be made automatically for you.

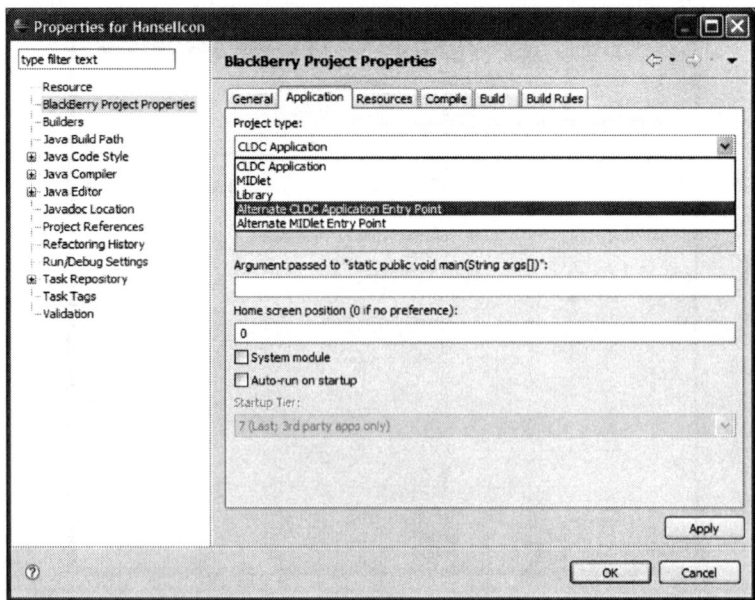

[296]

6. Assign a special value to the **Arguments** field, in this case use **Icon**.
7. Check the **System module** and the **Auto-run on startup** checkboxes.

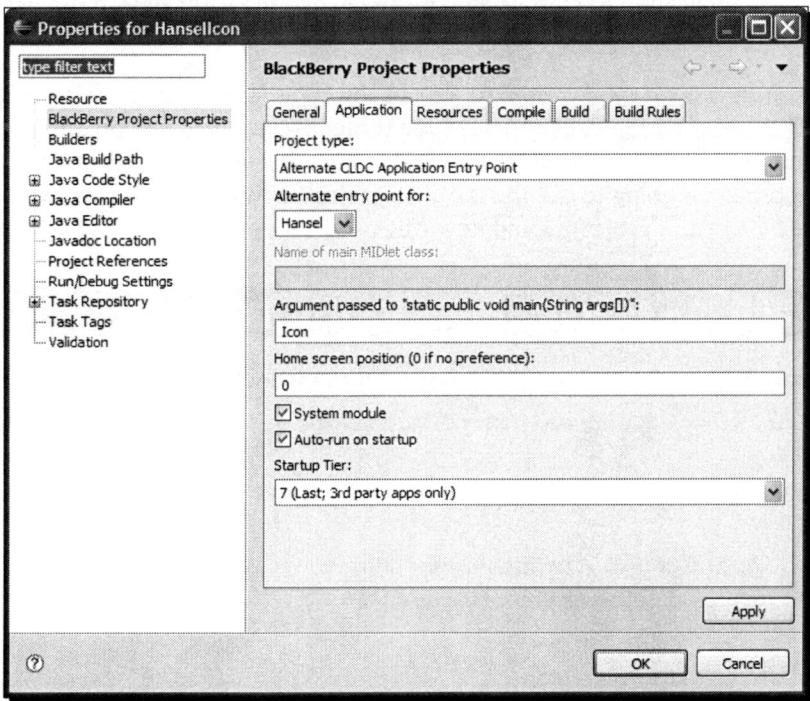

8. Dismiss the dialog by clicking on **OK**.

What just happened?

These steps create a new project in the workspace that has been configured to be the alternate entry point for the Hansel project. Notice that there is no difference in how the project is created. The only difference is how the project has been configured in the project's **Properties** dialog. As part of those configurations, we set some pretty important settings.

The most important setting for this is the argument passed to the `main` method. You may recall that the `main` method received a `String array` parameter, which the generated code called `args`. The `main` method will be called multiple times and needs to behave differently if it is being called because the `Hansel` application is being launched, or if it is being called because of the alternate entry point. By specifying different arguments for each project, the `main` method can know which project is calling it. In this case, as this alternate entry point project is intended to supply a focus icon, we set that parameter to the word **Icon**.

Advanced Topics

The other two checkboxes ensure that the new project is launched as soon as the device boots up. We've never changed the auto-run parameter because we don't want the application screen to be displayed as soon as the device boots up. In this case, though, we do want the new application to start so that it can change the icons before the user has a chance to see the screen.

Now that the project is set up, it's time to look at the code. Which code are we interested in? The code in the `Hansel` project of course! Even though Eclipse will let you add classes and other code to the `HanselIcon` project, this code won't be ever used. Remember that the `HanselIcon` project is going to call the `Hansel` project with a new parameter, and so any code in the `HanselIcon` project would never be used.

Time for action – adding a focus icon to Hansel

1. Replace the code in the `main` method with the following code.

   ```
   public static void main(String[] args)
   {
     if ( args != null && args.length > 0 && args[0].equals("Icon") )
     {
       UiApplication theApp = new HanselApp(true);
       theApp.enterEventDispatcher();
     }
     else
     {
       UiApplication theApp = new HanselApp(false);
       theApp.enterEventDispatcher();
     }
   }
   ```

2. Then, replace the constructor of the `HanselApp` with the next code snippet.

   ```
   public HanselApp(boolean setIcon)
   {
     if (setIcon)
     {
       invokeLater(new Runnable()
       {
         public void run()
         {
           ApplicationManager myApp =  ApplicationManager.
                                       getApplicationManager();
           boolean inStartup = true;
   ```

Chapter 10

```
            while (inStartup)
            {
              if (myApp.inStartup())
              {
                try
                {
                  Thread.sleep(1000);
                }
                catch (InterruptedException e)
                {
                  // TODO Auto-generated catch block
                  e.printStackTrace();
                }
              }
              else
              {
                  setIcons();
                  inStartup = false;
              }
            }
            //Exit the application.
            System.exit(0);
      }
    });

  }
     else
     {
       pushScreen(new HanselMainScreen());
     }
}
```

3. Also, add the following helper method to the `HanselApp` class.

```
private void setIcons()
{
 //Set the rollover icons.
 try
 {
    HomeScreen.updateIcon( Bitmap.getBitmapResource("Icon.PNG"),0);
```

Advanced Topics

```
        HomeScreen.setRolloverIcon(
        Bitmap.getBitmapResource("IconSelected.PNG"), 0);
      }
      catch(Exception e)
      {
      }
    }
```

4. Run the application and see that the icon changes when the application icon has focus.

What just happened?

This example shows how to add a focus icon, or roll-over icon, to your application. It will work for all versions of the SDK, which makes this technique a pretty popular one to follow. The code isn't too hard to follow either.

The first step of this code changes the `public static main` method to do some different processing if the argument passed in is the string "Icon". This is the `String` argument set in the previous section with the alternate entry point project that we created. If the argument is set to `Icon`, the application is created and the constructor is called with a parameter of `true` to indicate that this is being called by the `HanselIcon` project.

```
public static void main(String[] args)
{
  if ( args != null && args.length > 0 && args[0].equals("Icon") )
    {
    UiApplication theApp = new HanselApp(true);
    theApp.enterEventDispatcher();
    }
    else
    {
      UiApplication theApp = new HanselApp(false);
      theApp.enterEventDispatcher();
    }
}
```

The constructor to the application didn't take a parameter previously and our next set of changes adds this parameter and handles the processing. If the parameter is `false`, the `HanselMainScreen` is displayed in the same manner that it was done before. However, if the parameter is `true` some different processing takes place.

Chapter 10

Instead of simply displaying the screen, we set up some code to detect when the handheld has finished starting up. This code is needed only when working with version 4.1 of the SDK, but it works with all versions. With version 4.1, it was important not to try to change the icons before the device had fully started up.

```
invokeLater(new Runnable()
{
  public void run()
  {
      ...
  }
```

Once the `Runnable` is being executed, the code sets up a loop to wait until the device has finished starting up. Once it has finished, the `setIcons` method is called to perform the action.

```
boolean inStartup = true;
while (inStartup)
{
   if (myApp.inStartup())
   {
     try
     {
       Thread.sleep(1000);
     }
     catch (InterruptedException e)
     {
       // TODO Auto-generated catch block
       e.printStackTrace();
     }
   }
   else
   {
    setIcons();
     inStartup = false;
   }
}
```

The `setIcons` method wraps the actual calls to change the icons inside a `try/catch` block. Again, this is only necessary for working with version 4.1 of the SDK but it works fine for other versions as well. The parameter at the end of `updateIcon` and `setRolloverIcon` methods specifies the index of the entry point to update. As there can be many entry points, and even multiple entry points with a **HomeScreen** icon, this index is used to specify which one to update. In this case, the value is 0 and in most cases this will be true.

Advanced Topics

```
private void setIcons()
{
  //Set the rollover icons.
  try
  {
    HomeScreen.updateIcon( Bitmap.getBitmapResource("Icon.PNG"),0);
    HomeScreen.setRolloverIcon(
    Bitmap.getBitmapResource("IconSelected.PNG"),0);
  }
  catch(Exception e)
  {
  }
}
```

 The name of the image must be EXACTLY the same in the `getBitmapResource` method as it is on the file system, even the capitalization must be the same.

We've made a pretty big point of saying that this is necessary only for version 4.1 and that in version 4.7, you don't even need to use code to get a focus icon. What should be done for those versions in between 4.1 and 4.7?

It's actually much easier. The two methods to set the icons can be done right inside the `public static main` method. Additionally, all of the code to delay the processing until after the device has finished startup is no longer necessary. Because of this, the `HanselApp` class can go back to the original bland form we're used to and doesn't need any of the other code that was added.

```
if ( args != null && args.length > 0 && args[0].equals("Icon") )
{
  HomeScreen.updateIcon(Bitmap.getBitmapResource("Icon.PNG"),0);
  HomeScreen.setRolloverIcon(Bitmap.getBitmapResource(
                  "IconSelected.PNG"),0);
}
else
{
  UiApplication theApp = new HanselApp();
  theApp.enterEventDispatcher();
}
```

Pop quiz

1. What property of a project is used to differentiate one project from another when using alternate entry points?

    a. Entry Point

    b. Project name

    c. Command-line argument

2. Which versions of the BlackBerry SDK require a code-based technique to create rollover icons?

    a. versions 4.2 and lower

    b. Versions 4.7 and greater

    c. Versions lower than 4.7

3. For versions of the SDK that don't need a code-based technique, how is the rollover icon set?

    a. Through the project properties

    b. In the bitmap file properties

    c. With the Rollover icon dialog

Have a go hero – allowing the user to specify the filename

The `Hansel` application was a good way to get started using the `LocationProvider` for getting GPS data. One feature that would be nice to have is to modify the screen so that directions would be updated on a regular basis. In order to do this now, you would need to keep clicking the **Find Start Location** menu over and over again. In order to accomplish this, clicking the **Find Start Location** menu will need to start receiving location data on a regular basis. Once this starts there needs to be a way to stop it, so a new menu would also be needed.

Additionally, the bearing information is based on true north and not related to which direction the user is currently facing. It would be a lot clearer to inform the user to "bear 10 degrees to the right" instead of providing the bearing from true north. The `Location` object that we get from the `locationUpdated` method also contains a `getCourse` method, that can be used to convert the bearing we get from the `azimuthTo` method into a bearing relative to the user's current position. These small changes would go a long way to making `Hansel` a much better application.

Advanced Topics

Summary

This chapter focused on two rather distinct concepts—how to use the GPS to get location info and how to use an advanced project type, the alternate entry point project. While these topics didn't really go together, they are important in their own right for making applications.

After completing this chapter, you should understand:

- The basics of how the Global Position System works
- The three methods that a BlackBerry handheld can get location information
- How the `Criteria` class is used to specify which method you want to use
- How to get coordinates using the `Location` API
- What an alternate entry point project is and how it differs from a normal project
- How the static `main` method can be expanded to do different things for different entry points

It's been a wonderful and exciting journey so far, but there is still one more topic left to cover. Eventually, you will want to release your application for other people to use. You will need to put the finishing touches on that application first, and then when it's all ready, submit it to the BlackBerry AppWorld store for users to buy or download. These are the things we will talk about next!

11
Wrapping It All Up

Here we are, in the home stretch! In this chapter, we'll take the applications that we've just been working on and add the finishing touches in order to release it to the public through the BlackBerry App World. These finishing touches include adding localization through resource files, code-signing the application, and then completing the submission process.

If you've made a really great application that you want to sell online you want to be able to sell it to as many people as you can and make as much money as you can, right? BlackBerry handhelds are supported by and sold in many countries all over the world. It only makes sense that if your application can be created in such a way as to display the screen by using a language that is natural to a person; you are more likely to be able to sell it to them. This is accomplished through the use of a resource file that contains all of the language-specific words which are used in your application, and which can be easily changed. We'll cover this topic in more detail first.

Secondly, the BlackBerry SDK contains many powerful objects and methods that can be used to access private information of a user. This access could potentially be misused if the developer wanted to do so. Additionally, an application can access many low-level functions of the OS that could also be misused, such as deleting the user's data or sending spam e-mail. RIM recognizes this possibility, which is why you must code-sign your application before these functions can be used. We'll cover more about code-signing, what it means, and how to do it in the following section.

Lastly, you probably will want to distribute your application to the public. One of the best ways to do so is through the BlackBerry App World. The last section in this chapter will cover what steps are needed in order to do that. First, however, we need to finish polishing up the application by adding localization support.

Using resources for localization

No matter how good your application is, there are people who won't buy it or use it because of the language that is displayed on the screen. It just doesn't matter what your application does, if the user cannot read what is displayed on the screen they can't use it.

The solution to this problem is to make your application where the language being displayed on the screen can be easily and automatically changed to use the same language that the user's handheld has been configured to use. You can write a bunch of code to do this, but why bother? A solution has already been created and is part of the SDK already—that solution is a resource file. Using this solution you can distribute one application that can support multiple languages and change which one is displayed automatically as needed.

In a nutshell, a resource file is a lookup table where you can put all of the text being displayed on the screen and which can be easily swapped out with a different one. Now, you still have to do the translation of the text yourself, but the framework will help you out by swapping the resources when needed. Each bit of text is given an identifier that is used in the code when the text is needed.

As nice as this all is, there is one thing that is not so nice about it. The BlackBerry SDK is very good about avoiding things that work by "magic". That is to say, when "magic" is used, things work because you give something just the right name, or place a file in a specific location and as a result, the reasons why something works is lost. Unfortunately, resource files use a great deal of "magic" and this can lead to frustration if you don't do things "just right" and very little information is given when it does not work properly

In spite of these issues, it is still a technique that you should employ in every project. It is also worth noting that we haven't followed that directive in any of the applications we've created so far, and this is for a good reason. While it is a good technique to use in an application that you will be publishing and letting other people use, it makes for bad example code.

Time for action – adding a resource file

1. The first step to adding resources to a project is to add the resource file itself. This is done through the **New** right-click menu just like a class or project. However, a resource file isn't on the menu so you must find it by using the **Other...** menu item.

Chapter 11

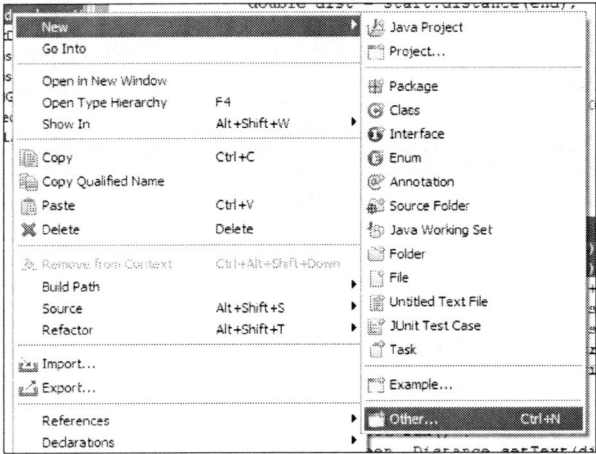

2. Selecting this menu will display the **New** wizard (like we've seen before) when creating a new BlackBerry project. This time, however, we want to choose the **BlackBerry Resource File** type before clicking on the **Next** button.

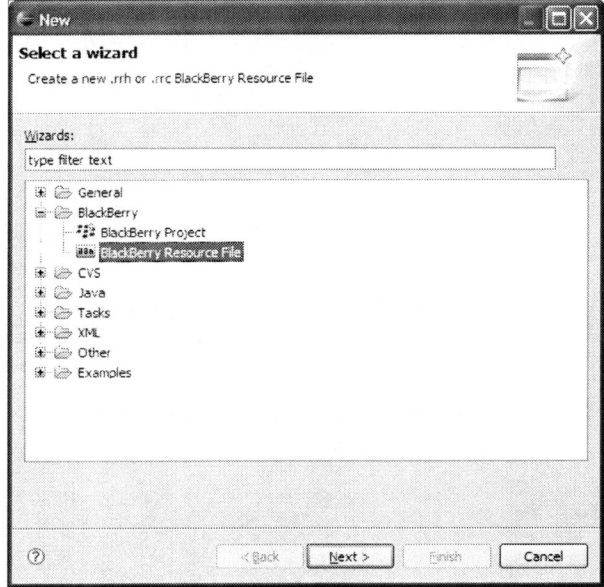

Wrapping It All Up

3. The next step in the wizard requires you to specify a location and a name for the new resource file. Select the location where the other Java files are at and enter the name `Hansel.rrh` as shown in the following screenshot:

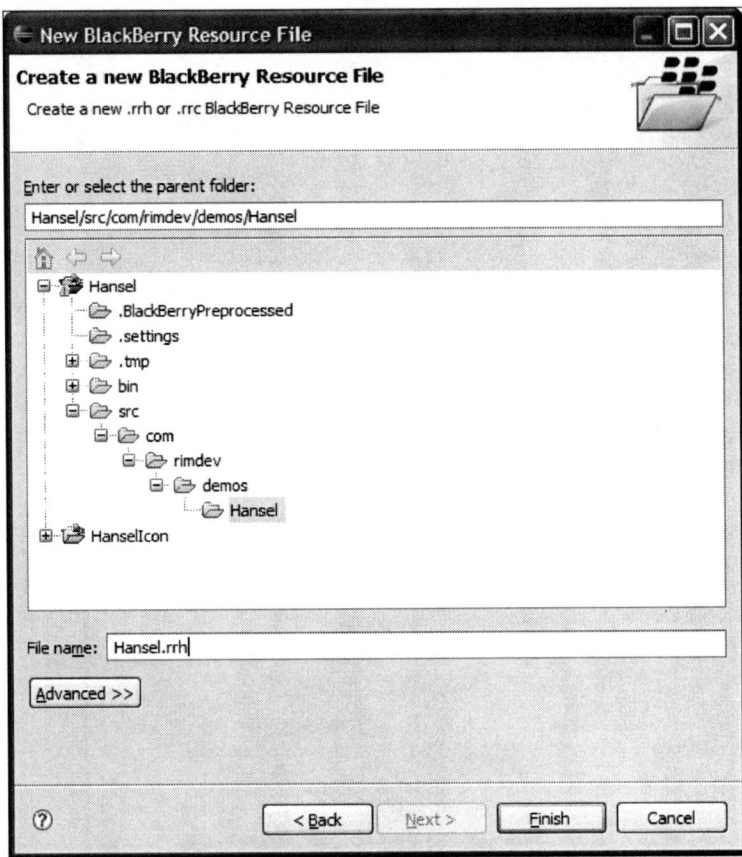

4. At this point, two new files have been added to the project—`Hansel.rrh` and `Hansel.rrc`. Double-click the file named `Hansel.rrc` to show it on the screen.

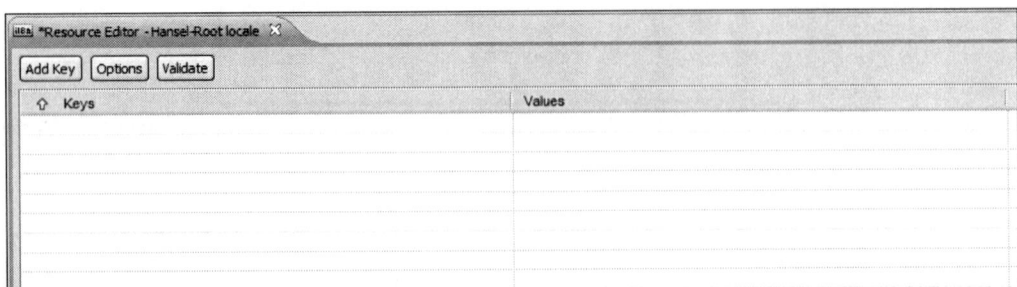

What just happened?

Adding a new resource file isn't very difficult, but there are some important things to note here. First is that adding a new resource file is somewhat hidden inside the **Other...** submenu. You may have remembered seeing it when you created a new project sometime earlier in the book.

The second thing is related to the funny naming requirements. The **New BlackBerry Resource File** wizard step does a good job of explaining the requirements. First, the file must be somewhere under the Eclipse `src` directory. Unlike images, which are often also considered resources, the BlackBerry resource file must exist in the `src` directory somewhere. This is because compiling the resource file will cause new code to be generated, which will be compiled with the application and become a class.

The last weirdness is that you are required to use either a `.rrc` or a `.rrh` extension for the filename when completing the wizard. For this file, it doesn't matter which one you enter and once the process is complete you will get *both* a `.rrc` and a `.rrh` file of the same name. Furthermore, clicking *either* of these files will display the same resource editor in the editor pane. This is because you can't directly edit the `.rrh` file, so attempting to open it will simply open the default `.rrc` file instead.

Resource bundles

You've already seen how we have multiple resource files that act together as one thing. This thing is called a resource bundle. As the name implies, a **resource bundle** is the term given to a collection of resource files that all work together. Why would you want more than one resource file? A single resource file can contain a set of values only for a specific language and locale. Therefore, if you want to support multiple languages and locales in your application, you will need multiple resource files—one for each language and locale.

In this case, so far, we have one resource file—the file named `Hansel.rrc`. The other file created, named `Hansel.rrh`, is the resource header file. This file stores the names of each resource key but not any values associated with that key. The resource file, the `.rrc` file, is what contains the actual values for each of the keys.

Why is this important? Remember that there are meant to be several resource files—one for each language and locale that is being supported. If we were to add another resource file to add support for another language, only the `.rrc` file would be created because the `.rrh` already exists. In short, you need only one `.rrh` file to be the master list of resources that are contained in each `.rrc` file.

So now that we've covered some of the background, let's add another resource file to the project to add support for both the Spanish language, in general, and more specifically, Spanish in Mexico.

Wrapping It All Up

Time for action – adding a second resource file

1. Create a new resource file by right-clicking on the project and selecting **New | Other...**.
2. Select **BlackBerry Resource** from the dialog.
3. Supply the filename `Hansel_es.rrc` and click on the **Finish** button.
4. Repeat steps 1 and 2.
5. Supply the filename `Hansel_es_mx.rrc` and click on the **Finish** button.

What just happened?

Once this is done, notice that there is still only one `.rrh` file, but we now have two more `.rrc` files in the project. This is because both files began with the name `Hansel`, and so were added to the already existing Hansel resource bundle. If you had chosen a different name, or perhaps misspelled the name, then another matching `.rrh` file would have been created as well.

The names of the files that are created as part of a resource bundle are very important. This is where we start to get into the "magic" part that I warned you about. When there are multiple resource files, the operating system will use the default language and locale of the handheld to determine which resource file to use. The names of these files are used to define what language and locale is supported by that particular resource file and by extension, which resource file to use on a particular handheld.

The resource file that we created first, the one without any kind of suffix to the name, is the language neutral resource file. This means that if the application is run on a handheld with a default language for which the application doesn't have a language-specific resource file, the language neutral resource file will be used.

The two new files that we just added provide language- and locale-specific resource files. By adding _es to the end of the name we are specifying that this file is the Spanish language resource file, which is locale neutral. The other resource file that we created had both a _es suffix and then also added a _mx suffix. The _mx suffix is the international country code for Mexico and denotes that the resource file is specific to the locale of Mexico.

So to bring it all together, a resource file that matches both the language and locale with the device settings will be used first. If a resource file has no locale suffix, but matches the language, it will be used next. And lastly, the language neutral resource file will be used if the device language and locale settings do not match any other resource file.

You can add as many resource files as you want to support. Some unusual combinations are possible with this system as well. For instance, you could have a resource file with the _en_mx suffix, which would specify an English language in Mexico. I call this unusual because most residents of Mexico will speak Spanish, so this combination would be uncommon.

There is no rule that says you can create only one resource bundle for your application. If your project uses multiple entry points, you might want to have a set of resource files for each entry point. Really, the system is very flexible and not very hard to use. The difficulty comes in knowing how to name your resource files correctly and there is little guidance on that topic.

Now that we have some resource files, let's add some values to them and set up the project to use our new resource file for perhaps the most important text to display—the name of the application!

Time for action – populating a resource file and configuring the project

1. Start off by opening the `Hansel.rrc` file by double-clicking it within the project.
2. Key values are added by using the **Add Key** button. Click on the **Add Key** button to add a new key value to the resource file.
3. Enter **APPLICATION_TITLE** into the **Add Key** dialog and press on the **OK** button.

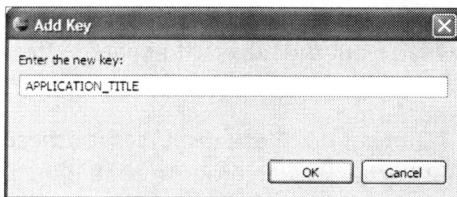

4. Repeat the previous steps to add an **APPLICATION_DESCRIPTION** key.

5. Setting the value of a key is done directly in the **Resource Editor** window. Double-click in the **Values** column next to the **APPLICATION_TITLE** key in the resource editor. When the cursor appears in the editor, type in the application name in this case, **Hansel**.

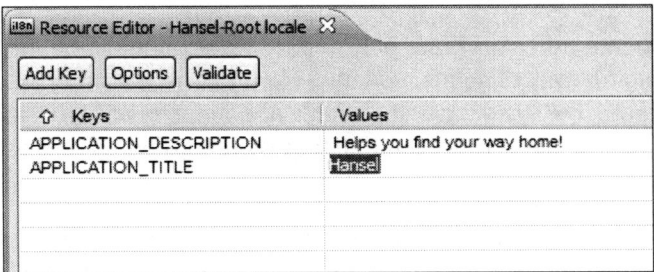

6. Open the Spanish version of the resource file by double-clicking the `Hansel_es.rrc` file. Notice that the values entered previously are not populated!

7. Enter a value for the keys in the Spanish resource. Set the application name to `Hansel` as before, but set the description key to `Le ayuda a encontrar tu camino a casa!`.

8. Now, change the project so that the name and description are shown. Right-click on the project node in the **Project Hierarchy** window and select **Preferences**.

9. Select the **BlackBerry Project Properties** item in the list on the left-hand side of the **Properties** dialog.

10. Select the **Resources** tab from the tabs that appear in the right-hand side of the dialog.

11. Initially, the project is not set up to use resources for these values. Check the **Title Resource Available** checkbox in order to enable the boxes below.

12. If you have more than one resource bundle in the application, select the proper one in the **Resource Bundle** List. In this case, you want to select **Hansel** from the **Resource Bundle** drop list.

13. Select the proper resource IDs from the **Title Id** and **Description Id** drop-down lists. These ID values are the same as a resource "key".

Chapter 11

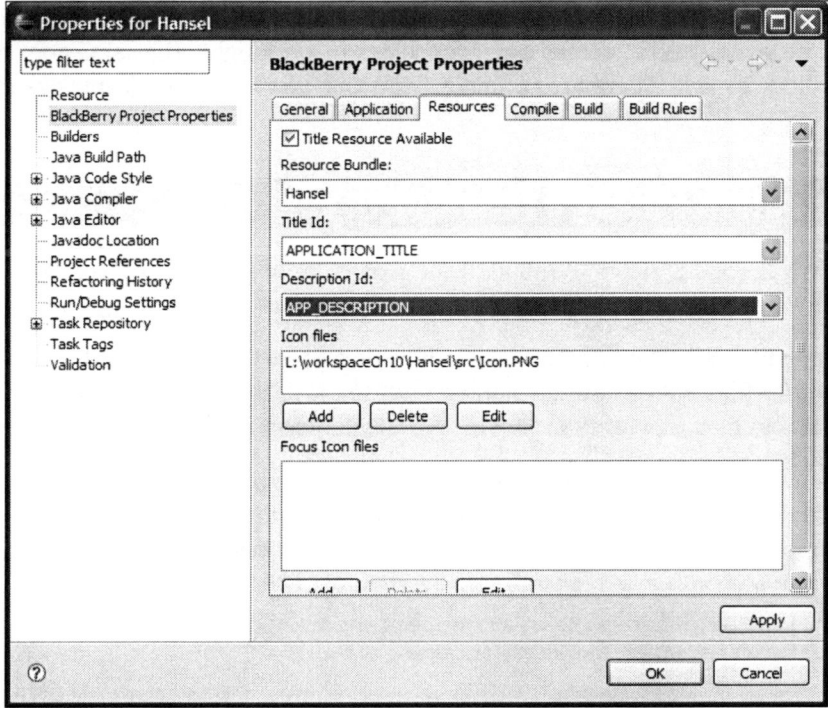

What just happened?

The steps that we just followed have done two things. First, we added new keys and values to the resource files that we have created in the project. It will be important to do this for every piece of text in the application that should be localized. What kind of text is that? Generally, any text that the user can see should be localized. This includes things such as date formatting strings, or even currency symbols.

Secondly, after creating two values for our keys, we changed the project settings to use those values. If the checkbox is unchecked, meaning that no resource values are used, the title and description from the first tab in the dialog, the **General** tab, will be used. However, once the checkbox on the **Resource** tab has been checked, the title and description that will be shown will come from the resource file instead.

These two values, the title and description, are pretty important. We have to handle these values in this special way though because these values are displayed before the application has started to run. Once the application has begun to execute, the process is completely different, and this is what we will focus on next.

Wrapping It All Up

We already saw how creating the resource files involved a little bit of "magic" in that the files have to be given specific names order for things to work right. The same goes for using resources in code as well. There are certain aspects that work only when you give the right name.

Time for action – using a resource in your code

1. First, it is good practice to rebuild your project before starting to work with a new resource file. Do this by selecting **Project | Build All**.

2. You need to add the new keys and values that you will be using to the resource files. Add a new key named SCREEN_NO_GPS_SUPPORT to the resources files and set the value to "No GPS Support is available".

3. The next step is to add an interface to the `HanselMainScreen` class where you will be using resources. Add the interface named `HanselResource` to the `implements` list in the class declaration next to the `LocationListener` so that the code looks like the following code.

   ```
   public class HanselMainScreen extends MainScreen implements
   LocationListener, HanselResource
   ```

4. Add a `ResourceBundle` object to the data members of the `HanselMainScreen`.

   ```
   ResourceBundle _resources;
   ```

5. In the constructor for the `HanselMainScreen`, create an instance of the `ResourceBundle` to use.

   ```
   _resources = ResourceBundle.getBundle(BUNDLE_ID, BUNDLE_NAME);
   ```

6. Change the code that displays the **No GPS Support** label to use the new resource that you just created.

   ```
   add (new LabelField (_resources.getString(
                   SCREEN_NO_GPS_SUPPORT)));
   ```

What just happened?

Congratulations, you're now using one resource in your application! OK, so there are a few dozen more to do, but you've got to start someplace! Using a resource really is pretty straightforward, but like most things there are still a few tricks to know and things to keep in mind when doing so. The first step is just one of them.

Remember, earlier we said that a resource bundle will actually get compiled into a class which will be part of your project? You don't get to see those generated classes, but they are there. Unfortunately, Eclipse doesn't seem to know that this is going to happen and so the automatic completion feature won't find the key values and the autodetection of problems will often erroneously report a problem which isn't really there.

If you try to use a newly created resource bundle, Eclipse will likely report anything related to that resource file as an error. When you compile the project, that error will most likely go away. In an attempt to avoid any confusion that might result from this erroneous error reporting, it's best to build the project first before trying to access it.

Even this isn't always going to work though. For that reason, I like to create all of my resource keys before trying to access them in the application. The most effective way to make sure that the automatic completion is in sync with the application is to build the project and then close and restart the workspace.

The first step to using a resource bundle is to first implement a special interface in the class that you want to use the resources in. Here, we see a bit more of the "magic" that happens behind the scenes in making resources work. The interface that we are implementing must be a special name, that is, the name of your resource bundle followed by the word "Resource". If you choose to create the resource files in a separate directory than where the rest of your source files are located, you may also need to include an `import` statement, but Eclipse should be able to do that for you through the menu of suggested fixes. If you wanted to include multiple resource bundles in your application, this step is where you would choose which bundle to use by implementing one interface name or the other.

Implementing the interface doesn't require any other methods to be implemented in your screen. It does provide access to some special constants that we will see in Step 5.

Step 5 is where we see some more of that "magic" of making resources work. This step is where we actually get the `ResourceBundle` object, which will be used later to get the actual text for displaying on the screen. The `getBundle` method takes two parameters filled in by the constants—BUNDLE_ID and BUNDLE_NAME.

Where did these constants come from? It's the last bit of "magic" we get to see. It doesn't matter much where they come from, but the bottom line is once you implement the resource interface, these constants are available. They always have the same name, too. As a result, the `getBundle` method call will always be the same.

```
_resources = ResourceBundle.getBundle(BUNDLE_ID, BUNDLE_NAME);
```

The hard part is out of the way at this point. The last task to be done is to actually get the text of a resource whenever you want to use it. That is done through the `getString` method on the `ResourceBundle` object you just retrieved. The `getString` method uses the resource key values, such as APPLICATION_TITLE and SCREEN_NO_GPS_SUPPORT, which we created and added using the **Resource Editor** pane.

```
add (new LabelField (_resources.getString(SCREEN_NO_GPS_SUPPORT)));
```

Many people like to use a specific prefix for resource key names that make it easier to identify or find in the autocompletion list. One might use some common prefixes such as RC or I18N or RES, but this is a personal matter, so the actual choice is left to you as the user. In this example we didn't follow a pattern, but I do believe that it is good practice to do so.

At this point we've shown doing this with only one resource string. Of course, every string in the application will need to be put into the resource bundle in order to be finished with the localization. For now, though, we will move on to the next topic, Code-signing!

Pop quiz

1. If a resource file has no language code or country code, when will it be used?

    a. When the user device has no language specified.

    b. It will not be used at all.

    c. When no other resource can be matched based on location or language settings.

2. What values are needed to create a Resource Bundle?

    a. BUNDLE_ID and BUNDLE_NAME

    b. The resource file name, language, and location

    c. BUNDLE_NAME

3. Which method is used to retrieve a resource from a resource bundle?

    a. `getResource`

    b. `getString`

    c. `getResourceString`

Code signing your application

Now that we have the application properly localized to use resource files, it's time to put the finishing stamp on it by code-signing the application.

Code signing is very similar to signing an important document in front of a **notary public**. The notary is there to make sure that you are the proper person who is supposed to sign the document and that you did in fact sign it by making you do it before them. In essence, the notary is a third party that verifies who you say you are and that you didn't fake the signature on the document.

In the case of Code signing, you are literally submitting the application that you have just created to RIM and, by entering your login and password, promising that your application doesn't do anything bad.

Most of the interesting objects and methods in the BlackBerry SDK require code signing in order to use them. They work fine in the simulator, but if you were to try to load the applications onto an actual device the loader would throw an error and prevent it. You may have noticed all of the little warnings that we've seen along the way indicating "Discouraged access". This is because we hadn't configured the projects to allow the use of methods that require code signing to use.

```
ServiceBook sb = ServiceBook.getSB();
ServiceRecord[] records = sb.findRecordsByCid("WPTCP");

for (int i = 0; i < records.l
    String uid = records[i].g
    if ( uid.indexOf("wifi")
        add(new LabelField ("
    }
}
```

> Discouraged access: The method findRecordsByCid(String) from the type ServiceBook is not accessible due to restriction on required library C:\Program Files\Eclipse\plugins\net.rim.eide.componentpack4.6.1_4.6.1.27\components\lib\net_rim_api.jar
>
> 1 quick fix available:
> Allow access to RIM Signed APIs

Making this change is very easy, so let's go ahead and make it now.

Time for action – configuring projects to allow access

1. Navigate to **BlackBerry | Configure BlackBerry Workspace**.
2. When the **Preferences** dialog appears, select **BlackBerry JDE | Code Signing** from the list on the left-hand side of the screen.

3. In the pane on the right-hand side of the dialog, check each checkbox listed in the **Code Signing** group.

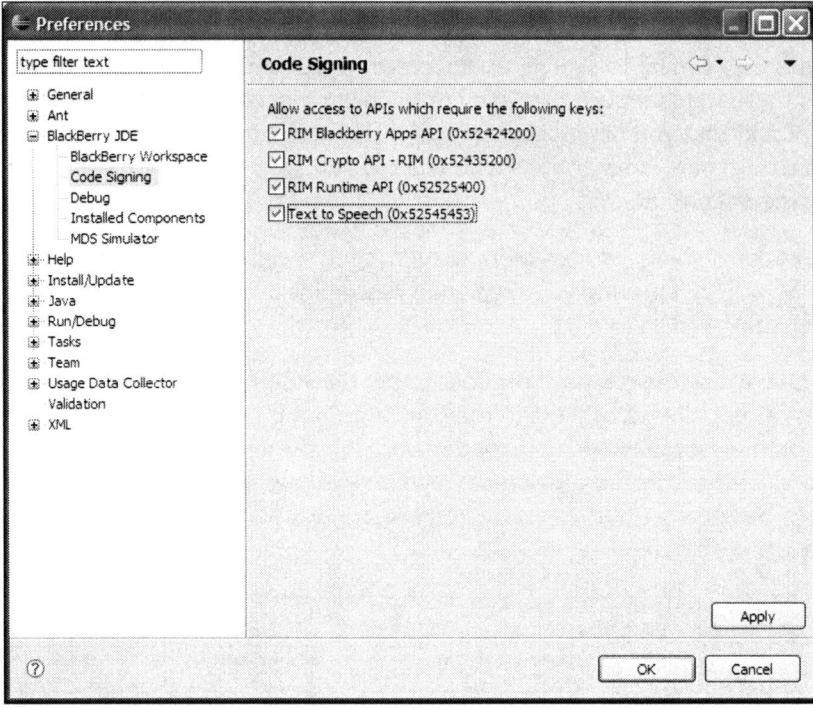

4. Finally, click on **OK** to close the dialog.

What just happened?

This simple task really did only one thing, and that is to make the little yellow warnings go away in the projects that we've already made. Making this setting is like saying "I plan to code-sign my application, so please don't bother me about it." It doesn't actually code-sign the application, and without the boxes checked, the applications still ran fine in the simulator.

 Note that SDK version 4.6 and higher have four checkboxes, while 4.5 and lower have only three. The fourth is for a new code-signed feature—the Speech to Text APIs.

Chapter 11

In order to actually code sign an application, we need to do a couple of more things. The first of which is to register with RIM and request some code signing keys. The registration process is easy and low cost. Simply fill out the web form at `https://www.blackberry.com/SignedKeys/` and pay the $20.00 fee with a credit card. Within a couple of days, you should get three email messages, each with a different code-signing key. The fourth, the Speech to Text APIs, is not part of the standard code-signing package and must be obtained separately from RIM.

Once you have the code signing keys in hand, I mean on disk, we need to install them into the BlackBerry SDK.

Time for action – installing the code-signing keys

1. Click on **BlackBerry | Install Signature Keys...** menu item on the BlackBerry menu in Eclipse.

   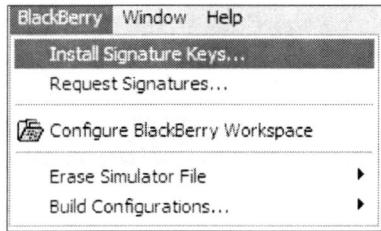

2. In the standard **File Open** dialog that appears, navigate to the location of the code-signing key files on your system. You will see three, but select only one for now.

3. Once the file is selected the **Signature Tool Registration** file is shown where you can enter the PIN and password that you provided when requesting the code-signing keys.

Wrapping It All Up

4. Once you've completed the registration for this key file, repeat the process for the other two files.

What just happened?

The registration process goes pretty smoothly assuming you can connect to the Internet and can remember your PIN and password. Be careful about guessing passwords if you can't remember them properly, as you can lock your account with too many wrong guesses. If that happens, you will have to call BlackBerry support at 1-877-255-2377 to request help with resetting the password attempts and or changing your password.

Also, if you can see that the **Signature Tool Registration** dialog has a button at the bottom for configuring a network proxy. You should know if you need to do this because this won't be the first application to require it. If you've never had to configure a proxy, then you probably don't need to worry about it, but if so, contact your IT support staff for help.

Now that the keys are installed, it's time to actually code-sign the application and put the final touch on it. After all the work we've done so far, this will seem anticlimactic because the process is so simple!

Time for action – code-signing the application

1. Launch the **Signature Tool** by selecting **BlackBerry | Request Signatures...**.
2. The **Signature Tool** dialog will be shown for each of the applications in your workspace. In this case, that is only the **Hansel** application.

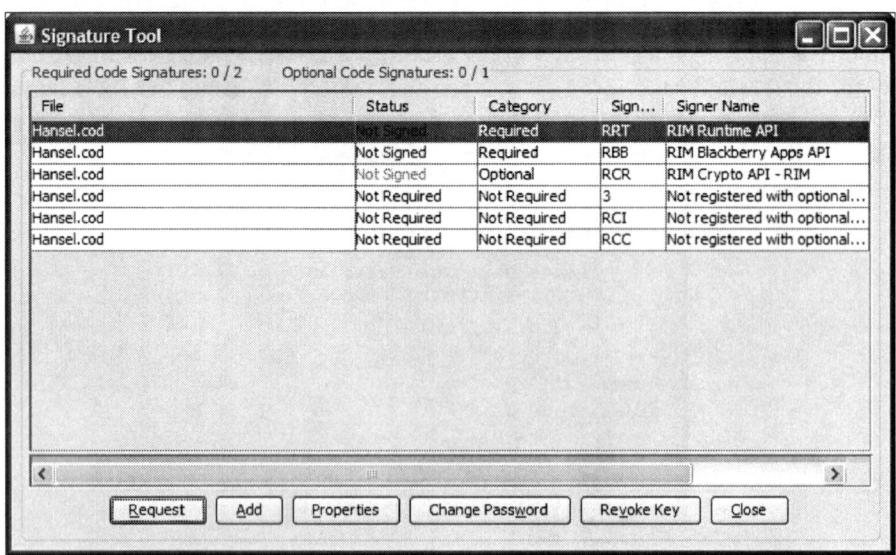

3. Click on the **Request** button and enter your password. This time, the PIN is not required.

4. When it is done, the **Status** column will change from a blue **Not Signed** to a green **Signed** when it is completed.

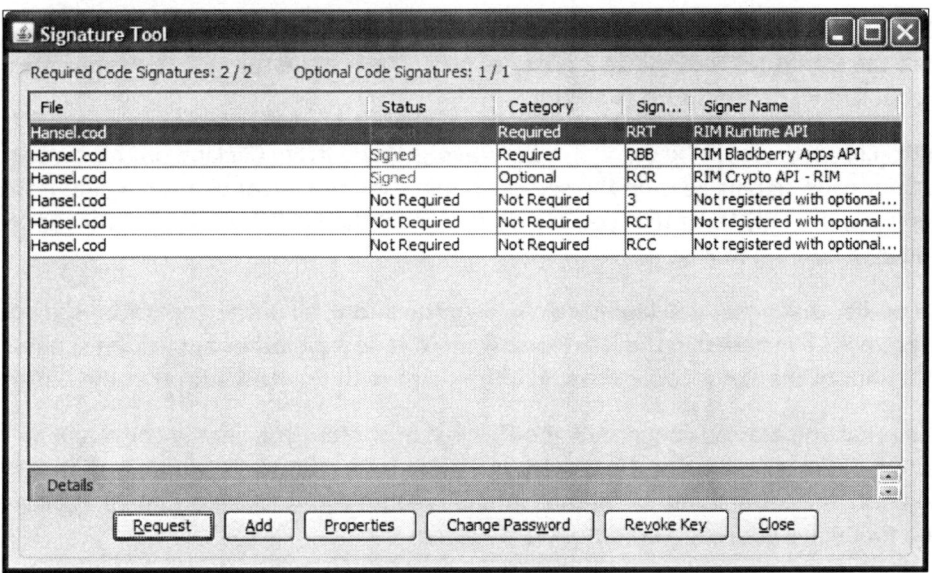

5. In addition to the visual cues that you get in the dialog, you also will get three e-mail messages immediately after doing anything with the **Signature Tool**.

What just happened?

The code-signing process isn't that difficult once all of the set up is done. This dialog itself is rather confusing though. This example was for the `Hansel` application, but yet we see that there are six lines in the **Signature Tool** list. There is a **details** pane under the list, but the information shown here is not useful.

The six lines shown in the tool are each for a separate signer and have a separate Signer ID. Some signers require a code signature and some do not. They are probably related to certain areas of the SDK and some specific functionality, but we aren't told what they are. The bottom line is that if you see lines indicating that the file is not signed, then you need to sign it and the software will take care of the rest.

Wrapping It All Up

Any time you use the **Signature Tool** you will get some e-mail messages from `websigner@ws-smtp.rim.net`. In the case of code-signing an application there will be three e-mail messages—one for each key that is invoked. Messages are also sent any time an incorrect password is entered and each attempt to install the keys on a system, whether it succeeds or not. The volume of traffic can get quite high at times and frankly, gets annoying.

If you had to set up a proxy when installing the code-signing keys, you will also have to configure the **Signature Tool** to use a proxy as well. This is done through the **Properties** button, but should be the same as before.

One button in particular to be wary of is the **Revoke Key** button. Clicking on this button will disable your code-signing keys on the server so that they can't ever be used again! If this ever happens, the only thing that you can do is contact the BlackBerry developer support and request a new set of keys.

We said earlier that when you launched the **Signature Tool**, all of the applications in your workspace will be included in the list. If you wanted to include other applications, possibly other versions of the same application, you can do so with the **Add** button at the bottom.

One thing that you may be concerned about is just how often you should code-sign an application. There is no hard and fast rule, and there is no limit to the number of times that you can do it. The general rule of thumb I would recommend is to code-sign an application any time that you need to load it onto a real device.

The simulator should be good enough for all of your initial testing and development, but there will be times when you must use a real device. Whether it is for testing or actual release of the application, it must be code-signed in order to be loaded onto a device, so that is the proper time to do the code-signing.

You should make sure to increment the version number of the application any time you code-sign it too. When testing in the simulator this won't make much difference, but the loader may refuse to load a new version of the application if the version number is the same.

There is a limit to the number of times that you can install a particular set of keys, usually just once. That isn't to say that you can't have the same set of keys in more than one place, but you can't use the **Install Keys** menu to do it. This may not seem like such a big problem, but when it comes to Eclipse each version of the SDK that you have installed uses a different **Signature Tool** program and expects the signature keys to be in a different location.

What this means is that if you installed the keys while working on a project using version 4.6 of the SDK, and later created another workspace that is using version 4.5 of the SDK, then you will not be able to use the **Request Signatures** menu item in order to sign it. This is because the two versions of the SDK are installed into different directories and each one has a separate **Signature Tool** program.

The result of this is that you MUST copy the signature keys around for each version of the SDK that you will be using. Fortunately the process is simple, and requires just a manual copy and paste of some files using Windows Explorer.

The first step is to find the key files for the keys that you have already installed. These will be in the component package directory of the SDK that you were using at the time the keys were installed. If you installed Eclipse into the default location and were using version 4.6 of the SDK, then the files should be located in `C:\Program Files\Eclipse\plugins\net.rim.eide.componentpack4.6.1_4.6.1.27\components\bin`. Even if you installed Eclipse or the SDK into a location, which is slightly different, the directory from `plugins` onwards should be the same.

There will be several files in the bin directory, but the ones we are interested in are `sigtool.db`, `sigtool.csk`, and `sigtool.set`. There is also a `sigtool.bat` there, but we do not need that file. Simply copy these files by using a standard file copy method.

Next, we have to find the directory of the other SDK version to copy them into. As version 4.5 should be installed as well, we can use that as an example. The path should be `C:\Program Files\Eclipse\plugins\net.rim.eide.componentpack4.5.0_4.5.0.16\components\bin` if you installed Eclipse into the default location. The two paths are very similar.

The three files we identified earlier should be copied into the `bin` directory of the destination SDK version. When this is done you will be able to use the **Request Signatures** menu when working with either version of the SDK in Eclipse.

While we have these files identified and the Windows Explorer windows open, it is probably also a good idea to back up these files onto a CD or flash drive or whatever preferred backup method you have. If for some reason you lose these files, you will need a new set of keys from RIM and must call them on the support number given earlier. It doesn't cost, but it is a hassle that a backup can avoid.

Now see, that wasn't so hard, was it? Now it's time to look at actually getting your application out for the rest of the world to see and use!

Distributing your application through BlackBerry App World

Now that we have everything coded, tested, polished, localized, and signed, we're ready to do what we set out to do from the very beginning, GET PAID! In order to do that, however, you have to sell the application to somebody. There are several avenues through which you can do this, but one of the best is to use the BlackBerry App World store. Now, this isn't to say that there aren't other great services out there. You should sell your application through as many different channels as possible. The BlackBerry App World though offers many advantages that make it easy for a user to use and purchase an application through, so we will focus on that first.

It does have one major disadvantage though, and that is the $200.00 that it takes to get registered. The fee is actually $20.00 per application that you submit, but they require that you purchase a package of ten at a time so once your vendor account is set up, you will be able to submit ten applications to the store. Hopefully, your applications sell well enough to recover that $200.00 investment!

To get started we must sign up and register as a vendor with the BlackBerry App World at `https://appworld.blackberry.com/isvportal/home/login.seam?cid=250514` by clicking on the **sign up** link or the **Get Started** button on the page. In true RIM fashion, you have to go through two legal agreements, both of which have scripting that forces you to scroll to the end of the agreement before you can check the **I agree** checkbox on that page. The first is a Research In Motion agreement but the second is for some other company called Digital River—a company that handles all of the sales transactions, so if you don't plan to sell your application, you don't need to complete the second agreement.

The next two pages are standard forms to collect your information and create an account. The page after that is where things get interesting. Just like any retail website, the next page is where you provide payment information followed up by a confirmation page. The payment information must use the PayPal service and no other methods are supported. This is because the PayPal account is used to both pay your fees and also to deposit any monies collected through the sale of your applications. PayPal has its own set of fees as well, but eliminates the need for any kind of credit card merchant accounts or for you to share bank account information with anyone else as well.

Once the vendor application is submitted it can take a few days to get set up, but the process is usually done in less than the ten days they suggest. You will also receive an e-mail asking for legal documentation that will need to be faxed as well. Overall, the process is pretty easy though.

Licensing models

One thing that you must think about while creating your application is how it will be licensed when you do go to sell it. The App World portal supports four different licensing models that you can use for your application. They offer some flexibility for securing your application and to prevent copying. You should understand each model and choose the right one for you before submitting your application.

- **Static License**: A static license model is the same as having no license key at all. The user doesn't have to do anything at all except start running the application. It is the easiest for the user, but using this method also doesn't do anything at all to protect your application once it is downloaded by the user.

- **Single License**: The Single License model supports the use of a license key, but uses the same license key for every user that downloads and installs your application. This model is more secure, but if the key is leaked out and the application is shared, it would be impossible to know who the responsible party is. It is easy to maintain however because you supply only a single key.

- **Pool of License**: This method randomly retrieves a key from a pool of keys that you had generated and uploaded previously. This model allows for each user to get a unique license key when purchasing your application. As each sale returns a new key, there is more maintenance required by you to make sure that the pool of keys is stocked with enough keys. This model is very effective when combined with a network-based registration model that returns the key along with user information back to you.

- **Dynamic License**: A dynamic license eliminates the need for maintaining a pool of license keys by making an `HTTP` request to a URL that is specified by you, each time a purchase is made and a license key is required. It requires more work in setting up the server that will be used to process the requests, but the long-term benefits may outweigh the upfront work needed for this model to work. It would also allow for the possibility of generating keys which contain a timestamp and could time-out if not used right away. Personally, this seems overkill, but the possibility is there.

There is one model which is not supported by any of these licensing models, and that is a way to create a device-specific key. By using a unique value from a specific device, such as the PIN, it is possible to create a license key that would work for that device only. This model is not supported for good reason though. A user expects to use the same software they had previously purchased each time they upgrade and get a new device. The BlackBerry App World does allow this by maintaining a list of all of the software purchased and downloaded through BlackBerry App World. A device-specific licensing model would prevent this support.

Submitting an application

Applications can be submitted in two ways but regardless of which method is used, any new applications or new versions of an already existing application must pass through an approval process. This approval process deducts one of your credits that you purchased upfront. Remember the $200.00 fee? That fee is good for ten application submissions. The good news is that an application that supports more than one OS and device target is still counted as only one submission. The bad news is that a new version will be treated as a new submission and deduct another credit from your account.

The first method for submitting an application is completely manual; meaning that you must upload the files needed for each OS Version and device combination as well as fill out the required information for each one. The process can be tedious if you have a large support matrix of devices and OS versions.

An alternative method is to put all of the versions together into a specially formatted ZIP file and upload the ZIP file in one step. This method removes some of the tedium of providing the information through the website, but requires more upfront work in preparing the ZIP file.

Once an application is uploaded and approved, you can configure other aspects of the application, such as licensing model, providing keys, and even excluding support for specific carriers. For instance, some carriers don't support some GPS modes, so for an application such as Hansel, it might make sense to exclude some carriers that don't support the mode you want to use. Another example might be related to networking. Some carriers don't support certain networking access models, so it may be beneficial to simply disallow purchases from users on those carriers.

The last step is to enable the application for download and then sit back and congratulate yourself on a job well done.

Summary

This chapter goes over how to put the finishing touches on an application by localizing the resources into resource files and properly code-signing the application so that it can be loaded onto a real device. As if that weren't enough, the last section covers the process for becoming a vendor with BlackBerry App World and how to submit an application.

After completing this chapter, you should understand:

- How to create a resource bundle in your application
- The "magic" gotchas that make resource bundles work
- How to get resource strings from within your application so that the proper strings can be displayed

- Why code-signing is important
- How to install code-signing keys and sign your application
- What it takes to get set up as a vendor on BlackBerry App World
- How to submit an application

There is still a lot left to be covered but at this point you are more than ready to get out there and start making some applications for yourself! Thanks for taking this journey with me! Now get out there and do something wonderful!

Pop Quiz Answers

Chapter 2

1	JDK and JRE	
	b	
2	Java Development Environment (JDE)	
	b	

Chapter 3

1	The project must be activated	
	a	
2	Perspective	
	c	
3	Javadoc	
	b	

Chapter 4

Pop Quiz 1

1	`UiApplication`
	b
2	static
	b

Pop Quiz 2

1	`LabelField`
	b
2	`add()`
	a

Pop Quiz 3

1	A large positive number
	c
2	A small positive number
	b

Chapter 5

Pop Quiz 1

1	Bitwise OR (|)
	a
2	Field
	a
3	`Bitmap` fields cannot be selected
	d

Pop Quiz 2

1	None of the above
	d
2	`DateField`
	b
3	`Field.EDITABLE`
	a

Pop Quiz 3

1	There is no limit
	d
2	The order in which radio button fields are added to the `RadioButtonGroup`
	b
3	False
	b

Pop Quiz 4

1	`getText()`
	b
2	Certain text can be clicked
	b
3	Either a period or ampersand as appropriate
	c

Pop Quiz 5

1	`ActiveRichTextField`
	b
2	`TextField`
	b

Chapter 6

Pop Quiz 1

1	Implement the `FieldChangeListener` interface
	c
2	`ListFieldCallback`
	a
3	`getCookie`
	c

Pop Quiz 2

1	`UiApplication`
	b
2	`pushScreen()`
	b

Pop Quiz 3

1	Constants with the `D_` prefix
	b
2	`Dialog.ask`
	a
3	`Dialog.LIST`
	c

Chapter 7

Pop Quiz 1

1	`RecordStore`
	a
2	`byte[]`
	b
3	`nextRecord`
	a

Pop Quiz 2

1	`PersistentStore`
	a
2	The store key
	b
3	`getContents`
	c

Pop Quiz 3

1	`Connector`
	c
2	`openDataOutputStream`
	b
3	`close`
	c

Chapter 8

Pop Quiz 1

1	`PIM`
	c
2	Use the method whose name matches the data type of the value, that is, `setString()`
	b
3	You can't set a single element in an array. You must replace the entire array with a new array of values.
	c

Pop Quiz 2

1	EventItem	
	a	
2	RepeatRule	
	b	
3	INTERVAL and FREQUENCY	
	b	

Pop Quiz 3

1	Address	
	c	
2	Transport.send()	
	c	

Chapter 9

Pop Quiz 1

1	getResponseCode	
	c	
2	HTTPConnection.GET	
	a	
3	TRUE	
	a	

Pop Quiz 2

1	It must be URL encoded
	c
2	Both content length and content type
	c
3	The name is defined in the web service definition
	a

Pop Quiz 3

1	`interface=WiFi`
	c
2	`deviceside=false`
	b
3	BIS-B
	c

Chapter 10

Pop Quiz 1

1	`LocationProvider`
	c
2	`QualifiedCoordinates` contain information about the accuracy of that reading
	b
3	`distance()`
	a

Pop Quiz 2

1	Command-line argument
	c
2	Versions lower than 4.7
	c
3	In the bitmap file properties
	b

Chapter 11

1	When no other resource can be matched based on location or language settings
	c
2	`BUNDLE_ID` and `BUNDLE_NAME`
	a
3	`getString`
	b

Index

Symbols

_AddTestAddressesAction menu item 206
_calculateAction 79
_en_mx suffix 311
_EntryList member 189
_es suffix 310
_mx suffix 310
_Output field 241
_PostData object 246
.rrc extension 309
.rrh extension 309
_StartAction menu item 280
_StartLocationCoordinate object 292
_StartLocation data member 292
_StopAction menu 281
_values 161

A

ActiveAutoTextEditField
  about 131
  creating 131
ActiveRichTextField
  about 136, 155, 157
  creating 137, 138
addChildNode 152
add method 213
addRecipient method 231
addRecord method 177, 179
address book
  embedding 220-223
  embedding, into application 220
Address object 231
addSiblingNode method 152

addStringArray method 210, 212
addString method 212
AddTestContacts menu item 212
AddTipCalc application 203
alternate entry point applications 13
alternate entry point project
  about 269, 294
  creating 296, 297
alternate entry points
  about 294, 295
  Alternate CLDC Application Entry Point type 296
  args 297
  Auto-run on startup checkboxes 297
  azimuthTo method 303
  CLDC Application 296
  Compose Message application 295
  focus icon, adding to Hansel 298-302
  focus icon, creating 295, 296
  getCourse method 303
  HanselApp class 299, 302
  HanselIcon project 298, 300
  HanselMainScreen 300
  locationUpdated method 303
  main method 294, 297
  Messages application 295
  project, creating 296, 297
  public static main method 300, 302
  Runnable 301
  Saved Messages application 295
  setIcons method 301
  setRolloverIcon method 301
  String argument 300
  String array parameter 297
  System module 297

UiApplication structure 294
updateIcon method 301
user, allowing to specify filename 303
amount field 77
amount.getText() 77
application
  distributing, through BlackBerry App World 324
  licensing models 325
  submitting 326
  debugger, starting 50
  debugging 49
  Debug toolbar button 50
  running 46
  running, in stimulator 47, 48
Application class 65
application development, BlackBerry handhelds
  BlackBerry web development approach 10
  Java application development approach 10
Application object 70, 175
args 297
assisted GPS 272, 273
ATTR_HOME phone number 214
attribute field 213
AUTOCAP_OFF disabled 130
autonomous GPS 272, 273
AUTOPERIOD_OFF disabled 130
AutoTextEditField
  about 129
  creating 129, 130
azimuthTo method 303

B

BasicEditField
  about 122
  creating 124, 125
BasicEditField.FILTER_EMAIL filter 126
BasicEditField.FILTER_PHONE style 125
Bill Amount field
  fixing 93
BIS-B transport 256
Bitmap class 103
BitmapField
  about 103
  Bitmap class 103
  Bitmap object 103
  creating 104

BitmapField object 104
Bitmap object 103
BlackBerry
  touchscreen, considerations 165, 166
  capabilities 9
  developer forums, URL 22
  developer knowledge base, URL 22
  tool and SDK downloads, URL 22
BlackBerry 5810
  features 11
BlackBerry 5820
  features 11
BlackBerry 6200 series
  features 11
BlackBerry 6500 series
  features 11
BlackBerry 6700 series
  features 11
BlackBerry 7100
  features 11
BlackBerry7100i
  features 12
BlackBerry 7130
  features 12
BlackBerry 7200 series
  features 11
BlackBerry 7290
  features 11
BlackBerry7510
  features 11
BlackBerry 7520
  features 11
BlackBerry 7700 series
  features 11
BlackBerry 8700
  features 12
BlackBerry 8800 series
  features 12
BlackBerry App World
  application, distributing 324
BlackBerry Bold
  features 12
BlackBerry Bold 9700
  features 12
BlackBerryContact class 210-213
BlackBerryContactList 208
BlackBerryCriteria class 273

BlackBerry Curve 8900
  features 12
BlackBerry developer documentation
  URL 22
BlackBerry developer zone
  about 22
  BlackBerry developer documentation 22
  developer forums 22
  developer knowledge base 22
  tool and SDK downloads 22
  URL 22
BlackBerry Eclipse plugin 16
BlackBerry Enterprise Server (BES) 256
BlackBerryEvent class 224
BlackBerry handhelds
  capabilities 9
BlackBerry Internet Service (BIS) 256
BlackBerry Java Development Environment. *See* JDE
BlackBerry Pearl
  features 12
BlackBerry Pearl 8110
  features 12
BlackBerry Pearl 8120
  features 12
BlackBerry Pearl 8130
  features 12
BlackBerry project
  Application class 65
  code 68
  MainScreen 71
  menu, adding to MainScreen 78, 79
  new application, running 84
  new project, creating 60-62
  package, adding to new project 63, 64
  right component package, selecting 81, 82
  screen requirements, determining 73
  SDK version, selecting 59
  SDK version, setting 81
  TipCalcApplication constructor 70
  TipCalcApplication, expanding 69
  UiApplication class, adding 65, 66
BlackBerry Storm
  features 12
BlackBerry Storm 2
  features 12

BlackBerry way
  persistent store 184
BlackBerry web development approach 10
BlackBerry widgets 10
BUNDLE_ID 315
BUNDLE_NAME 315
ButtonField
  about 142
  ChangeFieldListener 144
  CONSUME_CLICK style 145
  createFields method 143
  creating 142, 144
  fieldChanged method 144
  FieldChangeListener interface 144
  FieldSamplerMainScreen 144
  FieldSamplerMainScreen class 144
  getValue method 142
  implements clause 144
ByteArrayOutputStream 178

C

CalcDistanceLocationListener 287, 290
CalculateTip method 77
calendar
  addEvent method 225
  event, adding 224-227
callbacks 164
cell site 271, 273
ChangeFieldListener 144
characters 252
CheckboxField
  about 116, 117
  creating 117
CheckboxField class 118
CheckPathExists method 197
ChoiceField
  about 105, 106
  NumericChoiceField 108
  NumericChoiceField, creating 108
  ObjectChoiceField 106
  ObjectChoiceField, creating 106
choose method 222
classes
  Application class 65
  EditField class 74

TipCalcApplication class 68
TipCalcMainScreen class 71
code signing
  about 317
  application 320-323
  code-signing keys, installing 319, 320
  projects, configuring to allow access 317-319
Compose Message application 295
Conestoga Lake Conservation 290
Connection object 236
connection string 193
Connection types 236
ConnectionUID=<uid> parameter 265
Connector
  about 193
  data, reading from file 198
  data, storing to file 193-196
Connector class 193, 242 236
CONSUME_CLICK style 145
Contact class 209, 213
ContactList class 209
Content-type property 248
cookie 152
coordinates, Global Positioning System (GPS)
  _StartAction menu item 280
  _StopAction menu 281
  Criteria class 278
  data members 274
  getInstance method 278, 280
  getQualifiedCoordinates method 279
  getting 273
  GPS simulator 282
  HanselMainScreen class 280
  invokeLater method 279
  LabelField 278
  location, acquiring 274-277
  LocationListener interface 279, 280
  LocationListener interface, implementing 274
  LocationListener interface, updating 276
  Location object 279
  locationUpdated method 279
  makeMenu method 281
  makeMenu method, overriding 277
  menu objects, adding to menu 277
  menu objects, creating 276, 277
  new project, creating 274
  null parameter 278

  providerStateChanged method 279
  QualifiedCoordinates 279
  Screen class 280
  screen, setting up 274, 275
  setLocationListener 280, 281
  updateCoordinates method 279
coordinates object 154
CopyCat service 245
CopyMe 245
CopyMeHandler 253
CopyMe service 252
countValues method 215
CoverageInfo class 265
createContact method 209
createEvent method 226
createFields method 100, 110, 117, 119, 124,
    128, 137, 143, 146, 150, 151
create method 197
Criteria class 271, 272

D

data class
  creating 172
DataInputStream 200
DataOutputStream 178
Date class 178
DateField
  about 113
  creating 114
DateFormat class 113
Date object 115
Debug perspective
  about 52
DefaultHandler class 253
deleteRecord method 182
deleteRecordStore method 176
developer forums
  URL 22
DeviceInfo class 230, 264
devices, BlackBerry 11
Dialog.alert method 160
Dialog.ask method 160, 162
Dialog.ask() static method 161
Dialog class 159

dialog, displaying
    about 158
    information collecting, common dialog used 159
    information collecting, custom buttons on dialog used 160, 161
    information collecting, list on dialog used 162
Direct TCP/IP transport 255
Display.getWidth method 148
drawListRow method 147, 153
drawTreeItem method 153
dynamic license 325

E

Eclipse
    about 16
    downloading 23
    downloading, within JDE plugin 24, 25
    help, displaying 55, 57
    launching, steps 38
    OK button 39
    Use this as the default and do not ask again checkbox 39
    workbench 39, 41
    workspace 42
    Workspace Launcher dialog 40
Eclipse Full installer
    JDE plugin, installing 26, 27
Eclipse IDE
    starting 37, 38
Eclipse perspective
    advanced debugging tools 57
    changing 52, 53
    help, displaying 55-57
Eclipse src directory 309
EditField
    about 126
    creating 126
EditField class 74, 93
ELLIPSIS property 76
EmailAddressEditField
    about 128
    creating 128
EmailAddressEditField class 126
enterEventDispatcher method 70
Entry object 181

enumerateRecords method 181
ERROR. Bitmap object 103
event
    adding, to calendar 224-227
Event class 224
events
    e-mail, sending from application 230, 231
    recurring 227, 229
extends keyword 69

F

fieldChanged method 144
FieldChangeListener 164
FieldChangeListener interface 144
Field class 98
Field.EDITABLE 98
Field.FIELD_RIGHT 98
Field object 100
FIELD_RIGHT style 98, 118
FieldSampler application 119
    another listener, adding 168
FieldSamplerApplication 99
FieldSamplerMainField class 147
FieldSamplerMainScreen class 144-147
FieldSamplerScreen class 156, 157
FieldSampler skeleton application 102
FileConnection class 196
final keyword 292
FlowFieldManager 164
FOCUSABLE style 112
focus icon
    adding, to Hansel 298-302
    creating 295, 296
font family 135
FontFamily.forName() 135
FontFamily object 135
Font.getDefault() 135
Font.ITALIC style 135
Font object 135
fonts array 135
Font.UNDERLINED style 135
functions
    main function 67

G

GaugeField
  about 109, 110
  creating 110, 112
getAttributes method 215
getBundle method 315
getChoice method 108
getContents method 188
getCourse method 303
Get Data menu item 240
getData method 109, 110, 111
getEndLocation method 291
getEvent method 167
getFirstName method 205
getFont method 135
getGroup method 121
getInstance method 271, 280
getPersistentObject 188
getPredefinedBitmap method 103
getPreferedWidth method 148
getQualifiedCoordinates method 279
getRespsonseCode method 242
getSelectedIndex method 121
Get Start Location menu item 290
getStartLocation method 291
getString method 214, 316
getStyle method 98
getText method 77, 126
getTime() method 115
getValue method 100, 114, 115, 121, 142, 149, 150, 152
Global Positioning System (GPS)
  about 270
  coordinates, getting 273
  Hansel, expanding 285-290
  location, acquiring 274-277
  LocationProvider class 270
GPS data
  assisted GPS 272
  autonomous GPS 272
  cell site 271
  getting, ways 271
GPSInfo class 273
GPS receiver 270
GPS simulator
  about 282

Add button 283
Create a New Route dialog 284
Edit GPS Route dialog 283
Generate Random Route dialog 284
Locations radio button 283
NMEA extension 284
random route generator option 284
Simulate | GPS Location menu 282
Graphics drawText method 153

H

handhelds, BlackBerry
  capabilities 9
handler class 250, 254
Hansel
  _StartLocationCoordinate object 292
  _StartLocation data member 292
  about 270
  CalcDistanceLocationListener 287, 290
  Conestoga Lake Conservation 290
  expanding 285
  final keyword 292
  getEndLocation method 291
  Get Start Location menu item 290
  getStartLocation method 291
  MainScreen 285
  if (GPSSupported) block 287
  integer data type 293
  Location class 293
  LocationListener interface 287, 288
  LocationProvider instance 291
  locationUpdated method 288, 291
  MainScreen class 285
  menu items, adding to MainScreen class 285, 287
  menu items, adding to makeMenu method 287
  updateLocation method 292
HanselApp class 299, 302
Hansel_es.rrc file 312
HanselIcon project 298, 300
HanselMainScreen 285, 300
HanselMainScreen class 280, 314
hasCamera() method 264
HelloWorldDemo sample application
  importing 42-46

hello world project
  importing 42-46
help documentation 55
HorizontalFieldManager 164
HTTP basics
  about 237, 238
  HTTP GET requests 238
  HTTP POST requests 244
HttpBasicsMainScreen 246
HTTPBasicsMainScreen class 239
HttpBasics namespace 250
HttpConnection 244
HTTP Connection 267
HttpConnection class 242
HttpConnection object 237
HTTP connections 266, 267
HTTP GET requests
  _Output field 241
  about 238
  Connector class 242
  Get Data menu item 240
  getRespsonseCode method 242
  HTTP basics 238, 239, 240
  HTTPBasicsMainScreen class 239
  HttpConnection class 242
  HTTP_OK constant 242
  invokeLater method 241
  MainScreen derived class, creating 238
  run method 239
  ServiceRequestThread class 238-241
  setRequestMethod 242
  StringBuffer object 243
  Thread object 241
  UiApplication derived class, creating 238
  updateDestination 243
HTTP_OK constant 242
HTTP POST command 245
HTTP POST method 245
HTTP POST requests
  _PostData object 246
  about 244
  characters 252
  Content-type property 248
  CopyCat service 245
  CopyMe 245
  CopyMeHandler 253
  CopyMe service 252

  DefaultHandler class 253
  handler class 254
  Handler class 250
  HttpBasicsMainScreen 246
  HttpBasics namespace 250
  HttpConnection 244
  HTTP POST command 245
  HTTP POST method 245
  kSOAP2 library 254
  openOutputStream method 248
  POST method 248
  SAXParser class 253
  SAXParser object 253
  ServiceRequestThread class 246, 247
  setPostData method 249
  setPOSTData method 247
  Simple API for XML (SAX) parser 250
  StartElement 250
  startElement method 252, 253
  updateDestination method 251, 253
  URLEncodedPostData class 245, 247
  URLEncodedPostData object 248
  web service, calling 245
HttpsConnection object 266
HyperText Transfer Protocol (HTTP) 237

I

IDE 10, 16
implements clause 144
import statement 68, 73
indexOfList method 148
information, collecting
  common dialog used 159
  custom buttons on dialog used 160
  Dialog.alert method 160
  Dialog.ask method 160, 162
  Dialog.ask() static method 161
  Dialog class 159
  list on dialog used 162
  makeMenu method 159
  toString method 161
  _values 161
INFORMATION object 103
instanceof operator 100
integer data type 293

Integrated Development Environment. *See* IDE
INTERVAL field 228
invokeLater method 241, 279
isCoverageSufficient method 265
isInHolster() method 264
isSelected method 121
isSupportedArrayElement method 210
isSupportedField method 210

J

Java
  installing 17
Java application development approach 10
Java Development Environment. *See* JDE
Java Development Kit. *See* JDK
java.lang.Object class 66
Java Runtime Edition. *See* JRE
Java Runtime Environment. *See* JRE
Java SE SDK
  installing 17
Java way
  RMS 172
javax.microedition.lcdui.DateField package 113
javax.microedition.rms package 172
JDE
  about 16
  component package over-the-air, installing 28-34
  component package versions, installing 28
JDE component package versions
  installing 28
  installing, over-the-air 28-34
JDE plugin
  installing, for Eclipse Full installer 26, 27
JDK
  downloading 17-20
  installing 20, 21
Journal Entry class 179
JournalEntry class 177, 181, 194, 198
JournalEntry object 178, 189
JournalMainScreen class 174
JRE 17, 21

K

key-value pairing 204

L

LabelField
  about 102
  creating 102
layout managers
  about 164
  FlowFieldManager 164
  HorizontalFieldManager 164
  VerticalFieldManager 164
licensing, models
  dynamic license 325
  pool of license 325
  single license 325
  static license 325
listeners
  about 164
  FieldChangeListener 164
ListField
  about 145
  createFields method 146
  creating 145, 147
  Display.getWidth method 148
  drawListRow 147
  FieldSamplerMainField class 147
  FieldSamplerMainScreen class 145, 147
  getPreferedWidth method 148
  getValue method 149
  indexOfList method 148
  ListFieldCallback interface 145-149
ListFieldCallback drawListRow method 152
ListFieldCallback interface 145-149
LoadData method 199
LoadEntries method 181
LoadEntriesRMS method 180, 183
load method 179, 181, 198
localization
  resources, using 306
location-based service (LBS) 9
Location class 293
LocationListener interface 279, 280, 287, 288
Location object 279
LocationProvider class
  about 270
  Criteria class 271
  getInstance method 271
  GPS data getting, ways 271

GPS data receving, ways 273
LocationProvider.getInstance 291
LocationProvider instance 291
locationUpdated method 279, 288, 291, 303

M

main function 67
main method 69, 294, 297
MainScreen
  about 71
  adding 72
MainScreen class 76, 285
  VerticalFieldManager 165
MainScreen framework 101
makeMenu method 80, 85, 159, 220, 281
MapField
  about 154
  coordinates object 154
  creating 154
  moveTo method 154
MDS simulator
  debugging with 258, 260, 262
menus
  adding, to application 78
  adding, to MainScreen 78, 80
Message class 231
Message object 231
Messages application 295
methods
  CalculateTip method 77
  main method 69
  public static void main method 69
Mobile Data Services (MDS) 256
moveTo method 154
Multimedia Messaging Service (MMS) 266

N

NAME field 209
name parameter 193
names array 211
net.rim.device.api.i18n.DateFormat package 113
net.rim.device.api.ui.component.DateField package 113
net.rim.device.api.ui.UiApplication class 66

networking
  networkingabout 235
nextRecordId method 181
nextRecord method 181
NO_TEXT style 112
NumericChoiceField
  about 105
  and ObjectChoiceField, differences 109
  creating 108, 109
NumericTextFilter 93

O

ObjectChoiceField
  about 105, 106
  and NumericChoiceField, differences 109
  creating 106
offsets[8] 138
offsets array 135
onClose method 174-176, 197, 198
onSavePrompt 94
openDataInputStream method 200
openDataOutputStream method 198
open method 197, 236
openOutputStream method 248
openPIMList method 208, 226
openRecordStore method 176
operating system (OS) version 11

P

package
  adding, to new project 62, 63, 64
PasswordEditField
  about 127
  creating 127
PERCENT style 112
PersistentObject
  _EntryList member 189
  about 184, 185
  accessing 188
  data accessing 189
  data, storing 189
  getContents method 188
  getPersistentObject 188
  getting 186, 187
  JournalEntry object 189
  PersistentObject contents 190

PersistentObject method 190
setContents method 190
PersistentObject contents 190
PersistentObject method 190
PersistentStore
  about 184, 185
  advantages over RMS 185
persistent store, BlackBerry way
  persistable interface, implementation 184
  search capabilities 184
Personal Information Management (PIM) applications 202
perspective 52
PhoneTextFilter object 125
PIM applications 204
PIM class 205
PIMItem class 205
PIMItem method 210
PIMItems 205, 206
PIMList class 205
PIMList object 204
PIMLists 205
PIMList type 208
pool of license 325
pop quiz 35, 57
popScreen method 158
POST method 248
Priority 79
project. *See* **BlackBerry project**
providerStateChanged method 279
public keyword 69
public static main method 300, 302
public static void main method 69
pushScreen method 155

Q

QualifiedCoordinates 279

R

RadioButtonField 119
  about 118, 119
  creating 119
read methods 181
Record Management System (RMS) 171
RecordStore class 172
RecordStore instance 172

RecordStoreNotFound exception 176
recurring event 227
removable storage
  removing 192
removeValue method 214
RepeatingRule class 228
RepeatRule class 228
Research In Motion (RIM) 7
resource bundle
  about 309
  project, configuring 311-313
  resource file, populating 311-313
  second resource file, adding 310, 311
  using, in code 314, 316
ResourceBundle object 314, 315
resource file
  adding 306, 308
  Hansel.rrc 309
  Hansel.rrh 309
resources
  resource file, adding 306-309
  using, for localization 306
  using, in code 314-316
RichTextField
  about 133
  creating 133, 134
RMS
  about 172
  addRecord method 177, 179
  Application object 175
  backed up as one database 173
  ByteArrayOutputStream 178
  DataOutputStream 178
  Date class 178
  deleteRecord method 182
  deleteRecordStore method 176
  Entry object 181
  enumerateRecords method 181
  Java MIDP standard 172
  javax.microedition.rms package 172
  Journal Entry class 179
  JournalEntry class 177, 181
  JournalEntry object 178
  JournalMainScreen class 174
  LoadEntries method 181
  LoadEntriesRMS method 180, 183
  load method 179, 181

nextRecordId method 181
nextRecord method 181
onClose method 174-176
openRecordStore method 176
read methods 181
record, adding 177, 178
records contain no structure 172
records, deleting 182
records, retrieving 179, 180, 181
RecordStore class 172
RecordStore, creating 174, 175
RecordStore instance 172
RecordStoreNotFound exception 176
SaveEntriesRMS method 176
save method 178
share with no one or everyone 173
size limits 173
throws keyword 176
TODO comment 180
write method 178
run method 79, 212, 215, 239
Runnable 301

S

SaveData method 197, 200
save dialog
  disabling 94
Saved Messages application 295
SaveEntriesRMS method 176
save method 194, 197
save prompt
  fixing 94
SAXParser class 253
SAXParser object 253
screen
  About Screen, creating 156
  ActiveRichTextField 155, 157
  another screen, displaying 155
  FieldSamplerScreen class 156, 157
  popScreen method 158
  pushScreen method 155
  TipCalcApplication constructor 155
  UiApplication 155
Screen class 193, 280
screen requirements
  adding, to MainScreen 74

  determining 73
SDK
  other versions, installing 35
SDK, mangers
  FlowFieldManager 164
  HorizontalFieldManager 164
  VerticalFieldManager 164
SDK version
  about 11
  new project, creating 60
  package, adding to new project 63, 64
  right component package, selecting 81, 82
  selecting 10-12, 59
  setting 81
sendRequest method 230
SeparatorField
  about 101
  creating 101
service book 258, 265
ServiceRequestThread class 238, 239, 241, 246, 247
setArrayValue() method 219
setChecked methods 118
setChoices method 107
setContent method 232
setContents method 190
setDate method 115
setFilter method 125
setIcons method 301
setLocationListener 280, 281
setPostData method 249
setPOSTData method 247
setRepeat method 229
setRequestMethod 242
setRolloverIcon method 301
setSelectedIndex method 120
setSelected method 121
setStringArrayElement() method 219
setStringArray method 219
setString method 214, 216
setStyle method 98
setText method 224
setValue()method 219
Simple API for XML (SAX) parser 250
simulator
  about 16
  application, running 47, 48

single license 325
SOAP 249
SocketConnection object 267
StartElement 250
startElement method 252, 253
static keyword 69
static license 325
String argument 300
String array parameter 297
stringArraySize method 209, 218
StringArray type 212
StringBuffer object 243
String object 218
superclass 66
Superclass field 66
super.makeMenu 80
Swiss Army Knife wizard 62
system requirements 16

T

test contacts
  creating 206, 208
  e-mail addresses, adding 215-219
  expanding 212
  finishing 217, 218
  telephone numbers, adding 212, 214
TextField
  about 122
  ActiveAutoTextEditField 131
  ActiveRichTextField 136
  AutoTextEditField 129
  BasicEditField 122
  EditField 126
  EmailAddressEditField 128
  PasswordEditField 127
  RichTextField 133
TextFilter 93
The Font.BOLD style 135
threading 236
Thread object 241
throws keyword 176
TimeOff project 206
TipCalc
  application title, changing 92, 93
  expanding 95
  icon, adding 87-91

TipCalcApplication class 68
TipCalcApplication constructor 70, 155
TipCalcMainScreen class 71, 74
ToDo class 233
TODO comment 180
toHexString method 230
toString method 161
toString() method 106
TouchEvent class 167
TouchEvent method 167
TouchEvents 166
TouchGestures 167
touchscreen
  considerations 165, 166
transport
  about 255
  BIS-B 256
  ConnectionUID=<uid> parameter 265
  CoverageInfo class 265
  DeviceInfo class 264
  direct TCP/IP transport 255
  hasCamera() method 264
  isCoverageSufficient method 265
  isInHolster() method 264
  MDS/BES 256
  Multimedia Messaging Service (MMS) 266
  service book 265
  testing, for availability 262-264
  Wi-Fi 257
  Wireless Application Protocol (WAP) 257
Transport class 232
TreeField
  about 149, 150
  addChildNode 152
  addSiblingNode method 152
  cookie 152
  createFields method 150, 151
  creating 150
  drawListRow method 153
  drawTreeItem method 153
  getValue method 150, 152
  Graphics drawText method 153
  ListFieldCallback drawListRow method 152
triangulation 270
try-catch block 135

U

UiApplication 155
UiApplication class
  about 70, 99
  adding 65-68
UiApplication objects 67
UiApplication structure 294
UI development guidelines
  URL 73
Universal Resource Locator (URL) 193
updateCoordinates method 279
updateDestination 243
updateDestination method 251
updateIcon method 301
updateLocation method 292
URLEncodedPostData class 245, 247
URLEncodedPostData object 248
USE_ALL_WIDTH property 76
User Interface (UI) 65
using statement 68

V

VerticalFieldManager 164

W

WAP 1.X 257
WAP 2.0 258
WARNING object 103
websigner@ws-smtp.rim.net 322
Wi-Fi 257
Wireless Application Protocol (WAP)
  about 257
  WAP 1.X 257
  WAP 2.0 258
workbench 39, 41
workspace 42
Workspace Launcher dialog 40
write method 178

X

XML 250

Z

ZIP code 272

Thank you for buying
BlackBerry Java Application Development: Beginner's Guide

About Packt Publishing

Packt, pronounced 'packed', published its first book "Mastering phpMyAdmin for Effective MySQL Management" in April 2004 and subsequently continued to specialize in publishing highly focused books on specific technologies and solutions.

Our books and publications share the experiences of your fellow IT professionals in adapting and customizing today's systems, applications, and frameworks. Our solution-based books give you the knowledge and power to customize the software and technologies you're using to get the job done. Packt books are more specific and less general than the IT books you have seen in the past. Our unique business model allows us to bring you more focused information, giving you more of what you need to know, and less of what you don't.

Packt is a modern, yet unique publishing company, which focuses on producing quality, cutting-edge books for communities of developers, administrators, and newbies alike. For more information, please visit our website: www.PacktPub.com.

Writing for Packt

We welcome all inquiries from people who are interested in authoring. Book proposals should be sent to author@packtpub.com. If your book idea is still at an early stage and you would like to discuss it first before writing a formal book proposal, contact us; one of our commissioning editors will get in touch with you.

We're not just looking for published authors; if you have strong technical skills but no writing experience, our experienced editors can help you develop a writing career, or simply get some additional reward for your expertise.

BlackBerry Enterprise Server for Microsoft® Exchange

ISBN: 978-1-847192-46-2 Paperback:188 pages

Installation and Administration

1. Understand BlackBerry Enterprise Server architecture
2. Install and configure a BlackBerry Enterprise Server
3. Implement administrative policies for BlackBerry devices
4. Secure and plan for disaster recovery of your server

Grails 1.1 Web Application Development

ISBN: 978-1-847196-68-2 Paperback: 328 pages

Reclaiming Productivity for faster Java Web Development

1. Ideal for Java developers new to Groovy and Grails—this book will teach you all you need to create web applications with Grails
2. Create, develop, test, and deploy a web application in Grails
3. Take a step further into Web 2.0 using AJAX and the RichUI plug-in in Grails

Please check www.PacktPub.com for information on our titles

Lightning Source UK Ltd.
Milton Keynes UK
11 September 2010

159715UK00001B/111/P